W9-CIJ-732

Joan Winmill Brown

WITHDRAWN
by Unity Library

World Wide
Minneapolis, Minnesota 55403

JOY IN HIS PRESENCE, © 1982, Joan Winmill Brown.
Published by World Wide Publications, 1303 Hennepin Avenue,
Minneapolis, Minnesota, 55403.

All rights reserved.

Printed in U.S.A.

Library of Congress Cataloging in Publication Data:

Brown, Joan Winmill
  Joy In His Presence

    1. Devotional/Christian Life   I. Title
82-060307

ISBN 0-89066-041-7

*A*S I RESEARCHED MANY VOLUMES of early Christian literature, looking for passages to include in this devotional, I was extremely conscious of the dedication of these saints and their overwhelming desire to serve the Lord Jesus Christ with a constancy and commitment that was not shaken by tragedy and suffering. They found that the joy of His presence was with them through all their days as they spread the glorious news of the Gospel.

Today the message is the same—one of hope, love and forgiveness—and Christians all over the world attest to this same joy. It is found in the writings of modern-day believers, and it is my hope that the passages that I have included will continue to bless lives until our Lord returns.

Jesus Christ still needs consecrated men and women to reach the world, those who are strong in their faith. Each day we are bombarded with often horrendous news, causing many to wonder what the future will hold. But when we are committed to Jesus Christ, we have a joy that can never be taken away. It is not dependent on material or world events but on Him who has said, "These things have I spoken unto you, that my joy might remain in you, and that your joy might be full" (John 15:11). No matter how dire the circumstances, we know that His love and care are always with us.

While gathering this material, I imagined what it would be like if all these people, both past and present, could be assembled together. There would be dissertations on the doctrines of Scripture and probably many differences of opinion on many subjects, but I felt certain that all would be overshadowed by the centrality of the cross of our Savior. Each one would agree, "I am nothing without Jesus Christ."

My prayer is that this devotional will draw you closer to our Lord. As often as possible I have linked the past with the present in these devotionals so as to bring reassurance and a deeper consciousness of God's unfailing mercy and love. David said so long ago, "Restore unto me the joy of thy salvation..." (Psalm 51:12). Today we need to repeat those words when we allow the events of our time to mar our walk with Jesus Christ.

We can have the same joy that was with John Wesley, Augustine, Martin Luther, Dietrich Bonhoeffer, Fanny Crosby, Corrie ten Boom and all the saints who have lived for Jesus Christ, being sustained by His Holy Spirit.

If you are reading this book but have never known the joy of Jesus' forgiveness and love in your life, my hope is that you will find Him as Savior and Lord.

"Thou wilt show me the path of life: in thy presence is fullness of joy; at thy right hand there are pleasures for evermore" (Psalm 16:11).

My grateful thanks to all who have contributed to this book and especially to my husband Bill, Twila Knaack, Kathy Ganz and Fred Bauer. Their untiring help and encouragement are deeply appreciated.

Joan Winmill Brown

*So teach us to number our days, that we may
apply our hearts unto wisdom.* Psalm 90:12

THE PRAYER THAT ALL OF US SHOULD OFFER as we stand on
the threshold of another year is this: "So teach us to number our
days, that we may apply our hearts unto wisdom." Time actually
has little meaning in heaven. There are no calendars in eternity. Yet
because of the shortness of our time on earth, this prayer attributed
to Moses should become ours also. Why? Because, first of all, today is
the only hold we have on eternity.

No man can truly say, "I know that I will be living in the flesh tomorrow." The thread of life is so brittle, and the future is so uncertain, that none of us can boast that we own one second of the days
ahead. This moment, this one golden hour, is God's gift to us; and
the only segment of time that we can really call our own is the one
we are now living. *Billy Graham*

The world may be in turmoil and despair, but in the darkness the
light of Jesus Christ has all the more chance of shining brightly. Let
us ask Him to use us as His "light," as each day we come in contact
with so many who need the assurance of His love. *J.W.B.*

*Our Father and our God, we thank You for the gift of this new year.
Teach us to cherish each day that You give to us. Use our lives, Lord, to
minister to those we encounter so that we may share the hope and joy
that we have in You. May we glorify Your name in all that we do. In
Jesus' name, Amen.*

*...yield yourselves unto the Lord, and enter
into his sanctuary...* II Chronicles 30:8

HE ONLY ASKS THEE TO YIELD THYSELF TO HIM, that He may
work in thee to will and to do by His own mighty power. Thy
part is to yield thyself, His part is to work; and never, never will He
give thee any command which is not accompanied by ample power
to obey it. Take no thought for the morrow in the matter; but abandon thyself with a generous trust to thy loving Lord, who has promised never to call His own sheep out into any path without Himself
going before them to make the way easy and safe. Take each little

step as He makes it plain to thee. Bring all thy life in each of its details to Him to regulate and guide. Follow gladly and quickly the sweet suggestions of His Spirit in thy soul. And day by day thou wilt find Him bringing thee more and more into conformity with His will in all things; molding thee and fashioning thee, as thou art able to bear it, into a vessel unto His honor, sanctified and meet for His use, and fitted to every good work. *Hannah Whitall Smith*

> Oh, for a closer walk with God,
> A calm and heav'nly frame;
> A light to shine upon the road
> That leads me to the Lamb!
>
> *William Cowper*

(The Lord waits for us to yield our lives completely. We must search our hearts to see if there are any secret obstacles that block absolute surrender.)

Show me, Lord Jesus, whatever there is in me that hinders total consecration to You.

———➤ **JANUARY 3** ➤·———

Consecrate yourselves today to the Lord.... Exodus 32:29

◆————————————————————————————————◆

*T*HE CHRISTIAN *MUST* MAKE A BREAK WITH THE PAST so radical that his mind is filled with the thoughts of Christ Himself. A faith which does not do this, which stops with the belief that being "saved" is the whole Christian experience, is dead and denies Christ's concern for all mankind. It is like a baby dying in infancy; the child may be born healthy, but his life will have little or no impact on others.

Grasping this concept was a turning point for me, as it is, I suspect, for many Christians. God, I now understood, was working a powerful transformation in my thought habits and forcing me to *think* about what it really means to live as a disciple of God.

Charles W. Colson

> Take my life, and let it be
> Consecrated, Lord, to Thee.
> Take my moments and my days:
> Let them flow in ceaseless praise.
>
> *Frances Ridley Havergal*

Lord, all that I am is Yours. Teach me, through Your Word, to be a dedicated, consecrated disciple.

...forgetting those things which are behind,
and reaching forth unto those things which are before,
I press toward the mark for the prize of the
high calling of God in Christ Jesus. Philippians 3:13-14

*L*ETTING GO OF THE PAST AND BEGINNING HERE, now, where we are, to move again toward a reconciled life is one of the hardest things any human being is ever asked to do. Love is the power to do that.

God's love is our model. It keeps coming to us though we have fed a thousand offenses into His memory bank. God's love is also our power. We are enabled by a love that keeps no accounts since they were settled by Christ at His cross. From the cross, God moves on to new history. He does not wait until we have sifted and weighed all our faults. In love He begins where we are. Moved by this love, we have no need to savor past hurts caused by old enemies. Our ego has no need to nourish resentment, for it is supported, not by staying on top of personal relations, but by accepting forgiveness and freedom from God. We lose our masochistic taste for angry memories of the wrongs others have inflicted on us. We do not need to keep accurate score, for we do not need to be a moral winner. We forgive and start anew with what we now are and with what the other person now is.

Lewis B. Smedes

Put together all the tenderest love you know of, the deepest you have ever felt, and the strongest that has ever been poured out upon you, and heap upon it all the love of all the loving human hearts in the world, and then multiply it by infinity, and you will begin, perhaps, to have some faint glimpse of what the love of God is.

Hannah Whitall Smith

Our Father, invade our lives with the power of Your love, we pray.

Therefore if any man be in Christ, he is a
new creature: old things are passed away; behold,
all things are become new. II Corinthians 5:17

*O*NE DAY JOHN RUSKIN, the nineteenth-century writer, was walking in the streets of London and became fascinated with the mud left by a recent rainstorm. He began to wonder just what inorganic elements composed the substance and decided to have a sample analyzed. The report came back: sand, clay, soot, and water.

As he thought about the findings, it occurred to him that these were the very same elements from which jewels and gems are formed. From sand come the agate, onyx, carnelian, jasper, and amethyst; from clay come the ruby, emerald, topaz, and sapphire; and from soot comes the diamond. The London mud had the same elements as precious jewels!

Man cannot change the mud into priceless stones—only the Creator—and only He can change our lives from the seemingly worthless persons we are into those transformed by the love and forgiveness of Jesus Christ.   *J.W.B.*

An hour may come when you will never again hear Christ's
knock on your heart's door...
Everything that happens to you from now on—in this life and
throughout eternity—hinges on whether or not you stretch
out your hand to open the door to Him.
The latch is on the inside.

> Just one more step, Nicodemus.
> Just one more step to take.
> The dawn is coming.
> It must not come...too late!

Peter Marshall

Lord Jesus, whose love can change all hearts and lives as they are surrendered to You, we praise and glorify Your name.

————— ► JANUARY 6 ◄ —————

**The Spirit itself beareth witness with our spirit,
that we are the children of God....** Romans 8:16

◆———————————————————————————◆

RUTH GRAHAM, BILLY'S WIFE, was brought up in China as the daughter of a medical missionary. From childhood she knew the Gospel but failed to grasp that it was for her personally. One day while reading Isaiah, the Holy Spirit led her to personalize the words she was reading. She read Isaiah 53 like this: "He was wounded for *Ruth's* transgressions, he was bruised for *Ruth's* iniquities...and with his stripes *Ruth* is healed." The same Holy Spirit who brought Ruth Graham personal assurance can also convince you that you are no longer a stranger to God, nor even His slave, but one chosen to be His son or daughter.

Our effectiveness in sharing Jesus Christ depends not only on an initial experience of salvation and on our assurance but also on a life-long quest, a progressive, ever-deepening knowledge of Him. To reflect Christ in the marketplace, we need to be with Him in the quiet place. A daily devotional life of Bible reading, prayer and meditation is not some kind of legalistic regimen but a wonderful opportunity to fellowship with God and learn to know Him better.

Leighton Ford

Take time. Give God time to reveal Himself to you. Give yourself time to be silent and quiet before Him, waiting to receive through the Spirit the assurance of His presence with you, His power working in you. Take time to read His Word as in His presence; that from it you may know what He asks of you and what He promises you. Let the Word create around you, create within you, a holy heavenly light in which your soul will be refreshed and strengthened for the work of daily life.

Andrew Murray

Refresh me, Lord, with the light of Your Holy Word, so that I will be strengthened and ready to face whatever lies ahead.

————————— • **JANUARY 7** •—————————

The fear of the Lord is a fountain of life, to depart from the snares of death. Proverbs 14:27

I F WE HAVE REVERENCE FOR THE LORD, and if we value our relationship with Him, then we will spend a special time each day with Him in prayer. As we yield ourselves daily to Him in this way, seeking His face and bringing our praise, thanksgiving, and petitions, He will in turn shower us with blessings.

Someone once asked me, "Don't you think you might be bothering God with all the requests you make to Him for the things that aren't really so important? After all, He has more to think about than all the little details of *your* life."

It was my privilege to explain to this person that God delights in hearing from us and that we cannot bother Him too much. Because He is a loving Father, it gives Him great joy when His children come away from other interests for a special time alone with Him. In His Word He encourages us to ask, to seek, to knock. He promises that He will always answer us.

Mary C. Crowley

Prayer is not conquering God's reluctance, but taking hold of God's willingness.

Phillips Brooks

Thank You, our Father, that You care for the smallest detail in our lives. May we always realize that You are waiting for us to come to You and ask for that which is upon our hearts. This time of prayer, Lord, is one in which we would take time to adore You. In Jesus' name, Amen.

————————— **JANUARY 8** ————————

Be careful for nothing; but in everything by prayer and supplication with thanksgiving let your requests be made known unto God. Philippians 4:6

◆————————————————————————————————◆

*H*ERE ARE SOME SEED THOUGHTS to start you praying:
The great tragedy of life is not unanswered prayer but unoffered prayer.

Fall on your knees and grow there.

There is no burden of the spirit but is lighter by kneeling under it.

(Prayer means) not always talking to Him, but waiting before Him till the dust settles and the stream runs clear (F. B. Meyer).

Walker of Tinnevelly defined prayer as "the uplifting of empty hearts toward the divine supply."

We should not insist on our own ways when we pray. Remember Psalm 106:15: "He gave them their request; but sent leanness into their soul."

We must learn to pray far more for spiritual victory than for protection from battle wounds, or relief from their havoc, or rest from their pain (Amy Carmichael). *Ruth Bell Graham*

> Come, my soul, thy suit prepare,
> Jesus loves to answer prayer;
> He Himself has bid thee pray.
> Therefore will not say thee nay.
> Thou art coming to a King,
> Large petitions with thee bring;
> For His grace and power are such,
> None can ever ask too much.
>
> *John Newton*

Lord Jesus, we come with a joyous expectancy of Your answering our requests, if they are in Your plan for our lives.

————————— **JANUARY 9** ————————

...as for me, God forbid that I should sin against the Lord in ceasing to pray for you.... I Samuel 12:23

*W*HEN PEOPLE PRAY FOR EACH OTHER, beautiful things happen. No longer does it seem so important to us to hold on to a grudge. The love bubbles to the surface. God opens fresh channels of communication. Jesus Christ becomes an immediate, present Savior. The Holy Spirit becomes known as God Himself. Pride is punctured; hearts are humbled; attitudes change; homes are healed; holiness enters. The miracle of the Gospel occurs all over again as people become convinced that Christianity is real and that it works.

Many have wondered what Paul meant when he spoke of "all prayer" in Ephesians 6. Could it not be just another term for "supplication for the saints"—letting the power of God's love weld Christians in a spiritual bond as they hold up each other before the throne of Grace? Amazing things happened when our Lord prayed for people. Amazing things still happen when we follow His example.

Sherwood E. Wirt

It is sin against the Lord to cease praying for others. When once we begin to see how absolutely indispensable intercession is, just as much a duty as loving God or believing in Christ, and how we are called and bound to it as believers, we shall feel that to cease intercession is grievous sin. Let us ask for grace to take up our place as priests with joy, and give our life to bring down the blessing of heaven.

Andrew Murray

Father, we ask for Your grace as we pray for our loved ones and all those who need Your blessings.

JANUARY 10

...ye know him; for he dwelleth with you, and shall be in you. John 14:17

*I*T IS BY THE SPIRIT OF CHRIST that we can be transformed into the image of Christ, as we keep looking steadfastly toward Him. We thus have our part to play, in repentance, faith and discipline, but essentially holiness is the work of the Holy Spirit.

> And every virtue we possess
> And every victory won,
> And every thought of holiness,
> Are His alone.
> Spirit of purity and grace
> Our weakness, pitying, see;

O make our hearts Thy dwelling-place
And worthier Thee!

William Temple used to illustrate the point in this way. It is no good giving me a play like Hamlet or King Lear and telling me to write a play like that. Shakespeare could do it; I can't. And it is no good showing me a life like the life of Jesus and telling me to live a life like that. Jesus could do it; I can't. But if the genius of Shakespeare could come and live in me, then I could write plays like that. And if the Spirit of Jesus could come and live in me, then I could live a life like that. This is the secret of Christian sanctity. It is not that we should strive to live like Jesus, but that He by His Spirit should come and live in us. To have Him as our example is not enough; we need Him as our Savior. *John R. W. Stott*

(Let us adore the One who has given this perfect life for all our imperfections.)

Jesus, Savior, we praise Your name. Come into our flawed, unworthy lives and fill them with Your Holy Spirit.

───────────── •► **JANUARY 11** ◄•─────────────

Commit thy way unto the Lord; trust also in him; and he shall bring it to pass. Psalm 37:5

◆───◆

JESUS LOVES THE HEART UTTERLY AVAILABLE TO HIM, and He grieves over the heart totally closed to Him, and the heart that specializes in compromise to the exclusion of the other two possibilities is the heart in which He can never under any circumstances feel at home. Speaking to the Laodicean church, He said, "Would that you were either cold or hot! I will spue you out of my mouth!" (Revelation 3:15,16, *Amplified New Testament*). If you run away from any Christian experience, service or activity which entails a costly spiritual sacrifice and promptly seek refuge in compromise, be absolutely certain that your life is not the Great High Priest's idea of an ideal temple. Your responsibility is to make Him feel at home, and this He can never be if you prefer convenient, comfortable compromise to all-out abandoned availability. *D. Stuart Briscoe*

To believe is to commit.... In particular belief I commit myself spiritually to Jesus Christ and determine in that thing to be dominated by the Lord alone. When I stand face to face with Jesus Christ and He says to me, "Believest thou this?" I find that faith is as natural as breathing, and I am staggered that I was so stupid as not to trust Him before. *Oswald Chambers*

My Savior, into Your blessed hands I have committed my heart and life. Forgive the times my faith wavers and I allow doubts to cloud the joy of trusting You.

──────────── **JANUARY 12** ────────────

He restoreth my soul: he leadeth me in the paths of righteousness for his name's sake. Psalm 23:3

*J*ESUS NEVER SENDS A MAN AHEAD ALONE. He blazes a clear way through every thicket and woods, and then softly calls, "Follow Me. Let's go on together, you and I." He has been everywhere that we are called to go. His feet have trodden down smooth a path through every experience that comes to us. He knows each road, and knows it well: the valley road of disappointment with its dark shadows; the steep path of temptation down through the rocky ravines and slippery gullies; the narrow path of pain, with the brambly thorn bushes so close on each side, with their slash and sting; the dizzy road along the heights of victory; the old beaten road of commonplace daily routine. *Everyday paths He has trodden and glorified, and will walk anew with each of us. The only safe way to travel is with Him alongside and in control.* Dr. S. D. Gordon

It's good to remember that not even the Master Shepherd can lead if the sheep do not follow Him but insist on running ahead of Him or taking side paths. *Catherine Marshall*

Lord Jesus, how comforting to know You are leading me in all my ways. Forgive the times I forget.

──────────── **JANUARY 13** ────────────

And the stars of heaven shall fall, and the powers that are in heaven shall be shaken. And then shall they see the Son of man coming in the clouds with great power and glory. Mark 13:25,26

*H*OW OFTEN WE LONG FOR A WORLD WITHOUT WAR, hatred, or greed. Each day as we read the newspapers or watch television, it appears that everything is escalating so fast and there is no answer to the manifold problems that surround us. But beyond all this heartache there is an expectation—a promise that is going to be fulfilled—Jesus' return.

If our hope is based on earthly things, then we are bound to be disappointed and fearful. But to those of us who have experienced Jesus Christ's presence, we can live each day with hope in our hearts; knowing that whatever happens, when the time is perfect, as God has planned, His Son will return to rule this world.   *J.W.B.*

> There's a light upon the mountains,
>   And the day is at the spring,
> When our eyes shall see the beauty
>   And the glory of the King:
> Weary was our heart with waiting,
>   And the night-watch seemed so long,
> But His triumph-day is breaking,
>   And we hail it with a song....

Henry Burton

Lord Jesus, my hope is in You. The thought of Your return fills me with joy and brings the courage I need to live victoriously.

——•► JANUARY 14 ◄•——

The Lord is my strength and my shield; my heart trusted in him, and I am helped: therefore my heart greatly rejoiceth; and with my song will I praise him. Psalm 28:7

◆————————————————————————————————◆

*A*N AMAZING CHARACTERISTIC OF GOD'S NATURE that I have observed is: *He always comes in proportion to our needs.* The deeper the sorrow, the more comfort He gives; the larger the void, the more God fills it; the greater the need, the more we have of Him. "The Lord is *nigh* unto them that are of a broken heart" (Psalm 34:18).

I have found in my own life that God always comes in proportion to my need. It is more than just, "Lo, I am with you alway." That is God's "when"—always! But there are differences in my "whens." Difficult circumstances require an added measure of this strength and grace. At those times I can be sure He will be with me in that same proportion.

There is a quality and a seemingly quantity of His presence that changes with life's needs. It is like the "as" of Moses' beautiful promise to Asher during his final benediction to the 12 tribes which has been a comfort to every succeeding generation of believers: "As thy days, so shall thy strength be" (Deuteronomy 33:25). More strength is given where more strength is needed. *Evelyn Christenson*

> *I look to Thee in every need,*
>   *And never look in vain;*
> *I feel Thy touch, Eternal Love,*
>   *And all is well again:*
> *The thought of Thee is mightier far*
> *Than sin and pain and sorrow are.*
>
> S. *Longfellow*

JANUARY 15

...we are more than conquerors through him that loved us. Romans 8:37

---

*E*VERYONE DISCOVERS WITHIN HIMSELF AN AVERSION to what is good and a desire for what is evil.... Scripture takes particular notice of the heart and of the root and main source of all sins which is unbelief in the inmost heart.... Faith is a divine work in us. Oh, it is a living, creative, active, mighty thing, this faith.

Martin Luther

Luther shows that faith leads to love, and in the love of God we delight to keep all His laws with our new, regenerated nature. Then we experience the glorious liberty of the children of God, not because we are free of the law, but because the law of God now expresses how we want to act. We are at one with God and thus at one with the laws of His universe because the Spirit of Christ dwells in us.

Victory over sin depends upon our love for the Lord Jesus Christ. Love is power, and the love of Christ gives the power which makes a man competent, composed and serene, whatever the state in which he finds himself. To the end of life the struggle with temptation in one form or another goes on. Jesus warned us that each of us would need to take up his cross daily. Yet we, like Paul, can discover that through the love of Christ we can be adequate to every situation. We are not alone in the fight. His Spirit bears witness with our spirit.

Gordon Powell

Lord Jesus, each day may I remember the cross upon which You died for me. Such love is overwhelming, and I am deeply conscious of the many times mine is so shallow.

And the publican, standing afar off, would not lift up so much as his eyes unto heaven, but smote upon his breast, saying, God be merciful to me a sinner. Luke 18:13

S O MANY OF US HAVE COME TO FEEL that prayer, like the Christian life, is a moving passenger train that we ought to be aboard. We run and try to jump on, but through ineptness we fail to make the step. As in a nightmare we see that our efforts to cling are in vain, and we lose our grip. One by one we watch the cars pass us by. Other people find Jesus Christ, learn to pray, find victory in their lives, acquire a testimony, and move on, but we remain mute.

The prayers of others frequently frighten us, they are so artistically and fervently expressed; they fairly radiate joy and assurance. We become quite discouraged. Yet the one prayer that Jesus Christ honored above all others was the wail of a thieving tax collector: "God be merciful to me, a sinner." As Charles Spurgeon remarked from his London pulpit, "This publican had the soundest theology of any man in all England." He described himself as a sinner, and in the world of the Spirit what is a sinner? He is nothing. The New Testament was written not by men of spirit but by the Holy Spirit of God moving in men of nothing. *Sherwood Eliot Wirt*

I have sinned a great deal against my merciful heavenly Father since I was converted, and I have grieved Him a great deal during the many years that I have lived with Him. But the greatest sin that I have committed since my conversion, the way in which I have grieved my Lord the worst, is in connection with prayer, my neglect of prayer. This neglect is the cause of my many other sins of omission as well as of commission. *O. Hallesby*

Forgive me, Father, for neglecting so often my time of prayer. Help me to remember that wherever I am I can commune with You.

This is my commandment, that ye love one another, as I have loved you. John 15:12

*W*HERE DO YOU GET REPENTANCE? For me repentance comes as my response to overwhelming love from heaven. You put me in the light of Jesus Christ on the cross; then I can repent in reality.

The thief, newborn, experienced the "at homeness" of the cross. Because he was warmly accepted, he felt fully at home. We Christians —not Christ on the cross—are the ones who make it difficult for some to come into the family of God. We speak big words about love, but when it comes to putting our arms around someone we do not approve of, then it becomes another matter.

"That's different," you say.

But is it?

You give the excuse, "I don't like him."

No, you don't like him, but Jesus likes him. More than that, Jesus not only likes him, He loves him!

So you don't like someone whom Jesus loves. In a family it isn't a question of choosing the people you love or want there; you are stuck with them. The New Testament says that at the cross of Calvary you are brought by the power of Christ into a new relationship with all sorts of people—criminals, drunks, prostitutes. They all line up! You meet them because they are there.

If you find it hard to love another member of God's family, all you need is to make application to Headquarters and say, "Lord, I can't love that one, but I know You love him, so please give me Your love for him." If you do that, He will give you the love.   *Festo Kivengere*

> Love ever gives—
> Forgives—outlives—
> And ever stands
> With open hands.
> And while it loves,
> It gives.
> For this is Love's prerogative—
> To give, and give, and give.
>
> *John Oxenham*

Lord, at times I have not loved as You have commanded. Fill me with Your selfless love.

JANUARY 18

My meat is to do the will of him that sent me, and to finish his work. John 4:34

*I*F YOU GET A BIBLE AND START TO READ about Jesus Christ, you might be surprised to find in Him the true pattern for your own life. It happens to me many times. I get the feeling that I have goals that can be accomplished by my own efforts. Then I read about Jesus kneeling in prayer and realize that if Jesus—the Son of God, the Real Man—needed to pray, how much more do I. I am not sufficient without God. Or sometimes as a preacher I get lost in words and ideas and concepts. Then I look at Jesus, and what do I see? Jesus was involved with *people*. He didn't just preach about leprosy, He touched a leper. He didn't just lecture on hunger, He fed people who had empty stomachs.   *Leighton Ford*

Since my heart was touched at 17, I believe I have never awakened from sleep, in sickness or in health, by day or by night, without my first waking thought being how best I might serve my Lord.
                              Elizabeth Fry (English Victorian prison reformer)

Lord Jesus, help me to keep my eyes constantly on You, so that I may serve You and be sustained by Your Holy Spirit.

—→ JANUARY 19 —→

....be ye kind one to another.... Ephesians 4:32

---

*L*OOK AROUND YOU, FIRST IN YOUR OWN FAMILY, then among your friends and neighbors, and see whether there be not some one whose little burden you can lighten, whose little cares you may lessen, whose life pleasures you can promote, whose little wants and wishes you can gratify. Giving up cheerfully our own occupations to attend to others is one of the little kindnesses and self-denials. Doing little things that nobody likes to do, but which must be done by someone, is another. It may seem to many that if they avoid little unkindnesses they must necessarily be doing all that is right to their family and friends; but it is not enough to abstain from sharp words, sneering tones, petty contradiction, or daily little selfish cares; we must be active and earnest in kindness, not merely passive and inoffensive.   *Little Things*, 1852

Life is short. Who are the people in your life today who need to hear words of love rooted in current understanding of what is happening to and around them? The only way to keep our relationship with the Lord vital is to grasp the opportunities to express affirming love to others. Our prayers will soon become empty and shallow if we resist the impetus of His Spirit to love. *Lloyd John Ogilvie*

(Today let us think of the way we treat those close to us. Are we really Christlike in our everyday encounters?)

Father, help us to show our loved ones how much we care by our kindness and concern for them. Forgive the times we are short or unfeeling, Lord.

———————— • JANUARY 20 •———— ————

By pureness, by knowledge, by longsuffering, by kindness, by the Holy Ghost, by love unfeigned.... II Corinthians 6:6

◆————————————————————————◆

*D*EAR LORD, GIVE ME...THEM...SOMEBODY THE COURAGE to be kind.

That poor man who just got on the subway is so shabby, so talkative, so obviously confused. He doesn't know where to get off, but the woman he asked just gave him a cold stare and pointedly moved away. The man on the other side of him has turned his back.

Nobody will help him, Lord, and my heart hurts. It hurts so for him, but it's pounding for me too. I don't want to be conspicuous—to have them stare coldly at *me*. But oh, Lord, I know where he wants to go, and I can't stand it any longer. Please give me the courage to lean across the aisle, force a smile and signal with my lips and my fingers: "Three more stops."

And now, oh, Lord, give me even more courage, for he has lurched over to my side. He wants to talk—talk in a loud, eager voice about the job he's going to apply for and why it's important that he get there on time.

Yes, yes, he's been drinking, and he probably won't get it, poor guy. But thank You that I'm able to listen, to offer a little encouragement and to see that he doesn't miss his stop.

Thank You for his grateful handclasp at parting, his smile from the platform, his jaunty yet wistful wave. Thank You that I no longer care what the other passengers think, because my conscience is at rest and my heart is warm.

Please help him, Lord, and bless him. And thank You for giving me the simple courage to be kind. *Marjorie Holmes*

I am to become a Christ to my neighbor
and be for him what Christ is for me.

Martin Luther

Lord, sometimes I find my hesitancy to reach out to someone in need blocks Your love flowing through me. Forgive me, I pray.

—————————————→•→ **JANUARY 21** →•←————————————————

...the greatest of these is charity. I Corinthians 13:13

◆——◆

DO YOU REALLY WANT TO LOVE? Are you willing to be the "public utility," the town pump which is there for all to use? Do you really want to let Jesus be reincarnated in your humanity? Jesus is the "Man for others." If you give yourself to Him, He will immediately put you in the service of others in one way or another. Do you really want to volunteer for this life of loving? You can't do it on your own. He must do it in you. Will you have enough faith to release His power into your life? These are the only pertinent questions.

I am now deeply convinced that the power of love is from God. I believe that no one can truly love unless God is active within him. I hear Jesus say, "Without Me you can do nothing. You can bear no fruit. I am the vine, and you are the branches. Cut off from Me you are dead." I hear St. John say that only he who knows God can know the meaning of love. I hear St. Paul describe love as the highest and greatest gift of the Spirit. Wherever I have found love I have felt the presence of God, God at work in the minds and hearts and muscles of men. *John Powell, S.J.*

> May we and all who bear Thy name
> By gentle love Thy cross proclaim,
> The gift of peace on earth secure,
> And for Thy truth the world endure.
>
> *Author unknown*

Lord Jesus, invade my mind and heart and use me to help lessen another's sorrow.

—————————————→•→ **JANUARY 22** →•←————————————————

For I was an hungered, and ye gave me meat: I was thirsty, and ye gave me drink: I was a stranger, and ye took me in: naked, and ye clothed me: I was sick, and ye visited me: I was in prison, and ye came unto me. Matthew 25:35,36

◆——◆

VISITING THE SICK means that there will always be those who are sick. Feeding the hungry implies a personal involvement with someone who needs human and individual loving care, not just campaigning for a change of the political setup. Taking a stranger into one's home is quite different from giving money to keep a flophouse open. Going to a prison and visiting the people who are there is the only way we can visit the Lord in prison. The picture is powerful in its force, and we can't wiggle out of what it presents to us. However—with all there is to go on thinking about and praying about and searching our hearts and lives about in connection with this passage—we cannot miss the striking fact that Jesus says that the sick are to be cared for in some very personal way. We should check up on ourselves sometime: "Have I sent the Lord a card or a letter or a bunch of flowers in His sickness this week?" Day after day, week after week, instead of being tempted to say, "They shouldn't be so sick. What's *wrong* with their lives or their faith?" we are instead to be asking ourselves, "Have I failed to care *for the Lord* in some person's need when offered that opportunity?"   *Edith Schaeffer*

> I expect to pass through life but once.
> If, therefore, there be any kindness I
> can show, or any good thing I can do to
> any fellow-being, let me do it now, and
> not defer or neglect it, as I shall not
> pass this way again.   *William Penn*

(Each one of us can be used to minister to the needs of others. People are hurting and lonely in all communities.)

Lord, may I serve You in a very personal way through a soul who is in need today.

———————————— • **JANUARY 23** • ————————————

As we have therefore opportunity, let us do good unto all men.... Galatians 6:10

◆————————————————————————————————◆

*W*E MUST BE READY to allow ourselves to be interrupted by God. God will be constantly crossing our paths and canceling our plans by sending us people with claims and petitions. We may pass them by, preoccupied with our more important tasks, as the priest passed by the man who had fallen among thieves, perhaps—reading the Bible. When we do that we pass by the visible sign of the cross raised athwart our path to show us that, not our way, but God's way must be done. It is a strange fact that Christians and even ministers frequently consider their work so important and urgent that they will allow nothing to disturb them. They think they are doing God a service in this, but actually they are disdaining God's "crooked yet straight path" (Gottfried Arnold). They do not want a life that is crossed and balked. But it is part of the discipline of humility that we must not spare our hand where it can perform a service and that we do not assume that our schedule is our own to manage, but allow it to be arranged by God. *Dietrich Bonhoeffer*

It is thy duty oftentimes to do what thou wouldst not; thy duty, too, to leave undone what thou wouldst do. *Thomas à Kempis*

Almighty God, forgive me when I fail to see Your hand in the interruptions of the day. Teach me true humility, Lord.

➤ JANUARY 24 ◄

Not with eyeservice, as menpleasers; but as the servants of Christ, doing the will of God from the heart.... Ephesians 6:6

SEVERAL YEARS AGO MOTHER TERESA OF CALCUTTA, India, was introduced to an overflow congregation at Washington's National Presbyterian Church which included people from every part of Christendom. It was the first time this saintly Roman Catholic had ever spoken in a Protestant church.

A tiny Albanian woman of God, dressed in a simple unbleached muslin habit with bands of faded blue on the edges, Mother Teresa stood at the front of the sanctuary and spoke briefly on the work of the Sisters of Charity among the poorest of the poor who are dying each day in the slums of Calcutta. It was in the name of these same people that she would accept the Nobel Prize for Peace in 1979.

We were all melted down by the love that shone from the depths of her eyes and spread over her care-lined, yet joyful face. I was not the only one in the congregation with tears as I listened to her softly spoken words about how blessed it is to live in poverty and to share the suffering of God's children. And I'll never forget the perfect way she summed it up, putting to shame forever all "good works" that don't originate in the heart of God: "It is not that you serve the rich or the poor. It is the love you put into the doing." *Colleen Townsend Evans*

(Mother Teresa's example shines with the brilliance of Jesus' love. Might we give our lives to Him to serve the suffering in the world, especially those on our own doorsteps.)

Make us worthy, Lord, to serve our fellowman throughout the world who live and die in poverty and hunger. Give them through our hands their daily bread, and by our understanding give peace and joy.
Mother Teresa

⸺•► JANUARY 25 ◄•⸺

...that we should serve in newness of spirit....
Romans 7:6

*L*ET US BEGIN FROM THIS MOMENT to acknowledge Him in all our ways, and do everything, whatsoever we do, as service to Him and for His glory, depending upon Him alone for wisdom, and strength, and sweetness, and patience, and everything else that is necessary for the right accomplishing of all our living. It is not so much a change of acts that will be necessary, as a change of motive and of dependence. The house will be kept, or the children cared for, or the business transacted, perhaps, just the same as before as to the outward, but inwardly God will be acknowledged, and depended on, and served; and there will be all the difference between a life lived at ease in the glory of His presence, and a life lived painfully and with effort apart from Him. There will result also from this bringing of God into our affairs a wonderful accession of divine wisdom in the conduct of them, and a far greater quickness and despatch in their accomplishment, a surprising increase in the fertility of resource, and an enlargement on every side that will amaze the hitherto cramped and cabined soul. *Hannah Whitall Smith*

I once thought that my handicap had robbed me forever of a full life, but then I discovered that I had everything I needed to serve God. There is only one handicap in life I have learned. That is living without the knowledge of Jesus Christ. With Him, we have everything we need. *Joni Eareckson*

Lord Jesus, create in me a new awareness of my complete dependence on You.

⸺•► JANUARY 26 ◄•⸺

Jesus saith unto him, I am the way, the truth, and the life: no man cometh unto the Father, but by me. John 14:6

*H*E IS A PERSONAL CHRIST TO ME. He lives in me; and the way He walked, the way He lived, and the way He taught is a perfect example of the way I should walk, live and teach. I think the power He displayed on this earth can and will be displayed through those who have complete unity with Christ through the Holy Spirit. I believe that Jesus Christ is the Son of Man who came to earth to reconcile men to the Father. He is the Word, the answer to salvation, and the door to the Kingdom. Everything of any value in my life is surrounded by and tied up in Jesus Christ. The material things in life are valuable for a while, I guess, but that's not the value I'm looking for. I'm looking for the value of eternity and eternal life and salvation.

Hon. Harold E. Hughes

(Let us reaffirm our love and faith in Jesus Christ, our Savior and our Lord.)

Thanks be to Thee, my Lord Jesus Christ,
For all the benefits Thou hast given me,
For all the pains and insults Thou
hast borne for me.
O most merciful Redeemer, Friend, and
Brother,
May I know Thee more clearly,
May I love Thee more dearly,
May I follow Thee more nearly.

Twelfth-century prayer

JANUARY 27

He shall feed his flock like a shepherd.... Isaiah 40:11

---

*W*HO IS IT THAT IS YOUR SHEPHERD? The Lord! Oh, my friends, what a wonderful announcement! The Lord God of heaven and earth, the almighty Creator of all things, He who holds the universe in His hand as though it were a very little thing, He is your shepherd and has charged Himself with the care and keeping of you as a shepherd is charged with the care and keeping of his sheep. If your hearts could really take in this thought, you would never have a fear or a care again; for with such a shepherd, how could it be possible for you ever to want any good thing? *Hannah Whitall Smith*

When I was a small boy living in the San Joaquin Valley of California, my father brought home a little lamb. I think he bought it just for me. I used to get so exasperated with that lamb, trying to get it to lie down with its head in my lap. I learned that there is no way to get a sheep to lie down against its will. Yet if it has grass to eat and has its stomach filled, the sheep will automatically lie down.

The analogy is clear. The pasture to which our Great Shepherd leads us is the Word of God. When we feed on Him, we find contentment and rest of mind, of heart, of body. We confess our sin, we accept His forgiveness, He comes into our lives, we own Him as our Savior, and He gives us rest. Do you know that peace? It is not so much something that Christ gives as it is Christ Himself.

Cliff Barrows

Lord Jesus, tender Shepherd, I praise You for the peace You instill in me as You gently lead me.

━━━━ JANUARY 28 ━━━━

...walk in love, as Christ also hath loved us.... Ephesians 5:2

◆━━━━━━━━━━━━━━━━━━━━━━━━━━━━━━━━━━━━━━━◆

*I*F WE LIVE AS CHRIST LIVES, we will, as He did, give ourselves, for our whole life, to God, to be used by Him for men. When once we have done this, given ourselves, no more to seek anything for ourselves, but for men, and that to God, for Him to use us, and to impart to us what we can bestow on others, intercession will become to us, as it is in Christ in heaven, the great work of our life. And if ever the thought comes that the call is too high, or the work too great, the faith in Christ, the Interceding Christ, who lives in us, will give us the victory.

Andrew Murray

In 1895 Andrew Murray of South Africa was in England, and we were both guests in the same house. I knew that his books were very good, but was he as good as his books? He was better; for there was not only goodness, there was a delicious dry humor, dauntless courage, and the gentleness and simplicity of a dear child. And he was very loving. He never seemed to be tired of loving.

Amy Carmichael

(Andrew Murray reflected the love of his Savior. Do we, as loved ones, friends and neighbors encounter us?)

Lord Jesus, teach me to walk each step, each day, in Your love.

Who was delivered for our offenses, and was
raised again for our justification. Romans 4:25

J ESUS ENDURED GREAT HUMILIATION, and therefore there
was room for Him to be exalted. By that humiliation He accomplished and endured all the Father's will, and therefore He was rewarded by being raised to glory. He uses that exaltation on behalf of His people. Raise your eyes to these hills of glory, from where your help must come. Contemplate the high glories of the Prince and Savior. Is it not most hopeful for men that a Man is now on the throne of the universe? Is it not glorious that the Lord of all is the Savior of sinners? We have a Friend at court; yea, a Friend on the throne. He will use all His influence for those who entrust their affairs in His hands. Well does one of our poets sing:

> He ever lives to intercede
> Before His Father's face;
> Give Him, my soul, thy cause to plead,
> Nor doubt the Father's grace.

Come and commit your cause and your case to those once-pierced hands which are now glorified with the signet rings of royal power and honor. No suit ever failed which was left with this great Advocate.
C. H. Spurgeon

> What a friend we have in Jesus
> All our sins and griefs to bear!
> What a privilege to carry
> Everything to God in prayer!
> O what peace we often forfeit,
> O what needless pain we bear,
> All because we do not carry
> Everything to God in prayer. *Joseph Scriven*

Our Savior, we come to You to ask for Your intercession, knowing that You who have suffered such pain for us will hear and answer. Thank You, Lord.

...the very hairs of your head are all numbered. Matthew 10:30

I KNOW THAT CHRIST IS INTERESTED in every detail of my
daily life and of yours.
And why not?
If He has numbered the hairs of our heads...
   if He notes the sparrow's fall...
shall He not care about what we do every day and how we do it?
Most of us simply refuse to believe how practical God is.
He is ready to tell us what to say in an important conversation.
He is ready to help us make the right decision in a difficult choice.
He is ready to guide the hand of the surgeon,
   and the scissors of the housewife.
He is ready to give new strength to the tired servant standing over
   the kitchen sink.   *Peter Marshall*

He loves each one of us, as if there were
only one of us.   *Augustine*

*Lord Jesus Christ, we praise You for Your love that cares for all our
needs. The knowledge of this love strengthens our hearts.*

...he giveth more grace. James 4:6

O UR PAST, OUR CHILDHOOD, DOMINATES our future years—
how we react to certain situations, our ability to reach out to
others. But we cannot lean on our past; we should learn from it, but
not let it tear us down. All we confess to the Lord is forgiven and forgotten, just as David said in the Psalms:

As far as the east is from the west, so far
hath he removed our transgressions from us.
Like as a father pitieth his children, so
the Lord pitieth them that fear him. For
he knoweth our frame....   *Psalm 103:12-14*

Those last five words have been repeated by me over and over
again when stress has made me feel as if I were going to break again.
With a heart cry to God I have thanked Him that He is with me and

does know the extent to which this frame can be bent but not broken. I need to have His resiliency in my life so that the branches of my mind will not snap when the times come that make life difficult to bear.   *J.W.B.*

> Amazing grace! How sweet the sound—
> That saved a wretch like me!
> I once was lost but now am found,
> Was blind but now I see.
>
> 'Twas grace that taught my heart to fear,
> And grace my fears relieved;
> How precious did that grace appear
> The hour I first believed!
>
> The Lord has promised good to me,
> His word my hope secures;
> He will my shield and portion be
> As long as life endures.
>
> Through many dangers, toils, and snares,
> I have already come;
> 'Tis grace hath brought me safe thus far,
> And grace will lead me home.
>
> *John Newton*

Lord, when all around me at times seems so bleak, Your grace gives me hope and joy.

FEBRUARY 1

...in thy presence is fullness of joy.... Psalm 16:11

JOY DOESN'T MEAN WE ARE ALWAYS "UP." Second Corinthians 4:8-10 says, "We are pressed on every side by troubles, but not crushed and broken. We are perplexed because we don't know why things happen as they do, but we don't give up and quit. We are hunted down, but God never abandons us. We get knocked down, but we get up again and keep going. These bodies of ours are constantly facing death just as Jesus did; so it is clear to all that it is only the living Christ within [who keeps us safe]" (*TLB*).

Joy is knowing Him no matter what the circumstances of life. Let God make you new from the inside out. Let Him give you an indestructible joy. Let Him give you a quality of life so that you can enjoy all things.   *Jean Ford*

> He that comforts all that mourn
> Shall to joy your sorrow turn:
> Joy to know your sins forgiven,
> Joy to keep the way to heaven,
> Joy to win His welcome grace,
> Joy to see Him face to face.
>
> *Charles Wesley*

I praise You, Lord, for the abundance of Your joy that can never be destroyed. In times of sorrow and bereavement Your comfort brings me peace and hope.

———————— FEBRUARY 2 ————————

Rejoice evermore. I Thessalonians 5:16

◆——◆

*I*T IS EASY TO CONFUSE HAPPINESS WITH JOY. Happiness is produced by external circumstances; it can quickly disappear when someone bursts our bubble with an unkind word or deed. Joy comes from deep within, and no one can take it away. John 16:22 says, "You will rejoice; and no one can rob you of that joy" (*TLB*).

It's pretty hard to show happiness when a tooth aches or when a friend's death leaves a void in our lives, but even in such experiences we can know the joy of the Lord.

The British flag flies over Buckingham Palace to signify when the Queen is in residence. Joy should be the standard that identifies us as Christians and indicates that the King of kings resides within our hearts. Our joy should be so obvious to those around us that it is contagious. The face of the Christian should glow, to contrast sharply with the faces of despairing people who don't know Christ. "A joyful heart makes a cheery face," Solomon wrote in Proverbs 15:13. Complete joy is a 24-hour-a-day experience. Our zest for life should be evident from our waking moment on!   *Twila Knaack*

Joy is the gigantic secret of the Christian.   *G. K. Chesterton*

(Do others see the joy of Christ upon our face? Do we reflect this radiance to those we meet?)

Lord, no matter what the circumstances of this day, I know deep inside I have Your joy.

*When the Holy Spirit controls our lives
he will produce this kind of fruit in us:
love, joy, peace, patience, kindness, goodness,
faithfulness, gentleness and self-control.* Galatians 5:22-23 (TLB)

THOREAU WROTE, "IF A MAN DOES NOT KEEP PACE with his companions, perhaps it is because he hears a different drummer. Let him step to the music which he hears, however measured or far away." As Christians we have no alternative but to march to the drumbeat of the Holy Spirit, following the measured steps of goodness, which pleases God.

We can do good deeds, and by practicing principles of goodness can witness to those around us that we have something "different" in our lives—perhaps something they themselves would like to possess. We may even be able to show others how to practice the principles of goodness in their own lives. But the Bible says, "Your goodness is as a morning cloud, and as the early dew it goeth away" (Hosea 6:4). True goodness is a "fruit of the Spirit," and our efforts to achieve it in our own strength alone can never succeed.

We should be careful that any goodness the world may see in us is the genuine fruit of the Spirit and not a counterfeit substitute, lest we unwittingly lead someone astray.   *Billy Graham*

Every good gift is from God, and is given to many by the Holy Ghost. By nature there is in us no good thing. And there can be none: but so far as it is wrought in us by that good Spirit.   *John Wesley*

Lord, may I never forget that without Your Holy Spirit in my life I am nothing. Thank You for Your gifts that bring control to this wayward heart of mine.

...be filled with the Spirit.... Ephesians 5:18

I BELIEVE THAT THE DEVIL IS HAVING HIS HEYDAY NOW and although we see a mighty spiritual resurgence which has always been in history, there is the river of apostasy. The devil is on his last rampage before Jesus Christ comes back again.

Many years ago a man of God said, "Olford, remember this: Pray when you feel like it. Pray when you don't feel like it. Pray until you do feel like it." And I thank God for those wise words. That's warfare through the Holy Spirit.

My word to you is this: a Spirit-controlled worship; a Spirit-controlled welfare; a Spirit-controlled warfare; and a Spirit-controlled witness. Paul adds: "And (pray) for me, that utterance may be given unto me, that I may open my mouth boldly, to make known the mystery of the gospel, for which I am an ambassador in bonds: that therein I may speak boldly, as I ought to speak."

The Word of God commands a Spirit-filled life. Not to obey is a sin. The work of God demands it, whether it is in the church, in the home or in the world. The terms are simple: an initial acceptance of His control in my life, to be followed by a continued dependence upon His control in my life.

The tests? Your worship life will show it; your family life will show it; your warfare life will show it; your witness life will show it; and you will know what it is to be consciously, continuously and conspicuously filled with the Holy Spirit.   *Stephen F. Olford*

> Christ be with me, Christ before me, Christ behind me,
> Christ in me, Christ beneath me, Christ above me,
> Christ on my right, Christ on my left,
> Christ when I lie down, Christ when I sit down, Christ
>   when I arise.
> Christ in the heart of every man who thinks of me,
> Christ in the mouth of every one who speaks of me,
> Christ in every eye that sees me,
> Christ in every ear that hears me.
>
>   *St. Patrick*

Lord, I long for a completely Spirit-filled life. Help me shed the debris that impoverishes my soul.

———→ FEBRUARY 5 →———

...we are more than conquerors through him that loved us. Romans 8:37

◆————————————————————————◆

*B*EING FILLED WITH THE HOLY SPIRIT is just the opposite of sin. In Galatians 5:22 it says the fruit of the Holy Spirit is "love, joy, peace, longsuffering, gentleness, goodness, faith, meekness, temperance." This is the wonderful sanctification which the Holy Spirit is accomplishing in you and me.

In Ephesians 6 we read of the armor of God. This tells us that we do not have victory once and for all: we still need armor. But God's armor is so strong! If you read correctly you will see that it is the Lord Jesus Himself. He is our peace and our truth. He is in you, you in Him. There still will be battles to be fought, but now in a blessed circle: The devil attacks us and we may fall, but we rise again. We have forgiveness and cleansing. The path is leading upward and will be more and more victorious. The Lord Jesus is going to make you more than a conqueror! *Corrie ten Boom*

The Holy Spirit has been given to every child of God to be his life. He dwells in him, not as a separate Being in one part of his nature, but as his very life. He is the divine power or energy by which his life is maintained and strengthened. All that a believer is called to be or to do, the Holy Spirit can and will work in him. If he does not know or yield to the Holy Guest, the Blessed Spirit cannot work, and his life is a sickly one, full of failure and of sin. As he yields, and waits, and obeys the leading of the Spirit, God works in him all that is pleasing in His sight. *Andrew Murray*

Yielded lives are ones the Lord's power can flow through; Corrie ten Boom and Andrew Murray are shining examples. May *we* know such yieldedness.

Father, encircle me with Your Holy Spirit and search my heart, for I would be yielded to You. Thank You for the victory we have through Your presence.

FEBRUARY 6

...he saith unto him, Wilt thou be made whole? John 5:6

IN JESUS' LIFE HERE ON EARTH, there was always concern and love for the individual. "A certain man" who had been ill for 38 years had come to the pool of Bethesda at a time when an angel was supposed to "trouble" the waters. The people believed that whoever was lowered into the water first would be healed. Somehow this "certain man" had managed to get to the pool, but he had no one to help him into the water. Perhaps he had had someone who had been willing to take him there but could not wait for the angel. This man had been ill so long, they were probably tired of trying to help him—he was very much alone.

What a pathetic sight it must have been as Jesus approached that day. Crowds of people—sick, blind, lame, and paralyzed—all waiting, hoping that they would be healed. Into this assembly of desperate, heartweary, suffering people came Jesus and this lonely, seemingly forgotten man stood out to Him. He went over and healed him instantly—the love and concern of Jesus Christ for someone who had no one.   *J.W.B.*

> To those who fall, how kind Thou art;
> How good to those who seek;
> But what to those who find? Ah, this
> Nor tongue nor pen can show:
> The love of Jesus, what it is,
> None but His loved ones know.
>
> *Bernard of Clairvaux*

Lord Jesus, Your compassion for others humbles me. Your kindness and love fill me with a desire to help those who are alone and longing for love. Lead me to them, Lord.

FEBRUARY 7

Bear ye one another's burdens, and so fulfill the law of Christ. Galatians 6:2

JESUS SAID TO PETER, "Simon, Simon, behold, Satan hath desired to have you, that he may sift you as wheat: but I have prayed for thee, that thy faith fail not: and when thou art converted, strengthen thy brethren." In the composite life of the family of God we have resources that we don't have in any other way, and we are therefore to strengthen one another in the Lord. When we bear one another's burdens we are thus fulfilling the law of Christ. The emphasis is upon Christian love, bearing one another's burdens, living with sensitivity, and sharing that which people have to endure in this world.

"Bear ye one another's burdens, and so fulfill the law of Christ." "For every man shall bear his own burden." These are not contradictory; they are complementary and speak two sides of the same thing to us. In the family of God we need to be reminded of these basic spiritual principles. They are laws given to us by the Apostle Paul that bring us mutual self-support in the body of Christ. May it be so for His name's sake.   *Harold J. Ockenga*

Mutual love the token be,
Lord, that we belong to Thee:
Love, Thine image, love impart;
Stamp it on our face and heart....

Lord, make me more sensitive to the burdens of those around me who are hurting, I pray.

⟶ FEBRUARY 8 ⟵

...the Lord direct your hearts into the love of God.... II Thessalonians 3:5

T O LOVE AT ALL IS TO BE VULNERABLE. Love anything and your heart will certainly be wrung and possibly be broken. If you want to make sure of keeping it intact, you must give your heart to no one, not even to an animal. Wrap it carefully round with hobbies and little luxuries; avoid all entanglements; lock it up safe in the casket or coffin of your selfishness. But in that casket—safe, dark, motionless, airless—it will change. It will not be broken; it will become unbreakable, impenetrable, irredeemable....

The only place outside heaven where you can be perfectly safe from all the dangers and perturbations of love is hell.   *C. S. Lewis*

Strive to love your neighbor actively and indefatigably. In as far as you advance in love you will grow surer of the reality of God and of the immortality of your soul. If you attain to perfect self-forgetfulness in the love of your neighbor, then you will believe without doubt, and no doubt can possibly enter your soul....   *Feodor Dostoevski*

Father, Your heart was broken for us as You gave Your Son for our sin. May we not count the cost of loving in our own lives.

⟶ FEBRUARY 9 ⟵

Hatred stirreth up strifes: but love covereth all sins. Proverbs 10:12

T HERE ARE TIMES WHEN I BECOME SO ANGRY with a person that I want to say, "Get lost! You've had it!" That's the natural part of me—the limit of my human love. Then I remember how many times I've done some idiotic thing, the times I've hurt people, or the way I've misused the creation. Yet God still loves me. He hasn't crossed me off His list, so how can I cross anybody off my list? Can't I see that when a person hurts me, he does it out of his need, his insecurity, or his pain? What good will it do for me to react to his behavior? He needs some firm ground to stand on, some resources to fill his empty bucket. Something outside of me says, "There's another way to live—keep going back in love."

It isn't easy, it isn't natural to me, and I certainly can't claim the accomplishment for my own, but many times I am able to react in love when ordinarily I would reject in anger. The important thing is that my affirmation makes a difference not only in the life of the person who has hurt me but in my own life as well.   *Louis H. Evans, Jr.*

Instead of allowing yourself to be unhappy, just let your love grow as God wants it to grow. Seek goodness in others. Love more persons more. Love them more impersonally, more unselfishly, without thought of return. The return, never fear, will take care of itself.
Henry Drummond

God, take away the selfish motives in my relationships with others and let me love them unrestrainedly.

FEBRUARY 10

Beloved, let us love one another: for love is of God.... I John 4:7

---

*O*NE OF THE MOST BEAUTIFUL WOMEN I HAVE EVER KNOWN was my husband's grandmother. When I first met her she was almost 90 years old...tiny, fragile, with one of the most elegantly boned faces I've ever seen. But at 90 it's not your face or your frame that counts. It's your soul...the way you've lived, the feelings you've known, the thoughts that have passed through your mind. They're what show. And Grandmother Egly's beauty came from deep inside her.

I can picture her now the way she was when I first saw her...sitting in the kitchen, which was the busiest place in the house, darning a sock for someone. And as any of the family members passed by, she would look up and say, "And what can I do for *you* today?" This was not just a chance remark—it was the theme of her life.

When I think of love being constructive, I think of Grandmother Egly. She didn't just sit back, waiting for someone's need to fall into her lap. She was eager to love...she wanted to help...and she looked for the things that needed doing. This is the way Paul describes God's love for us, and he urges the Corinthians—and us—to let this love work its way through us and into the lives of others. Too often human love says, "You got yourself into this, now get yourself out!"... "Help yourself!"..."You can do it if you try." God's love knows no such limitations. It is love on the offensive...love offering itself, not waiting to be asked. It asks, "What can I do for *you* today?"

Colleen Townsend Evans

No one is useless in the world who lightens the burden of it for anyone else.

Charles Dickens

Lord, what can I do for You today? Whatever the task, may it be done with the eagerness and purity of Your love.

FEBRUARY 11

Owe no man any thing, but to love one another: for he that loveth another hath fulfilled the law. Romans 13:8

---

*I*N THE NEW TESTAMENT, Christians are told to love those who treat them badly. That's because our world is starving for the taste of genuine love. I'm not talking about soap-opera love where "I love you" usually means "I love me and want what you can give." I'm not even talking about "brotherly love." For "If you love those who love you, what credit is that to you?...Even 'sinners' do that" (Luke 6:32-33). What I *am* talking about is love that costs, love that gives until it hurts—even when it knows it won't get anything in return. In order for the world to see that kind of love, they need to see Christians who dare to follow Christ's example. And what was the example Christ set? He loved even those who flogged Him and beat Him.

Joni Eareckson

Contemplate the love of Christ, and you will love. Stand before that mirror, reflect Christ's character, and you will be changed into the same image from tenderness to tenderness. There is no other way. You cannot love to order. You can only look at the lovely object, and fall in love with it, and grow into likeness to it. And to look at this Perfect Character, this Perfect Life. Look at the great sacrifice as He laid down Himself, all through life, and upon the cross of Calvary; and you must love Him. And loving Him, you must become like Him. Love begets love.

Henry Drummond

Lord Jesus, You gave of Yourself all Your life, even the supreme sacrifice of the cross. Such love demands mine, and I love You wholeheartedly, beloved Savior.

Herein is love, not that we loved God,
but that he loved us, and sent his Son
to be the propitiation for our sins. I John 4:10

*I*S IT TRUE THAT GOD IS LOVE to me as a Christian? And does
the love of God mean all that has been said? If so, certain questions arise.

Why do I ever grumble and show discontent and resentment at the
circumstances in which God has placed me?

Why am I ever distrustful, fearful, or depressed?

Why do I ever allow myself to grow cool, formal, and halfhearted
in the service of the God who loves me so?

Why do I ever allow my loyalties to be divided so that God has not
all my heart?

John wrote that "God is love" in order to make an ethical point, "if
God so loved us, we also ought to love one another" (I John 4:11).
Could an observer learn from the quality and degree of love that I
show to others—my wife? my husband? my family? my neighbors?
people at church? people at work?—anything at all about the greatness of God's love to me?

Meditate upon these things. Examine yourself. *J. I. Packer*

The measure of a Christian is not in the height of his grasp, but in
the depth of his love. *Clarence Jordan*

Lord, I know I am "found wanting" when I look at the depth of my
love for others. Forgive me and fill me with Your love and grace.

Jesus said unto him, Thou shalt love the Lord
thy God with all thy heart, and with
all thy soul, and with all thy mind. Matthew 22:37

*F*RANKLY, I SEE NO PROSPECT of our even wanting to obey the
second commandment seriously until we have begun to obey
the first. We don't really see other men and women as our brothers
and sisters simply by talking airily about the brotherhood of man.
We only see them as such when we begin to get a vision of God the
Father. It is so fatally easy to talk highfalutin' hot air about all the
world being "one big family" and yet fail to "get on" with the mem-

bers of our own families, or with those who live next door, or in the (apartment) above us. In sober fact, men do not really love their fellows, except their own particular friends, until they have seriously begun to love God. It is only then that we learn to drop the destructive attitude of hatred and contempt and criticism, and begin to adopt the constructive attitude of Christian love. So, then, the second reason for the command to love God being "the first and great commandment" is that we don't really keep the second until we have obeyed the first.   *J. B. Phillips*

> Love is the lesson which the
> Lord us taught.   *Edmund Spenser*

Almighty God, teach me in all my ways to love You. May others see Your love in me as I minister through the power of my heavenly Father.

--------------------- **FEBRUARY 14** ---------------------

In whom we have redemption through his blood, even the forgiveness of sins.... Colossians 1:14

◆ ─── ◆

*T*O BE A LOVER IS TO LET GOD FORGIVE US! We hold the awesome power to refuse or receive. Our forgiveness has been settled once and for all on the cross. We do not confess in order to be forgiven, but because we have been already. If we allow God to forgive us, we will feel a burst of gratitude. How can we thank Him for forgiving us? Jesus told us. What we do and say to others we do and say to Him. The way the woman cared for Jesus is the way we are to care for people. We will never be able to do enough. Costly involvement, listening with love, forgiveness as we have been forgiven, second chances when they are least deserved, sacrificial giving of our resources for practical help, sharing the hope we have discovered in the Gospel—all are ways to anoint the feet of Jesus.

That's how to be a lover. The more our Lord forgives us, the more we will become sensitive, compassionate, open and forgiving lovers. Our world desperately needs people whose gratitude has made them communicators of grace.   *Lloyd John Ogilvie*

(May we always be grateful for Jesus' love and forgiveness.)

> *I praise Thee while my days go on;*
> *I love Thee while my days go on:*
> *Through dark and dearth, through fire and frost,*
> *With emptied arms and treasure lost,*
> *I thank Thee while my days go on.*
>
>   *E. B. Browning*

These things I command you, that you
love one another. John 15:17

◆——◆

*C*HRIST'S LOVE IS THE INITIATORY KIND OF LOVE. We must work creatively to find ways to express that kind of caring to those people with whom we are supposed to be in love.

Another love aid that I have established is the regular habit of praying for our family members before I fall to sleep each night. It is an activity that insures loving feelings. I remember their little crises as well as their large ones. I concentrate on their personality development, their spiritual, emotional, physical, and social growth. I talk to the Lord about my attitudes toward them.

Regularly, He gives me a tender heart. I love my husband more each night when I fall asleep than I have loved him that day. I am reminded of the special beauties of each of these my family members. I know something more of the commendation in Ephesians—why husbands were told to love their wives as Christ loved the church. There must be something sacramental in all our extended relationships, something of God, lest they fail. My evening prayers are the time when I implore God to be with me in my loving.

Karen Burton Mains

We ought daily or weekly to dedicate a little time to the reckoning up of the virtues of our belongings—wife, children, friends—and contemplating them then in a beautiful collection. And we should do so now, that we may not pardon and love in vain and too late, after the beloved one has been taken away from us to a better world.

Jean Paul Richter

My Lord Jesus, help me to find opportunities to love more deeply
and expressively those who mean so much to me.

———————————•→ **FEBRUARY 16** →•———————————

And thou shalt love the Lord thy God
with all thine heart, and with all thy soul,
and with all thy might. Deuteronomy 6:5

◆——◆

*Y*OU CANNOT KNOW GOD AND NOT LOVE HIM. To know Him is to love Him. The person who is born of the Spirit takes hold of the Spirit, appreciates the Spirit, and knows God; and the knowledge of God is always the birth of love in the soul.

The man born of the Spirit holds with a loose hand the things of the world. He is not careless about flowers; he loves them because they are sacramental symbols of the infinite touch of his Father. He is not careless of the birds; he loves them because they sound in his listening ear tones of the music of the Father's home.

G. Campbell Morgan

> Let us with a gladsome mind
> Praise the Lord, for He is kind:
> For His mercies aye endure,
> Ever faithful, ever sure.
>
> All things living He doth feed;
> His full hand supplies their need:
> For His mercies aye endure,
> Ever faithful, ever sure.

John Milton

Lord God, how we love You and Your creation. Each day we see evidence of the glory of Your faithfulness and provision.

FEBRUARY 17

I am come that they might have life, and that they might have it more abundantly. John 10:10

◆───◆

*T*O LOVE ABUNDANTLY IS TO LIVE ABUNDANTLY, and to love for ever is to live for ever. Hence, eternal life is inextricably bound up with Love. We want to live for ever for the same reason that we want to live tomorrow. Why do you want to live tomorrow? It is because there is someone who loves you and whom you want to see tomorrow, and be with, and love back. There is no other reason why we should live on than that we love and are beloved. It is when a man has no one to love him that he commits suicide. So long as he has friends, those who love him and whom he loves, he will live; because to live is to love. Be it but the love of a dog, it will keep him in life; but let that go and he has no contact with life, no reason to live. The "energy of life" has failed. Eternal life also is to know God, and God is Love. This is Christ's own definition. Ponder it. "This is life eternal, that they might know Thee the only true God, and Jesus Christ whom Thou hast sent." Love must be eternal. It is what God is.

Henry Drummond

His love for me is greater far
Than distance to a shining star,
Priceless as a golden treasure,
Scopeless and beyond all measure,
Deeper than the deepest sea,
Timeless as eternity.

Fred Bauer

Lord Jesus, I praise You for Your eternal love that encircles me and brings me indescribable joy.

FEBRUARY 18

...the Lord stood with me, and strengthened me....
II Timothy 4:17

T HE GOD WHO MADE OUR BODIES IS CONCERNED about the needs of our bodies, and He is anxious for us to talk with Him about our physical needs.

Every morning the sun rises to warm the earth. If it were to fail to shine for just one minute, all life on the earth would die. The rains come to water the earth. There is fertility in the soil, life in the seeds, oxygen in the air. The providence of God is about us in unbelievable abundance every moment. But so often we just take it for granted.

With infinite love and compassion our Lord understood the human predicament. He had deep empathy with people; He saw their needs, their weaknesses, their desires, and their hurts. He understood and was concerned for people. Every word He spoke was uttered because He saw a need for that word in some human life. His concern was always to uplift and never to tear down, to heal and never hurt, to save and not condemn. *Charles L. Allen*

He is so infinitely blessed, that every perception of His blissful presence imparts a vital gladness to the heart. Every degree of approach to Him is, in the same proportion, a degree of happiness. And I often think that were He always present to our mind, as we are present to Him, there would be no pain, nor sense of misery.
Susanna Wesley

Thank You, God, for being with me whenever I need Your strength. I know I am not alone, and my heart rejoices.

FEBRUARY 19

In the multitude of my thoughts within me thy comforts delight my soul. Psalm 94:19

*H*OW BIG IS GOD? He is the *God of destiny*. It is He who determines the outcome of history and who stands in the shadows keeping watch over His own.

Men and nations may parade grandly across the stage of history, but they do not determine the course of either life or death. The curtain of history will be drawn, not by man, but by God.

How big is God? Look about you and see the evidence of His wisdom and power. If a man claims to be an artist, one has the right to ask to see his pictures. If he says he is an architect, one wants to see something he has designed; if an athlete, to see his prowess; if an inventor, to see his product.

Look at the heavens, the moon and the stars. Look at the earth, all the marvels of God's creative power. Look at His Son and Calvary. Look in His Word and all it reveals. Look into the innermost reaches of your troubled soul and hear Him speak peace. You will get an inkling of how great He is.

How big is God? He can never be measured by earthly standards, but on every hand we see signs of His glory. God is a Spirit, and we can grasp what this means only when we worship Him in spirit and in truth. Although He is nearer than hands or feet, yet He encompasses all of time and eternity.

Staggering? Of course. But, oh, how comforting to those who know Him!

L. Nelson Bell

Where there is faith, there is love;
Where there is love, there is peace;
Where there is peace, there is God;
And where there is God, there is no need.

Leo Tolstoy

Our Father, the knowledge of the enormity of Your power and creation amazes me! You, who have made heaven and earth, love me and the wonder of this fact comforts and brings joy to my soul.

FEBRUARY 20

He said, "I am the true vine, and my Father is the husbandman. ...Abide in me, and I in you. As the branch cannot bear fruit of itself, except it abide in the vine, no more can ye, except ye abide in me." John 15:1,4

*T*O ABIDE IN HIM IS TO LIVE, but to be separated is to dry up and die. Peace is part of abiding. It is a by-product. He calls us to that resting position in Himself not to dominate us but to live through us. The One who does not panic or fear wants to live in us. He is the same One who is coming again. What He gives now is forever. It doesn't diminish, it increases.

Getting peace and keeping it is not luck or a gift that only some have, or something determined by "fate." It centers on one truth—Jesus Christ. He is the source of it. To have Him is to have peace, and to have peace is to enjoy the daily walk that means abundant living with all the purpose and happiness that He intended us to have. Some people will miss it, and that's too bad because no one has to.

One thing is certain—you don't have to miss it. And maybe it's time now to find a quiet place alone where you can drop to your knees and tell Him what He has been waiting too long already to hear: "Take me, Lord Jesus, into the center of Your will."

Living in Jesus you will not only know the will of God for your life, you will have Life itself in the center of His will. There really is no other place to be.   *Roger C. Palms*

"Rest in the Lord; wait patiently for Him." In Hebrew, "Be silent to God, and let Him mold thee." Keep still, and He will mold thee to the right shape.   *Martin Luther*

Lord, teach me to be still. Bring me into a deeper walk with You, where I can be completely in Your will. Mold me, Lord.

FEBRUARY 21

Henceforth I call you not servants; for the servant knoweth not what his lord doeth: but I have called you friends.... John 15:15

I HAVE FOUND A GREAT MANY KIND FRIENDS, but Jesus is the best. He understands me so well, and has such a way of putting up with my frailties, and has promised to do so much for me, when all other loved ones swim away from my vision, and I can no more laugh with them over their joys or cry with them over their sorrows. Oh! when a man has trouble, he needs friends. When a man loses property, he needs all those of his acquaintances who have lost property to come in with their sympathy. When bereavement comes to a household, it is a comfort to have others who have been bereaved come in and sympathize. God is a sympathetic Friend. Oh, the tenderness of divine friendship.

Thomas De Witt Talmadge

The Christian should never forget that he has a Friend who stands by him, a Friend who knows all about fear because He "set His face to go to Jerusalem," aware that the cross and death were waiting for Him there. The faith that this risen Christ is beside him and that He is quite capable of controlling the future whatever evil may come, is a source of serenity and courage to many a humble Christian believer.

Gordon Powell

Jesus, thank You for the peace that Your friendship brings. You, having suffered for my sin, know the depths of my heartache. I praise You for Your love which brings solace to my soul.

--------- **FEBRUARY 22** --------

[The Father]...*hath delivered us from the power of darkness, and hath translated us into the kingdom of his dear Son....*

Colossians 1:13

*I*T IS THE KINGDOM OF LIGHT. We are no longer in the old realm of confusion separating us from each other.

The rule of that Kingdom is love, for God is love. Fences we had built are smashed down by the power of the Holy Spirit. We find that we are closer to one another, having our hearts tuned to the love of Christ and our eyes focused on the person of Christ.

The shortest way to each other is through the cross of our Lord and Savior Jesus Christ.

Let us read on. In this Christ "we have redemption and forgiveness of sin." There you are. The forgiving attitude is the rule of the Kingdom.

This is how you keep fresh, dear brethren. You keep fresh by repenting of the things which tend to isolate brothers and sisters in this Kingdom. Forgiveness is provided.

There is forgiveness of sins, and there is redemption. He puts them both together. It is a provision made for you and for me.

Festo Kivengere

Thou hast made us for Thyself, and our hearts are restless until they rest in Thee.

Augustine

Lord Jesus, forgive me for so many things, especially for not loving or forgiving others. Cleanse my heart, Lord, and let me find rest in the light of Your abiding love.

***...ye shall know that I am in my Father,
and ye in me, and I in you.*** John 14:20

*I*N A MISSIONARY GROUP IN INDIA was a young American woman who testified: "I came to India because my husband was called, but inwardly I rebelled, and when I went on board ship I felt I was leaving life behind me in the States. But one evening while out walking I found Christ on the Indian road. From that day to this I have felt that I would not mind if He sent me to the loneliest island of the South Seas. *He* is life. I didn't leave life behind me in America. I have it."

Certainly she had it, because she had *Him*—and He had her! Now she could say with Paul, "The love of Christ constraineth me." She had tapped the power of the extra motive. And the result? Life was no longer mean, stunted, frustrated, but released, abounding, overflowing.

"What more are you doing than others?" It's that "more" which Christ supplies. It's that "more" for which the world is looking.

Paul S. Rees

> Him evermore I behold
> Walking in Galilee,
> Through the cornfield's waving gold,
> In hamlet or grassy wold,
> By the shores of the Beautiful Sea.
> He toucheth the sightless eyes;
> Before Him the demons flee;
> To the dead He sayeth: Arise!
> To the living: Follow Me!
> And that voice still soundeth on
> From the centuries that are gone,
> To the centuries that shall be!

Henry Wadsworth Longfellow

Lord Jesus Christ, I would follow You no matter where You lead. If it means being content where I am or serving You in a distant place, make me completely surrendered to Your will.

***...where the Spirit of the Lord is,
there is liberty.*** II Corinthians 3:17

*A*LL DURING HIS MINISTRY, PAUL BATTLED "the false brethren who come to spy out our liberty in Christ Jesus" by setting up moral and ritualistic restrictions.

Augustine was right:

Christ's way is "Love God, and do as you please."

As you grow to love God, what you "please" will change. This is where the surprise comes in. God gives the inner man a new set of goals and passions. It would be bondage indeed to obey God when we do not want to; it is delightful freedom to do what we most want to do. And that is the wonderful way that God works it out for us.

Peter Marshall

> Consider
> The lilies of the field, whose bloom is brief—
> We are like they;
> Like them we fade away,
> As doth a leaf.
>
> Consider
> The sparrows of the air, of small account:
> Our God doth view
> Whether they fall or mount—
> He guards us too.
>
> Consider
> The lilies, that do neither spin nor toil,
> Yet are most fair—
> What profits all His care,
> And all this toil?
>
> Consider
> The birds, that have no barn nor harvest-weeks:
> God gives them food—
> Much more our Father seeks
> To do us good.

Christina Rossetti

Lord, thank You for the freedom of being in Your will.

FEBRUARY 25

...Go in peace: and the God of Israel grant thee thy petition that thou hast asked of him. I Samuel 1:17

*F*AITH IS THE HELP AGAINST ALL DISCOURAGEMENTS. Hoping, trusting, waiting on God, is the special, if not the only, means appointed against all discouragements. "I had fainted," says David, "unless I had believed to see the goodness of the Lord in the land of the living." Faith bears up the heart against all discouragements.

What is it to hope in God, to trust in God, and to wait on Him? I answer that to hope in God is to expect help from God; to trust in God is to rely or rest upon God for help; and to wait on Him is to continue and abide in this expectation or reliance. Trusting in God is the recumbency of the soul upon God in Christ for some good thing that lies out of sight.

You know how it was with Hannah, when she had received a word from God: "She went away" (says the text) "and looked no more sorrowful." Her heart was quieted, for she had a word from God; and though before she was a woman of sorrowful spirit, yet having received a word from God, and believing that word, her heart was quiet. *William Bridge*

Open all the doors and windows of your soul to the Lord. Don't keep any rooms locked or closed off to Him. Let Jesus take over. The depth of the faith that releases the power of God is measured by your willingness to let God direct your life. Raise yourself up to Him as a gift. Surrender your life and your heart to Him. *John Powell, S.J.*

Almighty God, may this life of mine be completely surrendered to Your Son; then my heart, like Hannah's, will be at peace.

FEBRUARY 26

For God so loved the world, that he gave his only begotten Son, that whosoever believeth in him should not perish, but have everlasting life. John 3:16

*I*T'S A TERRIBLE WORLD TO LOOK OUT ON TODAY if you see only the human factors, only men and nations desperately trying to work out a precarious salvation. What a lost and crazy world it is, with its strange mingling of technological affluence and achievement on the one hand and spiritual impoverishment and famine on the other, and with its demonic playing with nuclear fire and the devilry of biological warfare! Certainly there would seem to be ample grounds for fatalism, cynicism, despair.

But a Christian, looking out on the darkened scene, retains unshadowed confidence because he knows there is another factor in the field and a greater will constantly and unwearyingly at work: the immense pressure of a transcendent penetrating energy that fills the universe and every detail of creation. "God so loved," said Jesus—not just one favored segment of the human race, not Israel or the Church, not the well-meaning or the spiritually minded—"God so loved the world." Time enough to despair of history when the Creator God who brought history into being has abdicated the throne. Time enough to start losing heart when Christ the Word incarnate confesses that His passion was a blunder and the truth He taught a lie. Till then, son of man, stand upon your feet, believing in the divine initiative and recognizing the unslumbering pressure in every instant of a supreme and sovereign Grace. For God has chosen this world to be at last the Kingdom of His Son. *James S. Stewart*

...The real hinge of history is Jesus Christ. *Charles Malik*

Father, thank You for loving this world so much that You gave Your Son. I am at peace in this turbulent time of history because one day I know He is coming back. Praise His name!

———————————•— **FEBRUARY 27** —•———————————

I beseech you therefore, brethren, by the mercies of God, that ye present your bodies a living sacrifice, holy, acceptable unto God.... Romans 12:1

◆——————————————————————————————◆

*W*HEN WE ANTICIPATE SEEING SOMEONE WE LOVE who has been separated from us, how wonderful it is to know that we are going to be with that person again. We have so much to look forward to—there is something in the future that is going to bring us happiness. The *great* promise is that each day we can expect Jesus to return. We should always have that expectancy, that hope of seeing Him.

I often meet people who say, "Life is meaningless and empty. I have nothing to look forward to." I can empathize with these people, for once I felt like they do. Then the living Christ came into my life and brought His joy. Now no matter what problems there are to face, no matter how desperate the situation, there is the underlying knowledge that He is with me and one day I shall see Him face to face.

With Jesus Christ, life is no longer meaningless! His anticipated return is *fact!* Because of this, there are questions that none of us can avoid if we want to be ready for His arrival:

Is He Master and Lord of my life?
Will we be ready for that day when "every knee shall bow"?

J.W.B.

> *Teach us, Master, how to give*
> *All we have and are to Thee;*
> *Grant us, Savior, while we live,*
> *Wholly, only Thine to be.*

Frances Ridley Havergal

FEBRUARY 28

...*by love serve one another.* Galatians 5:13

THERE IS THE SERVICE OF BEARING THE BURDENS of each other. "Bear one another's burdens, and so fulfill the law of Christ" (Galatians 6:2). The "law of Christ" is the law of love, the "royal law" as James called it (James 2:8). Love is most perfectly fulfilled when we bear the hurts and sufferings of each other, weeping with those who weep.

If we care we will learn to bear their sorrows. I say "learn" because this, too, is a discipline to be mastered. Most of us too easily assume that all we need to do is decide to bear the burdens of others and we can do it. Then we try it for a time and soon the joy of life has left and we are heavy with the sorrows of others. It does not need to be so. We can learn to uphold the burdens of others without ourselves being destroyed by them. Jesus, who bore the burdens of the whole world, could say, "My yoke is easy, and my burden is light" (Matthew 11:30). Can we learn to lift the sorrows and pains of others into the tender arms of Jesus so that our burden is lighter? Of course we can. But it takes some practice, so rather than dashing out to bear the burdens of the whole world, let's begin more humbly. Begin in some small corner somewhere and learn. Jesus will be your Teacher.

Richard J. Foster

The glory is not in the task, but in the doing of it for Him.

Jean Ingelow

So often, Lord, our eyes are on distant multitudes when we should also be constantly aware of the needy, lonely people nearby. Show me them, Lord.

*For therefore we both labor and suffer
reproach, because we trust in the living
God, who is the Savior of all men....* I Timothy 4:10

◆————————————————————————◆

HOW MANY TIMES HAVE WE FELT OUR HEARTS PIERCED with deep sorrow as we have endeavored to serve our Lord? We have felt wounded, misunderstood. To abandon our task seemed desirable, the easy way out tempting.

As we read of the lives of the saints, we see that they too experienced hardships as they ministered for Jesus Christ. Amy Carmichael's poem "No Scars?" speaks to us today. Her ministry in India was paved with sorrows and conflicts, yet she saw in them the gentle discipling of her Lord and identified with His suffering. She knew that when she had been through the crucible of suffering like Job, she would "come forth like gold." *J.W.B.*

Hast thou no scar?
No hidden scar on foot, or side, or hand?
I hear thee sung as mighty in the land,
I hear them hail thy bright ascendant star,
Hast thou no scar?

Hast thou no wound?
Yet I was wounded by the archers, spent,
Leaned Me against a tree to die; and rent
By ravening beasts that compassed Me, I swooned:
Hast thou no wound?

No wound? no scar?
Yet, as the Master shall the servant be,
And pierced are the feet that follow Me.
But thine are whole: can he have followed far
Who has nor wound nor scar?

Amy Carmichael

Lord Jesus, when I consider Your scars for me, the "wounds" I experience as I labor to serve You are superficial. Gladly will I serve You, loving Savior.

———————•→ **MARCH 1** ←•———————

**Withhold not good from them to whom
it is due....** Proverbs 3:27

*W*E ARE LIVING IN A DAY when the Lord's people need encouragement—in the world, in the church, and in our own lives. Discouragement is one of the weapons the enemy uses to blunt our effectiveness in Christian service and to hinder our progress in our Christian discipleship.

There is scriptural support for this ministry of encouragement. Barnabas is the outstanding example in the Word of God of one who encouraged. He was the "son of encouragement." *Paraklesis* is the Greek word. It is translated "consolation" or "comfort," but its basic meaning is this: "one who is called to the side of another to give comfort and encouragement."

If you will study the life of Barnabas, you will find that this is true throughout his life. Even when he failed he was still trying to encourage. We find that in every relationship he was a man who lived true to his name, who encouraged.   A. Jack Dain

Count That Day Lost

If you sit down at set of sun
And count the acts that you have done,
   And counting find
One self-denying deed, one word
That eased the heart of him who heard;
   One glance most kind,
That fell like sunshine where it went—
Then you may count that day well spent.

George Eliot

Father, help me to be like Barnabas—encouraging, loving, caring. There are so many opportunities; do not let me fail You.

―――――――――――――――― **MARCH 2** ―――――――――――――――

And you also are joined with him and with each other by the Spirit, and are part of this dwelling place of God. Ephesians 2:22, *TLB*

*A*FTER WORLD WAR II, German students volunteered to help rebuild a cathedral in England, one of many casualties of the Luftwaffe bombings. As the work progressed, debate broke out on how to best restore a large statue of Jesus with His arms outstretched and bearing the familiar inscription, "Come unto Me." Careful patching could repair all damage to the statue except for Christ's hands, which had been destroyed by bomb fragments. Should they attempt the delicate task of reshaping those hands?

Finally the workers reached a decision that still stands today. The statue of Jesus has no hands, and the inscription now reads, "Christ has no hands but ours." *Paul Brand and Philip Yancey*

(We may feel there is so little we can accomplish for our Lord, when all the time He is waiting patiently for our willingness to serve Him.)

Take my hands, and let them move
At the impulse of Thy love.

Take my feet, and let them be
Swift and "beautiful" for Thee.

Take my intellect, and use
Every power as Thou shalt choose.

Frances Ridley Havergal

MARCH 3

He hath showed thee, O man, what is good; ; and what doth the Lord require of thee, but to do justly, and to love mercy, and to walk humbly with thy God? Micah 6:8

◆————————————————————————————————◆

T HE TRUE MARK OF THE MAN AND WOMAN in whom God's life flows freely is their innocence of their own inspiration. There is a beautiful, relaxed, quiet gentleness about the personality permeated by God's Spirit. One of the most outstanding hallmarks is the absence of abrasiveness or pride of personal prestige. Instead the attitude of mercy and compassion to others, accompanied by a genuine empathy, marks such people.

God places enormous emphasis upon this aspect of the Christian's behavior. Not only does He desire to see it expressed in the conduct of His followers, but, even more than that, *He insists on it.*

W. Phillip Keller

There is no true and constant gentleness without humility; while we are so fond of ourselves, we are easily offended with others. Let us be persuaded that nothing is due to us, and then nothing will disturb us. Let us often think of our own infirmities, and we shall become indulgent toward those of others. *Fénelon*

Lord Jesus, may my eyes always be upon You and may Your gentle, loving, compassionate nature infill my longing heart.

*In whom we have redemption through his blood,
the forgiveness of sins, according to the
riches of his grace....* Ephesians 1:7

◆ ———————————————————————————— ◆

*J*ESUS CHRIST WAS TOO REALISTIC...
             knew human nature too well,
not to realize that each of us is tempted.
Not one of us remains untainted by impurity of deed or thought.

And so in God's eyes the pure vessel is not only that which
remains untouched.
Pure is the vessel also which the Master has cleansed...
   in whom His Spirit abides to keep us cleansed.
Else He could never have forgiven and accepted
                 Mary of Magdala...
             Zacchaeus...
           the woman taken in adultery...
          the Gadarene demoniac...
        Joanna, the wife of Herod's steward, Chuza,
         the woman with the alabaster box of ointment....
He is the only One who claims to be able to forgive and to cleanse.

Peter Marshall

         He bought me:
         body, soul, all,
         and I am so free
         in my captivity
         that I hardly can believe
         He bought me.

         Not with gold or silver,
         nor even with kingdoms,
         but body for body,
         soul for soul,
         He bought me.

         So not as the world loves
         do I love Him
         but with the love
         that He gave
         when He bought me.

Janice Barfield

Lord, forgive the many times my actions do not deserve Your great sacrifice. Your love shines into my often capricious heart and shows me my willfulness.

Hereby perceive we the love of God,
because he laid down his life for us.... I John 3:16

---

*H*E WAS HOLY, HUMBLE, harmless, meek and merciful when among us, to teach us what we should be when He was gone. And yet He is among us still, and in us too, a living and perpetual preacher of the same grace by His Spirit in our consciences.

To be like Christ, then, is to be a Christian. And regeneration is the only way to the Kingdom of God, which we pray for. Let us today therefore hear His voice and not harden our hearts, who speaks to us in many ways: in the Scriptures, in our hearts, by His servants and providences. And the sum of all is holiness and charity.

Men may tire themselves in a labyrinth of search, and talk of God; but if we would know Him indeed it must be from the impressions we receive of Him; and the softer our hearts are, the deeper and livelier those will be upon us. Some folk think they may scold, rail, hate, rob, and kill too, so it be but for God's sake. But nothing in us unlike Him can please Him.

Let us then try what love will do. For if men do once see we love them, we should soon find they would not harm us. Force may subdue, but love gains; and he that forgives first wins the laurel. If I am even with my enemy, the debt is paid; but if I forgive it I oblige him forever. He that lives in love lives in God, says the beloved disciple. And to be sure a man can live nowhere better. Love is above all; and when it prevails in us all we shall all be lovely, and in love with God and one with another.   *William Penn*

Love is the one thing that still stands when all else has fallen.... Love has no equal as a spiritual gift. Tongues cease, knowledge becomes obsolete, wisdom passes away, as do all other gifts. Only love goes with us from this world into the next...because God is love. Love is stronger than death...it transcends death...yes, love is eternal!

Eternal...but not impossible...for this *agape* love is meant to be part of our lives now, here on earth, as well as hereafter. It is not beyond our mortal reach...it is the meaning and the mission of life itself...it makes possible our communication with each other...it enables us to understand what is going on in the heart of another person...it provides us with the spiritual energy to live our lives as He wants us to live—in spite of stress, without bitterness, seeking only to give more because we are receiving so much. *Colleen Townsend Evans*

Lord Jesus, whenever my thoughts return to the days when You walked this earth, I see You loving. Lord, teach me to love, I pray.

MARCH 6

To the praise of the glory of his grace, wherein he hath made us accepted in the beloved. Ephesians 1:6

THE STORY IS TOLD OF A MAN who once booked his passage on a steamer to Florida. It cost him nearly all he had and being, as he thought, a wise man, he laid out his money in provisions. He purchased bread and cheese, it was all he could afford, to see him through the journey. It was a meagre fare, but beggars cannot be choosers, and he made the best of the situation. But after a few days the bread became stale and the cheese moldy, and, worse, still three times a day he inhaled appetizing odours from the kitchen which nearly drove him frantic. Finally, the day before the journey ended, he met a steward carrying a great plate of roast turkey.

The very sight of it made him reckless. "See here," he cried, "how much will a dinner like that cost?" "Cost, sir," replied the steward, "why nothing, it's all paid for in your passage!"

And if someone says, "What a silly story," my reply is that I can tell you something far more foolish. There are Christians living on spiritual stale bread and moldy cheese when they might be enjoying roast turkey from heaven! It's all included in the passage. Then lay hold, why live below your privileges? Read the first chapter of the Epistle to the Ephesians and see what an inheritance is yours. Go through the New Testament and underline the promises and then lay hold of them. *A. Lindsay Glegg*

A man can accept what Christ has done without knowing how it works; indeed, he certainly won't know how it works until he's accepted it. *C. S. Lewis*

Lord Jesus, I thank You for the costly inheritance given to me, unworthy as I am. Your promises of love, forgiveness and eternal life I accept gratefully.

*What the law could not do because human nature
was weak, God did.* Romans 8:3 *(TEV)*

•————————————————————————————•

G OD HAS DONE IT! That is the whole point of Christianity! *God has done it!* The law could not do it because it was "weak through the flesh." If one remembers nothing else, he must remember this—that *God has done it.* The flesh could not do it. The Bible holds out no encouragement whatever to the flesh. There is not a verse, not a sentence, not a line, not a word, in Scripture that will generate confidence in the flesh. "The flesh profiteth nothing." The life God requires is more than difficult to live; it is *impossible* to live.

There is no man or woman who by his own effort can live the Christian life. The only one who is able to live the life required by God is the Son of God Himself. The whole point of Christian faith is that He will live this life in and through the man who consents to Him. By the farthest reach of the imagination, by all the struggle and effort of which a man is capable, he himself will never come close to living the life or following the example of Jesus Christ. The man who is trying to live the Christian life by his own power is failing by the very fact that he is trying to do so.

From Genesis to Revelation, from cover to cover, the Bible declares that God is the initiator, the aggressor in redemption, but it does not stop there. He also is the sustainer and the finisher of redemption. Paul sums it up in these words: "Being confident of this very thing, that he which hath begun a good work in you will perform it until the day of Jesus Christ" (Philippians 1:6).   *Richard C. Halverson*

Let one more attest:
I have seen God's hand through a lifetime
And all was for best.

Robert Browning

Lord Jesus, how thankful I am that I do not have to try to live the Christian life. It is by Your strength that I can achieve it.

*And this gospel of the kingdom shall be preached
in all the world for a witness unto all nations;
and then shall the end come.* Matthew 24:14

A MISSIONARY ACQUAINTANCE OF MINE was working in Indochina shortly before the fall of Dien Bien Phu. He was taken captive by a band of Communist guerrillas and held for several weeks. During this period he became very friendly with their young officer and taught him English by means of the Bible.

Toward the end of this time they sat discussing an impending operation in which the guerrillas were going up against tremendous odds. When the missionary pointed out that he might die, the officer thought for a moment and then said quietly, "I would gladly die if I could advance the cause of Communism one more mile." Then he made this telling comment, "You know, as you have read to me from the Bible I have come to believe that you Christians have a greater message than that of Communism. But I believe that we are going to win the world, for Christianity means something to you, but Communism means everything to us."

Such dedication should strike us to the heart. While the emissaries of big business, the missionaries of Islam and other resurgent religions, and the evangelists of Communism are probing the ends of the earth, how long can we who know Christ hold our peace?

Leighton Ford

(We need total dedication to win our world for Jesus Christ. Some have given their lives. As we read the words of one, Betty Scott Stam, who was martyred for her belief, let us rededicate all we are and ever will be to our Savior.)

Open my eyes, that I may see
This one and that one needing Thee:
Hearts that are dumb, unsatisfied;
Lives that are dark, for whom Christ died.
Open my eyes in sympathy
Clear into man's deep soul to see;
Wise with Thy wisdom to discern,
And with Thy heart of love to yearn.
Open my eyes in power, I pray.
Give me the strength to speak today,
Someone to bring, dear Lord, to Thee;
Use me, O Lord, use even me.

But **there is** *forgiveness with thee....* Psalm 130:4

*I*N ENGLAND A SENSITIVE BOY JOINED THE BRITISH ARMY, but when the shot and shell began to fly, he deserted. In time he became a great astronomer and discovered a new planet. He was sent for by King George, but the man realized that his life was forfeit to the king for his desertion. The king knew him too; what would he do? Before the king would see him, the man was requested to open an envelope. It was his royal pardon. The king brought him in and said, "Now we can talk, and you shall come up and live at Windsor Castle." He was Sir William Herschel.

William Herschel was guilty and did not deny it! But King George had mercy upon him and made him a member of the royal household. That is what God promises to do for us. "And he will have mercy upon him...for he will abundantly pardon." To all of us poor, lost, wanton sinners the Bible says, "For God sent not his Son into the world to condemn the world; but that the world through him might be saved."

Billy Graham

> Long my imprisoned spirit lay
> Fast bound in sin and nature's night;
> Thine eye diffused a quickening ray—
> I woke, the dungeon flamed with light:
> My chains fell off, my heart was free,
> I rose, went forth, and followed Thee.
>
> *Charles Wesley*

Lord Jesus, for the weight of guilt that has been lifted from my burdened soul, I praise You.

Let your light so shine before men, that they may see your good works, and glorify your Father which is in heaven. Matthew 5:16

*W*E CAN SAY ONE OF TWO THINGS when we hit a difficult spot. We can pray, "Save me from" or "Glorify Thyself." If we learn to ask God to help us to glorify Him in life's situations instead of seeking escape, life takes on purpose and meaning.

James 1 says, "Let patience have her perfect work." William Barclay points out that the word *patience* is much too weak a translation. It means literally "the ability to take a tragedy and turn it into a glory." Perhaps that is what God is asking you to do, and by His grace you can. Not only that, but if you will be an eager pupil and take notes on the things that He is teaching you through each experience, you will come out like Moses who after 120 years could say: "O Lord God, thou hast begun to show thy servant thy greatness." Think of it! After 120 years things were just beginning for Moses. *Ruth Bell Graham*

The crosses of the present moment always bring their own special grace and consequent comfort with them; we see the hand of God in them when it is laid upon us. But the crosses of anxious foreboding are seen out of the dispensation of God; we see them without grace to bear them; we see them indeed through a faithless spirit which banishes grace. So, everything in them is bitter and unendurable; all seems dark and helpless. Let us throw self aside; no more self-interest, and then God's will, unfolding every moment in everything, will console us also every moment for all that He shall do around us, or within us, for our discipline. *Fénelon*

Almighty God, help me to transcend the sorrows in my life and turn them into glories for You.

MARCH 11

The Lord is my shepherd; I shall not want. Psalm 23:1

SHORTLY BEFORE HER DEATH in February of 1971, my mother did an oil painting for me. It has become a silent "friend" of mine, a mute yet eloquent expression of my calling. It is a picture of a shepherd with his sheep. The man is standing all alone with his crook in his hand, facing the hillside with sheep here and there. You cannot see the shepherd's face, but the little woolies surrounding him have personalities all their own. Some have the appearance of being devoted and loving, one looks independent and stubborn, another is starting to wander in the distance. But the shepherd is there with his flock, faithfully and diligently tending them.

The rather large piece of art hangs in my study with a light above it. There are occasions when I am bone weary after a huge day of people demands, preaching, and close contact with the Fullerton flock. Occasionally on days like this, I will turn off my desk lamp and my light overhead and leave on only the light on that unique painting. It helps me keep my perspective. It is a reminder...a simple, silent affirmation that I am right where God wants me, doing the very things He wants me to do. There is something very encouraging about taking a final look at the shepherd with his sheep at the end of my day. *Charles R. Swindoll*

> The little sharp vexations
>   And the briars that cut the feet,
> Why not take all to the Helper
>   Who has never failed us yet?
> Tell Him about the heartache,
>   And tell Him the longings too,
> Tell Him the baffled purpose
>   When we scarce know what to do.
> Then, leaving all our weakness
>   With the One divinely strong,
> Forget that we bore the burden
>   And carry away the song.
>
> *Phillips Brooks*

My Lord, my Shepherd, I rest content within Your loving care.

MARCH 12

Great peace have they which love thy law: and nothing shall offend them. Psalm 119:165

◆———————————————————————————◆

*W*E ARE TOLD IN PSALM 119:165 that peace is the gift of God. He has a formula for peace. His formula is in the Person of His Son, Jesus Christ, whom He has designated as Prince of Peace. The nations of this world have rejected the peace that God offers. They plan and build for war. Yet there are millions of people around the world who do have peace at this moment because they have found the secret of peace. They have peace in their hearts, as the Bible teaches: "Being justified by faith, we have peace with God through our Lord Jesus Christ."

The real war in which men are engaged is a war of rebellion against God. This rebellion has brought about destruction, suffering, misery, frustration and a thousand and one ills to the population of the world. God longs to see this rebellion cease. He has sent His Son, Jesus Christ, to the cross as a demonstration of His love and mercy. He asks us to come to that cross in repentance of our sins and submission of our will to Him. He promises a peace treaty for all who will come by faith. *Billy Graham*

Be still, my soul! thy God doth undertake
To guide the future as He has the past.
Thy hope, thy confidence let nothing shake;
All now mysterious shall be bright at last.
Be still, my soul! the waves and winds still know
His voice who ruled them while He dwelt below.

Katharina von Schlegel

Lord, Your peace turns this turbulent soul of mine into one that knows the calm of Your love and mercy.

━━•► MARCH 13 ◄•━━

God will tenderly comfort you when you undergo these same sufferings. II Corinthians 1:7 (*TLB*)

◆━━◆

C. H. SPURGEON, PRINCE OF PREACHERS, wrote and preached a great deal about suffering, merited and unmerited, and of the sufficiency of God's grace when the godly are called upon to suffer. Yet this marvelous winner of souls, toward the close of his remarkable ministry, never knew a day without physical pain. On the large pulpit of his London church was a couch where he lay during the preliminary part of the service conducted by a helper and prayed for strength and grace from on high to preach the Gospel as only he could. Then, having delivered his soul, back to the couch he went. We can imagine hundreds of the congregation asking why God allowed His most faithful and useful servant to suffer so, when he was so bent on honoring Him by life, lip, and literature.

How true it is that some of the choicest saints on earth are often among the greatest sufferers! Fanny Crosby, the famous hymn writer, had to sit in darkness during nearly all of her long, devoted life. Yet the unforgettable hymns of this blind hymnist reveal no sign of complaint. *Herbert Lockyer*

O what a happy soul am I!
Although I cannot see,
I am resolved that in this world
Contented I will be;
How many blessings I enjoy
That other people don't!
To weep and sigh because I'm blind,
I cannot, and I won't.

Fanny Crosby

Father, thank You for the tender comfort that comes during suffering. May we always be content in You.

Well done, thou good and faithful servant.... Matthew 25:21

*W*HEN WE MEET HIM FACE TO FACE, our suffering will have given us at least a *tiny* taste of what He went through to purchase our redemption. We will appreciate Him so much more. And our loyalty in those sufferings will give us something to offer Him in return. For what proof could we bring of our love and faithfulness if this life had left us totally unscarred? What shame would we feel if our Christianity had cost us nothing? Suffering prepares us to meet God.

And suffering does one more thing. If in our trials we are faithful, *they win for us rich rewards in heaven.* "For our light and momentary troubles are achieving for us an eternal glory that far outweighs them all" (II Corinthians 4:17). It's not merely that heaven will be a wonderful place *in spite* of all our sufferings while on earth. Actually, it will be that way *because* of them. My wheelchair, unpleasant as it may be, is what God uses to change my attitudes and make me more faithful to Him. The more faithful I am to Him, the more rewards will be stored up for me in heaven. And so our earthly sufferings don't just aid us today; they will serve us in eternity.   *Joni Eareckson*

> Face to face with Christ my Savior,
> Face to face—what will it be—
> When with rapture I behold Him,
> Jesus Christ who died for me?

> Face to face I shall behold Him,
> Far beyond the starry sky;
> Face to face in all His glory,
> I shall see Him by and by!
>
> *Carrie E. Beck*

Lord Jesus, it is enough to know I shall see You. My sufferings are worth the joy I shall one day know. Even now there is joy serving You, my Savior.

Watch ye, stand fast in the faith,
quit you like men, be strong. I Corinthians 16:13

*O*UR CROSS IS THE PAIN involved in doing the will of God. That aspect is being lost sight of: we say that after sanctification all is a delight. Was Paul's life all delight? Was our Lord's life all delight? Discipleship means we are identified with His interests, and we have to "fill up that which is behind of the afflictions of Christ." Only when we have been identified with our Lord can we begin to understand what our cross means.

Matthew 10:16-39 needs to be re-read because we are apt to think that Jesus Christ took all the bitterness and we get all the blessing. It is true that we get the blessing, but we must never forget that the wine of life is made out of crushed grapes. To follow Jesus will involve bruising in the lives of the disciples as the purpose of God did in His own life. The thing that makes us whimper is that we will look for justice. If you look for justice in your Christian work you will soon put yourself in a bandage and give way to self-pity and discouragement. Never look for justice, but never cease to give it; and never allow anything you meet with to sour your relationship to people through Jesus Christ. "Love...as I have loved you."   *Oswald Chambers*

Jesus hath many lovers of His Kingdom, but few bearers of His cross. All are disposed to rejoice with Him, but few suffer sorrow for His sake. Many follow Him to the breaking of the bread, but few to the drinking of His bitter cup.   *Thomas à Kempis*

Lord, let me continually remember how You were treated, for my sake, as each day I encounter "bruising" in my relationship with others. Forgive any self-pity, Jesus.

―――――――――――――――•◦ **MARCH 16** ◦•―――――――――――――――

Is not this the carpenter...? Mark 6:3

*W*HAT WAS CHRIST DOING in the carpenter's shop? Practicing. Though perfect, we read that He *learned* obedience, He *increased* in wisdom and in favor with God and man. Do not quarrel therefore with your lot in life. Do not complain of its never ceasing cares, its petty environment, the vexations you have to stand, the small and sordid souls you have to live and work with. Above all, do not resent temptations; do not be perplexed because it seems to thicken round you more and more, and ceases neither for effort nor for agony nor prayer. That is the practice which God appoints you; and it is having its work in making you patient, and humble, and generous, and unselfish, and kind and courteous. Do not grudge the hand that is molding the still too shapeless image within you.   *Henry Drummond*

> Earth changes, but thy soul and God stand sure:
>> What entered into thee,
>> That was, is, and shall be:
> Time's wheel runs back or stops:
>> Potter and clay endure.

Robert Browning

Lord Jesus, mold me and make me a vessel worthy of Your love.

⊷ MARCH 17 ⊶

...be thankful unto him, and bless his name. Psalm 100:4

◆───◆

*A*T THE LAST SUPPER OUR LORD TOOK A CUP and said, "...Drink of it, all of you; for this is my blood of the covenant, which is poured out for many for the forgiveness of sins" (Matthew 26:27,28, *RSV*).

He was fulfilling the first great covenant God made with mankind —that one day out of the seed of Abraham every nation on earth should be blessed. Thank God for that covenant!

And He was fulfilling a new covenant that God had promised through Jeremiah when He said, "And no longer shall each man teach his neighbor and each his brother, saying, 'Know the Lord,' for they shall all know me, from the least of them to the greatest, says the Lord; for I will forgive their iniquity, and I will remember their sin no more" (31:32, *RSV*). Thank God for *that* covenant-making God! He desires all of us to drink of the same cup—to be a covenant-making people.

"By this all men will know that you are my disciples, if you have love for one another" (John 13:35, *RSV*). I know of nothing that the world is more hungry for than covenant love. This is our chance! "The whole creation is on tiptoe to see the wonderful sight of the sons of God coming into their own" (Romans 8:19, *Phillips*).

Thank God for His creative love!   *Louis H. Evans, Jr.*

(May we pledge to love others with an affirming love as Jesus loved us. In doing so we will delight Him. First, let us look within our lives and ask the Lord for true gratitude.)

> *O Thou who has given so much to us,*
> *give us one thing more, a grateful*
> *heart; for Christ's sake. Amen.*

George Herbert (1593-1633)

I sought the Lord, and he heard me.... Psalm 34:4

*A*NDREW MURRAY SAYS: It is one of the terrible marks of the diseased state of the Christian life in these days, *that there are so many that rest content without the distinct experience of answered prayer.* They *pray daily*, but know little of direct, definite *answer to prayer as the rule of their daily life.*

And it is this the Father wills. He seeks daily intercourse with His children in *listening to and granting* their petitions. He wills that I should come to Him day by day with distinct requests. He wills day by day to do for me what I ask.

There may be cases in which the answer is a refusal, but our Father lets His child know when He cannot give him what he requests, and like the Son in Gethsemane, he will withdraw his petition.

Whether the request be according to His will or not, God will by His Word and His Spirit *teach those who are teachable* and who will give Him time. Let us withdraw our requests, if they are not according to God's mind, or persevere until the answer comes.

Prayer is appointed to obtain the answer!

It is in prayer and its answer that *the interchange of love between the Father and His child takes place.*

Are *your* prayers answered?　　　　　　　　　*Mrs. Charles E. Cowman*

Prayer is not flight; prayer is power. Prayer does not deliver a man from some terrible situation; prayer enables a man to face and to master the situation.　　　　　　　　　　　　　　*William Barclay*

My Father, this time of prayer with You is very dear to my heart. I know I am Your child and whatever is best for me You will give in answer to my requests.

And when they had plaited a crown of thorns,
they put it upon his head.... Matthew 27:29

*A*S THE DAYS APPROACHED THAT FIRST GOOD FRIDAY, Jesus suffered indescribable agony. In the garden of Gethsemane He wrestled in prayer to God: "Father, if thou be willing, remove this cup from me: nevertheless not my will, but thine, be done" (Luke 22:42). The Scripture continues: "And being in agony he prayed more earnestly: and his sweat was as it were great drops of blood falling down to the ground" (v. 44).

Jesus knew the suffering He would have to face upon that cross. He knew He would have to endure the reviling, the cruel taunts of the mob, the unbelievable suffering at the hands of the soldiers. He also knew that this was why He had come into the world—that there was no one else who could pay the price of our sin and, in one of the greatest acts of humility, He willingly went to a shameful death for you and me.   *J.W.B.*

> But His lone cross and crown of thorns
> Endure when crowns and empires fall.
> The might of His undying love
> In dying conquered all.
>
> *John Oxenham*

Beloved Savior, even though You knew the suffering You would face upon the cross, You went willingly for us. Our hearts are awed by such love.

MARCH 20

I pray for them: I pray not for the world, but for them which thou hast given me; for they are thine. John 17:9

*H*EROES ARE PARADIGMS. They show us what strength or courage or purity actually *looks* like.

Jesus was a hero in that sense. He showed us, in ordinary, everyday terms, what courage looked like. Consider a moment on His last night before the crucifixion. After praying the great prayer of John 17 —a prayer for all of us—He had gone with the disciples to the accustomed place, a peaceful garden, where Judas knew he could find Him. Judas arrived with the guard and officers provided by Jesus' archenemies, the chief priests and Pharisees. They came with lanterns and torches and weapons. A man's natural instinct would be to flee or hide.

Jesus, fully realizing all that was going to happen to Him, went forward and said to them, "'Who are you looking for?'" It was a demonstration of quiet courage, born of the knowledge that He was held by the sovereign will of His Father. It was a purely and thoroughly *manly* act.

Jesus was far more than a hero. He was Himself the Way, the Truth, and the Life. "For me to live," Paul said, "is Christ...." That truth is radical and transforming. *Elisabeth Elliot*

The fact of Jesus' coming is the final and unanswerable proof that God cares. *William Barclay*

Savior, Your transforming sacrifice for me gives courage to confront the daily cares of this life. I am victorious in You, Lord. I praise Your name!

➤ MARCH 21 ◆

...he will guide you.... John 16:13

◆—————————————————————————————————◆

*J*ESUS SUFFERED *TEMPTATION AND PAIN* before us; our *sicknesses* He bare; *weariness*—He has endured it, for, weary He sat by the well; *poverty*—He knows it, for sometimes He had not bread to eat, save that bread of which the world knows nothing; *to be houseless*—He knew that, too, for the foxes had holes and the birds of the air had nests, but He had not where to lay His head.

My fellow Christian, there is no place where thou canst go, where Christ has not been before thee—sinful place alone excepted. *He hath been before thee;* He hath smoothed the way; He hath entered the grave, that He might make the tomb the royal bedchamber of the ransomed race, the closet where they lay beside the garments of labour to put on the vestments of eternal rest.

In all places whithersoever we go, the Angel of the covenant has been our forerunner. Each burden we have to carry has once been laid on the shoulders of Immanuel. *Charles H. Spurgeon*

> All those who journey, soon or late,
> Must pass within the garden's gate;
> Must kneel alone in darkness there,
> And battle with some fierce despair.
> God pity those who cannot say:
> "Not mine but thine"; who only pray:
> "Let this cup pass," and cannot see
> The purpose in Gethsemane.
> *Ella Wheeler Wilcox*

Guide me, Lord, as I come to You in prayer. Teach me true, unquestioning obedience as I seek Your will.

I have been crucified with Christ: and I myself
no longer live, but Christ lives in me. Galatians 2:20 (*TLB*)

*W*HETHER IT IS THE NEW BIRTH or a return to the Father after falling away, the child coming home does just that, he comes home. With nothing in his hand, like a child, he waits, ready to receive forgiveness.

And when we receive that forgiveness, we become people for God to love when once we were people to oppose. And, being people loved, we love Him with everything that is within us.

Never again will we want to do anything that will separate us from His love. That's why having been close and wandered away and then returned again, we know that He and He alone is our source of love, joy and peace. We will no longer try to determine the direction of our own lives. It is the living God and Him alone who plans our lives and lives within us each day.

Believing that makes us new people.

We are no longer confused about who we are. We are His.

We no longer wonder were we are going; we are going with Him. And that puts depth to the query, "What about my tomorrows?"

Roger C. Palms

You have trusted Him in a few things, and He has not failed you. Trust Him now for everything, and see if He does not do for you exceedingly abundantly above all that you could ever have asked for or thought, not according to your power or capacity, but according to His own mighty power, that will work in you all the good pleasure of His most blessed will. *Hannah Whitall Smith*

Father, teach me to trust You in everything. Help me to comprehend Your amazing love that is guiding me each and every day. I will not fear tomorrow.

...and yet I am not alone, because the
Father is with me. John 16:32

*I*T WAS WHILE SUFFERING ON HIS CROSS that Jesus had a sense of being forsaken that will never be experienced by any true follower of His. The Father was always with Him—until that excruciating moment when Jesus cried with a loud voice, "My God, my God, why hast thou forsaken me?" (Matthew 27:46). As Jesus hung on that cross, the Father had to turn from His Son in order that the Son could experience and bear our sins in His death.

That forsakenness will never be ours. We who deserve to be forsaken by the holy God will never be — because Jesus, who had never sinned, undeservedly bore that sin for us. We will never be forsaken as Jesus was — for us.

Evelyn Christenson

> I come to the garden alone,
> While the dew is still on the roses;
> And the voice I hear falling on my ear,
> The Son of God discloses.
>
> And He walks with me, and He talks with me,
> And He tells me I am His own;
> And the joy we share as we tarry there,
> None other has ever known.

C. Austin Miles

Father, thank You for never forsaking me. When clouds come into my life I will remember You have not left me alone. Your holy presence remains.

———————— **MARCH 24** ————————

Then Jesus, crying with a loud voice, said, "Father, into thy hands I commit my spirit!" Luke 23:46 (*RSV*)

CARROLL S. RINGGOLD WRITES OF A WHITE CROSS which stood on the outskirts of a city. A young boy was lost in the city. A policeman asked, "Where do you live? Just tell me where you live." But the boy did not know his address. Finally, upon further questioning, the small boy said, "Take me to the cross on the hillside, and I can find my way home from there."

So God has placed a cross at the center of the centuries. And as we find the cross we find our way home again, here and hereafter. The cross is the bulletin board on which God nailed His message of redemption.

John M. Drescher

The thing that steadied Christ's life was the thought that He was going to His Father. This one thing gave it unity, and harmony, and success. During His whole life He never forgot His Word for one moment. There is no sermon of His where it does not occur; there is no prayer, however brief, where it is missed.... "The Great Name" was always hovering on His lips, or bursting out of His heart.

Henry Drummond

Father, each day brings me closer to my heavenly home, and I see before me the cross of Jesus. It is in His name I know I will be worthy to stand before You.

MARCH 25

...and the Lord hath laid on him the iniquity of us all. Isaiah 53:6

◆ ── ◆

T HE INIQUITY OF US ALL LAID ON HIM! That's what was so totally finished on the cross. That's why Christ cried out, "It is finished." The full payment for sin rested upon Christ.

And in that moment, Christ, separated from God the Father by our sins, cried out, "My God, my God, why hast thou forsaken me?" God can have no fellowship with sin, even when it is His only begotten Son hanging there beneath sin's monstrous burden. That's what Christ did for us. Divine atonement. We accept that when we accept Him as Lord.

Jeannette Clift

There is a green hill far away,
    Outside a city wall,
Where the dear Lord was crucified,
    Who died to save us all.

We may not know, we cannot tell
    What pains He had to bear,
But we believe it was for us
    He hung and suffered there.

Oh, dearly, dearly He has loved,
    And we must love Him too,
And trust in His redeeming blood,
    And try His works to do.

He died that we might be forgiven,
    He died to make us good,
That we might go at last to heaven,
    Saved by His precious blood.

There was no other good enough
    To pay the price of sin;
He only could unlock the gate
    Of heaven and let us in.

Cecil Frances Alexander

Lord Jesus, Your cross brings me forgiveness, and I am humbled by Your suffering for my atonement.

Blessed are the poor in spirit: for theirs
is the kingdom of heaven. Matthew 5:3

*T*HE MORE WE CONCENTRATE our gaze on the cross, the more clearly this beatitude speaks to us. The way of the cross is not a velvet carpet for a prince of the Church, nor is it a *Via Appia* for the triumphant conqueror. It is a poor way, an unfriendly and deserted way, soiled with blood, sweat, and tears. It is a way that breaks down even a man's spiritual vitality and leaves him at the end of his tether. It leads not to self-realization but to self-sacrifice, to the wolves and the Roman execution squad. To walk this way is not to be filled with the Spirit but to be emptied by the Spirit.

When we have reached that crucifixion point—call it high or low—when we recognize that we are unprofitable servants, the divine blessing is released. How else could God work? He cannot fill our cups with the Water of Life until they have been drained of all other waters. That is why the blessed ones are those who are poor in spirit. It is their poverty, their insolvency, that gives them the capacity for taking on treasure.   *— Sherwood E. Wirt*

God sometimes passes us into the valley of shadow that we may learn the way and know how to lead others through it into the light. To get comfort, we must comfort with the comfort wherewith we ourselves have been comforted. In wiping the tears of others our own will cease to fall.   *F. B. Meyer*

Father, in the valley of suffering my soul is empty, drained, but I praise You that Your Holy Spirit fills me with the Water of Life and I find comfort once more. May I comfort another with this glorious truth.

But God forbid that I should glory, save
*in the cross of our Lord Jesus Christ....*Galatians 6:14

*A*S WE TAKE TIME TO GAZE INTENTLY AT THE CROSS of Jesus Christ, a complete change should come over us. Then our attitudes, our priorities, will experience a radical change. We see the emptiness of our accomplishments if they are not achieved for our Lord. All that we regard as being important in our lives becomes secondary, for we realize the sacrificial Love that hung there for us.

Let us quietly and reverently read these words of Isaac Watts and let their beauty pour into our souls so that we may worship our Savior in a deeper, more consecrated way. *J.W.B.*

When I survey the wondrous cross
On which the Prince of glory died,
My richest gain I count but loss,
And pour contempt on all my pride.

Forbid it, Lord, that I should boast,
Save in the death of Christ my God;
All the vain things that charm me most,
I sacrifice them to His blood.

See, from His head, His hands, His feet,
Sorrow and love flow mingled down:
Did e'er such love and sorrow meet,
Or thorns compose so rich a crown?

Were the whole realm of nature mine,
That were a present far too small:
Love so amazing, so divine,
Demands my soul, my life, my all.

Isaac Watts

My Lord Jesus, humbly I come to You, and from a contrite and grateful heart I worship You, my Savior and my Redeemer.

———————————— **MARCH 28** ————————————

....the angel of the Lord descended from heaven, and came and rolled back the stone.... Matthew 28:2

◆——————————————————————————————————◆

THE ANGEL WHO CAME TO THE GARDEN where Jesus' body lay rolled away the stone and permitted fresh air and morning light to fill His tomb. The sepulcher was no longer an empty vault or dreary dormitory; rather it was a life-affirming place that radiated the glory of the living God. No longer was it a dark prison but a transformed reminder of the celestial light that sweeps aside the shadows of death. Jesus' resurrection changed it.

An unknown poet has said of the tomb, "'Tis now a cell where angels used to come and go with heavenly news." No words of men or angels can adequately describe the height and depth, the length and breadth of the glory to which the world awakened when Jesus came forth to life from the pall of death. *Billy Graham*

'Tis mystery all! Th' Immortal dies!
Who can explore His strange design?
In vain the first-born seraph tries
To sound the depths of love Divine!
'Tis mercy all! Let earth adore!
Let angel minds inquire no more.

Charles Wesley

How we adore You, Lord! From sorrow we turn to the triumph of Your resurrection, and our hearts rejoice.

➤ MARCH 29 ➤

And the angel...said unto the women, Fear not ye: for I know that ye seek Jesus, which was crucified. He is not here: for he is risen, as he said. Come, see the place where the Lord lay. And go quickly, and tell his disciples that he is risen from the dead; and, behold, he goeth before you into Galilee; there shall ye see him.... Matthew 28:5-7

◆————————————————————◆

CHRIST IS ALIVE. To thousands upon thousands at the present hour this is no mere theory or vague, uncertain rumor, but proved, inviolable experience; and if they are facing life victoriously now where once they were defeated, it is because they have found the same risen Lord who walked among the flowers of the garden on the morning of the first Easter Day.

James S. Stewart

And He departed from our sight that we might return to our heart, and there find Him. For He departed, and behold, He is here.

Augustine

Lord Jesus, we know You are alive and that You walk with us each day. May our lives reflect this joy.

➤ MARCH 30 ➤

Death is swallowed up in victory. I Corinthians 15:54

◆————————————————————◆

ON WHICH SIDE OF EASTER ARE YOU LIVING? Are you on the dark, dreary, defeated side where the powers of evil still reign and death still has the final word? Or are you living on the blessed, beautiful side of the resurrection with an assurance that Christ has won, death has been defeated and eternal life has begun in a way that no mere cessation of physical life can hinder?

Jesus Christ said, "I am the resurrection and the life; he who lives and believes in me shall never die." But He followed this profound statement with a penetrating question: "Do you believe this?" (John 11:25).

Lloyd John Ogilvie

I serve a risen Savior, He's in the world today;
I know that He is living, whatever men may say;
I see His hand of mercy, I hear His voice of cheer,
And just the time I need Him He's always near.

He lives, He lives, Christ Jesus lives today!
He walks with me and talks with me along life's narrow way.
He lives, He lives, salvation to impart!
You ask me how I know He lives? He lives within my heart.

In all the world around me I see His loving care;
And though my heart grows weary I never will despair;
I know that He is leading through all the stormy blast,
The day of His appearing will come at last.

Alfred H. Ackley

Lord Jesus, I do believe that through You I have eternal life! May I serve You with assurance and victory, I pray.

◆ MARCH 31 ◆

God hath sent forth the Spirit of his Son into your hearts.... Galatians 4:6

◆———————————————————————◆

W HEN JESUS TOLD HIS DISCIPLES of His imminent departure, how they must have grieved and panicked! To think they would no longer be able to rely on Him each day to guide them. No more would they know the warmth and compassion of His friendship and love. So often this happens in our own lives when someone we care for deeply either has to leave us for a long time or—the ultimate sorrow—dies.

But Jesus promised that the disciples would not be alone. God would send a Comforter. He said, "I will not leave you comfortless: I will come to you" (John 14:18).

I once visited a woman in a very poor neighborhood, whose room was filled with joy. She had been ill for years, but her face was radiant as she spoke of the comfort that Jesus Christ gave her each minute of every hour of every day. "I know I am not alone," she said. "Jesus is with me, and His love and comfort are all I need." She was suffering greatly, but she could see beyond all the suffering to the day when she would not only feel His presence, she would be able to see Him face to face.

We can all know this Comforter, the Holy Spirit, in our lives. When we give ourselves completely to Jesus, His presence comes to be with us and we never have to face another day without His divine guidance and strength.   *J.W.B.*

> All the way my Savior leads me—
> What have I to ask beside?
> Can I doubt His tender mercy,
> Who through life has been my guide?
>
> Heavenly peace, divinest comfort,
> Here by faith in Him to dwell!
> For I know, whate'er befall me,
> Jesus doeth all things well.
>
> *Fanny Crosby*

Lord Jesus, Your Holy Spirit, the Comforter, abides with me and I praise You that wherever my life takes me, I am not alone.

APRIL 1

But to all who received him, he gave the right to become children of God. All they needed to do was to trust him to save them. John 1:12 (TLB)

WE MUST BELIEVE IN PEOPLE AS JESUS DID. He showed faith in the most hopeless characters. He believed in those who were called "publicans and sinners." If we describe them as "stand-over men and down-and-out" it would probably conjure up a more exact picture of the kind of people with whom He chose to associate. Yet He did associate with them because He knew there was still good that could be called forth. He believed in rough, hard-swearing, half-educated fishermen like Peter, James and John and made them the foundation of His Church. He believed in people who seemed to be incurably selfish like Zacchaeus and Matthew. He believed in people whose lives and whose mental health had been wrecked by lust, people like Mary of Magdala and the woman taken in sin. To such people He said, "Neither do I condemn you, go and sin no more." If He could accept people like that, surely you and I can accept people who sin against us!

More than that, if He believed that they could still do great things with their lives, as they did when inspired by Him, surely we can look for the buried treasure in the problem people we have to deal with and enter into the great Christian adventure of bringing forth that treasure. It probably only needs a little encouragement, a little faith, forbearance and forgiveness to produce wonderful results.

Gordon Powell

Life that ever needs forgiveness has for its first duty to forgive.

Edward Bulwer-Lytton

Lord Jesus, forgive me for the times I judge another when I should be seeing a person You love.

APRIL 2

For in him we live and move and are! Acts 17:28 (TLB)

CLINGING TO A SLOPE AT THE NORTHERN TIP of this Sea of Galilee is Bethsaida, and close by Bethsaida was the place where Jesus fed the 5,000. It was Andrew, "a local boy," who came to Jesus that day and said, "There is a lad here, which hath five barley loaves, and two small fishes..." (John 6:9). And He fed them. I used to wonder about that miracle when I was young and full of doubts—but no more, since He has fed me. Stop wondering! Isn't it enough to know that we can never get beyond His love and care?

And there's another thing to remember about this day of feeding: Jesus fed them with the help of a boy's hand. A hand like yours and mine. *Use my hand, Lord...*

> Take my hands, and let them move
> At the impulse of Thy love.

Use me and lead me, Master, lest someone die of hunger!

Dale Evans Rogers

Depend upon it, God's work done in God's way will never lack God's supplies.   *J. Hudson Taylor*

Lord, I look at these hands of mine and ask You to use them in loving service for mankind.

APRIL 3

...Father, if thou be willing, remove this cup from me: nevertheless not my will, but thine, be done. Luke 22:42

IF JESUS NEEDED THAT GETHSEMANE PRAYER TIME, it goes without saying that we do! And we need it when the crowd is singing hosannas! Don't be deceived, crowds change, and we don't know if there'll be a hostile group and a cross tomorrow. There will be some opportunity to die to our selfishness, that is for sure, and to overcome that test we need to be prepared!

As I read this passage of Scripture, I cannot believe the concern of the Lord Jesus! With all that He had on His mind, He kept coming back to shake His dopey disciples awake—all to no avail. Then it was too late. The crowd was back, the hosannas had gone, and in their place the discordant notes of hatred and hostility were heard. We see Judas approaching his Master in cold anger, giving Him his kiss of death, and we hear Jesus' response: *"Friend!"* Friend? Yes, the Man who taught the Sermon on the Mount was beautifully demonstrating His own revolutionary teaching—"Love your enemies, do good to those who hate you, and pray for those who despitefully use you." Judas, Judas, why are you doing this? Friend! See Jesus reaching out; this is what you do when you've watched and prayed your way through to deciding the will of God is all there is left to do!

Jill Briscoe

Take God on thy route and thou shalt banish wrinkles from thy brow. Gethsemane itself shall not age thee if thou tread by the side of Jesus; for it is not the place of thy travel that makes thee weary—it is the heaviness of thy step.
George Matheson

Father, how I need this time of prayer with You! People change, circumstances change, but my communion with You brings constancy and revival.

————— **APRIL 4** —————

***And the Word was made flesh, and dwelt among us,
(and we beheld his glory, the glory as of the
only begotten of the Father,) full of grace
and truth.*** John 1:14

◆————————————————————————————◆

*N*EVER HAS ANYONE GIVEN UP SO MUCH. It is claimed (by Him as well as by us) that He renounced the joys of heaven for the sorrows of earth, exchanging an eternal immunity to the approach of sin for painful contact with evil in this world. He was born of a lowly Hebrew mother in a dirty stable in the insignificant village of Bethlehem. He became a refugee baby in Egypt. He was brought up in the obscure hamlet of Nazareth, and toiled at a carpenter's bench to support His mother and the other children in their home. In due time He became an itinerant preacher, with few possessions, small comforts and no home. He made friends with simple fishermen and publicans. He touched lepers and allowed harlots to touch Him. He gave Himself in a ministry of healing, helping, teaching and preaching.

John R. W. Stott

In fancy I stood by the shore, one day,
　　Of the beautiful murm'ring sea;
I saw the great crowds as they thronged the way
　　Of the Stranger of Galilee.

I saw how the man who was blind from birth
　　In a moment was made to see;
The lame were made whole by the matchless skill
　　Of the Stranger of Galilee.

And I felt I could love Him forever,
　　So gracious and tender was He!
I claim'd Him that day as my Savior,
　　This Stranger of Galilee.

Mrs. C. H. Morris

My Lord Jesus, Your tender love for all has touched my heart. Lead me to those who need today that same love, I pray.

---------------------------•— **APRIL 5** —•------------------------

For we have not a high priest which cannot be touched with the feeling of our infirmities.... Hebrews 4:15

◆——◆

*J*ESUS SPOKE, BUT HE ALSO HEALED. The two went together; they were the equipoise between loving God and loving one's neighbor—the two duties into which Jesus resolved all that the Law laid down and the prophets had proclaimed. Even in the garden of Gethsemane He healed, restoring the man's ear that Peter had impulsively hacked off with his sword. For that matter, even on the cross He offered healing words to the penitent thief crucified beside Him, making a rendezvous with him in paradise. Jesus never for one moment forgot our human need for bodies and minds in working order; for eyes that truly see and ears that truly hear. His compassion for the maimed, whether they were physically, mentally or spiritually disabled, was fathomless.

Malcolm Muggeridge

Christ pitied because He loved, because He saw through all the wretchedness, and darkness, and bondage of evil; that there was in every human soul a possibility of repentance, of restoration; a germ of good which, however stifled and overlaid, yet was capable of recovery, of health, of freedom, of perfection. *Dean Stanley*

Lord Jesus, thank You for Your compassionate love that reaches out and heals our troubled minds and bodies and brings forgiveness to a repentant soul.

———————————————— • **APRIL 6** • ————————————————

Thus the heavens and the earth were finished.... Genesis 2:1

◆———◆

MAN CAN MAKE; ONLY GOD CAN CREATE. Creative power being a divine prerogative, it was exercised by the Spirit at creation. As a mother bird, He brooded over a chaotic condition and produced this beautiful world of ours (Genesis 1:2). As the result of the Spirit's energy, the beauty of the earth, the glory of the sky, and the wonders of oceans came into being. Thus, Cowper in "The Task" expressed it:

> One Spirit—His
> Who wore the platted thorns with bleeding brow,
> Rules universal nature. Not a flower
> But shares some touch, in freckle, streak or stain,
> Of His unrivaled pencil.

Inscribed upon Ruskin's Memorial at Friar's Crag, Keswick, England, are the words, "The Spirit of God is around you in the air you breathe. His glory in the light that you see, and in the fruitfulness of the earth and joy of His creatures. He has written for you day by day His revelation, as He has granted you day by day your daily bread."
Herbert Lockyer

God is He without whom one cannot live. *Leo Tolstoy*

Almighty God, Your Holy Spirit makes me conscious of all the beauty You have created and the provision You have given for our welfare. I praise You, Lord God.

———————————————— • **APRIL 7** • ————————————————

Behold your King! John 19:14

◆———◆

ALONE...JESUS STOOD IN THE HALL OF JUDGMENT,
                alone...
        There were no witnesses for the defense...
        No concerned family or friends...

The only voice was for the prosecution...
    The jury, a howling mob bent on crucifixion.

As I see Him standing there, with His noble brow
    bleeding from the crown of thorns...
        the "royal" purple robe, draped over Him in mockery,
           bloodstained from the leaden whip...
I see His love...for He stood there—*alone*—
    for you and me.

J.W.B.

Fairest Lord Jesus,
Ruler of all nature,
O thou of God and man the Son!
Thee will I cherish,
Thee will I honor,
Thou, my soul's glory, joy and crown.

Seventeenth-century German hymn

Beloved Lord Jesus, Your love for me as You stood alone, accused for my sin, brings me to my knees in repentance for all the selfish and thoughtless deeds of my life.

APRIL 8

...he was wounded for our transgressions, he was bruised for our iniquities: the chastisement of our peace was upon him; and with his stripes we are healed. Isaiah 53:5

---

*W*HEN WE LOOK AT THE CROSS, without sentimentality, but with a little thought and imagination, we realize that what we could never do, what we are always powerless to do, *has been done* by Christ. This is the Act of Reconciliation which we could never make, the bridge which we could never build. No longer do we see God as the Fearful Judge isolated in splendid majesty, but right down among us, taking upon Him our flesh and plunging into the heart of our insoluble difficulty. When we see what sort of a God the cross reveals to us, it is no exaggeration to say that a revolution takes place in our thinking and our feeling. It is not too difficult to hurl defiance at a high and mighty God who, secure in His majesty, makes us mortals feel guilty and afraid. But it is impossible to be unmoved when we see our very Creator down in the sweat and dust of the arena, going to that awe-inspiring length to make the reconciliation.

It may come quietly into our hearts, or it may break over us like a wave, that the nature of God is not, as we supposed, that of a tyrant, a spoilsport, or a jesting fate, but Love—not sentimental love, but real Love that would face the grim degradation of the cross to reconcile us to Himself. *J. B. Phillips*

A Christian is one who never forgets for a moment what God has done for him in Christ. *John Baillie*

My Lord Jesus, may I never forget Your love, which took You into the vilest arena of suffering for my sake.

APRIL 9

Father, forgive them; for they know not what they do. Luke 23:34

---

*T*HE PARABLE THAT JESUS TOLD of the lost sheep again speaks of His love for each one of us. The shepherd leaves the 99 sheep safe in the fold and goes out to find that lost one. Finding it, he lays the animal on his shoulders and comes back rejoicing. It would have been easy to say, "I have 99 others, I am too busy and too tired to bother finding this one," but the shepherd cares for each one of his sheep.

With Jesus' love in our lives, we can rise above the grudging spirit and love one another as he or she should be loved. It is a love that has been through difficult places itself, a love that has known rejections but now has been lifted up into the magnificence of the light of Christ's love.

When we have this love in us we can face today, tomorrow, the days ahead, knowing we are being shepherded by our Savior, who loved us so much that He was willing to die for us. The cross illustrates that God is all love, for He sent His Son to die, taking our guilt upon Him—the sacrificial Lamb.

Even when Jesus faced the cross, He prayed for *us,* "Father, forgive them...." These words of His as He speaks to the Father are the embodiment of His true self-sacrificing love for you and me. *J.W.B.*

> The King of love my shepherd is,
> Whose goodness faileth never;
> I nothing lack if I am His,
> And He is mine forever.
>
> *Henry W. Baker*

(The greatest need in our world today is love. Love for our family, our friends; for the people who are lonely, misunderstood. Jesus needs us to convey His love.)

Lord Jesus, Your sacrificial love burns deep within my soul. May I, in turn, give such love to another.

APRIL 10

We love him, because he first loved us. I John 4:19

---

*T*HERE IS ONE WHO CAN SYMPATHIZE WITH US in our sufferings, because there is not an experience in our lives about which He does not know. Every valley that we are called upon to pass through, He has passed through ahead of us. He knew what it was to be poor. He knew what it was to be forsaken of friends and left alone. He knew what it was to be thirsty and to be weary. He knew what it was to have enemies revile Him. He knew what it was to spend sleepless nights as He wrestled in prayer for those who did not appreciate Him.

He knew what it was to be tempted and yet to be victorious. He knew what it was to suffer pain as they hung Him upon the cruel cross of Calvary and drove the wicked nails through His precious hands and His precious feet until He cried out, "My God, my God, why hast thou forsaken me?" He knew what it meant to go through the valley of the shadow, to taste death for every man. There is not a thing which is not known to Him.

O suffering, weary one, look now to the Lord Jesus Christ and receive His comfort.   M. R. DeHaan

> O the deep, deep love of Jesus,
> Vast, unmeasured, boundless, free!
> Rolling as a mighty ocean
> In its fullness over me!
> Underneath me, all around me
> Is the current of Thy love—
> Leading onward, leaning homeward,
> To Thy glorious rest above!
>
> O the deep, deep love of Jesus—
> Spread His praise from shore to shore!
> How He loveth, ever loveth,
> Changeth never, nevermore!

How He watches o'er His loved ones,
Died to call them all His own;
How for them He intercedeth,
Watcheth o'er them from the throne!

Samuel Trevor Francis

Jesus, in Your suffering for me You have given an example of selfless love. Please know I love You.

APRIL 11

Then said Jesus unto his disciples, If any man will come after me, let him deny himself, and take up his cross, and follow me. Matthew 16:24

*T*O BE A FOLLOWER OF THE CRUCIFIED means, sooner or later, a personal encounter with the cross. And the cross always entails loss. The great symbol of Christianity means sacrifice, and no one who calls himself a Christian can evade this stark fact. It is not by any means an easy thing to recognize, within a given instance of personal loss, the opportunity it affords for participation in Christ's own loss. What, we ask ourselves, can this possibly have to do with *that*? We are not by nature inclined to think spiritually. We are ready to assign almost any other explanation to the things that happen to us. There is a certain reticence to infer that our little troubles may actually be the vehicles to bring us to God. Most of us simply grin and bear them, knowing they are the lot of all human beings, and our memories being marvelously selective, we simply cancel them out, none the better for the lessons we might have learned.

Elisabeth Elliot

There are some who would have Christ cheap. They would have Him without the cross. But the price will not come down.

Samuel Rutherford

Show me, Lord, the lessons to be learned in times of distress. Let me not be blind to Your teachings.

APRIL 12

And he that taketh not his cross, and followeth after me, is not worthy of me. Matthew 10:38

*N*EXT TO THE ROMANS COMMENTARY ON MY DESK was the volume that had become almost a Christian textbook for me: Bonhoeffer's *The Cost of Discipleship*. Sacrifice and suffering, a costly break with the pre-Christian life, nothing less than death to self, to Bonhoeffer were indispensable elements of the Christian life, and his own life was lived true to his preaching. Though an outspoken foe of Hitler, Bonhoeffer in 1939 chose to return to Germany from his safe haven in America. If he did not join his people to suffer with them through the war, he reasoned, he could not pastor to them in their recovery afterward. He spent most of the war years in prison until his execution in 1945. It was not that he chose martyrdom—his letters from prison make that plain—rather he was simply obedient to Christ's call. "Only he who is obedient can believe," Bonhoeffer wrote....

Charles W. Colson

> *Lord, whatever this day may bring,*
>   *Thy name be praised...*
> *O God, be gracious unto me and help me.*
> *Give me strength to bear what Thou dost send,*
>   *and do not let fear rule over me...*
> *I trust in Thy grace,*
>   *and commit my life wholly into Thy hands.*
> *Do with me according to Thy will*
>   *and as is best for me.*
> *Whether I live or I die, I am with Thee,*
>   *and Thou, my God, art with me.*
> *Lord, I wait for Thy salvation*
>   *and for Thy Kingdom.*
> *Amen.*

Dietrich Bonhoeffer
(Letters and Papers from Prison)

APRIL 13

He that spared not his own Son, but delivered him up for us all, how shall he not with him also freely give us all things? Romans 8:32

---

*H*IS HAND IS STILL REACHING OUT to transform lives. He takes us even if our faith is as small as "a grain of mustard seed," then helps us grow each day to the full beauty of discipleship.

I often wonder what His thoughts must have been the day He left His home in Nazareth for the last time, to face an angry, hostile world on a mission He knew He had been born for—to die for us. But until that time, three years later, He would accomplish more than any man has ever done in a whole lifetime.

Little is written of Jesus' life before He began those three power-packed years of His ministry. The account of His life in the Gospels is sketchy. What a beautiful Child He must have been! Playing with His friends in the fields around His home, loving nature, which would be used to illustrate His parables in the years to come. As He worked with Joseph in the carpentry shop, did He think—as He picked up the nails and hammered them into the wood—of that day when His hands would be pierced by nails as men stretched Him on a cross?

J.W.B.

Jesus was crucified by the ordinary sins of every day. We are all in this together. Our heart and conscience tell us, when we stand on Calvary, that what we see there is our own work and that the sins we so lightly condone result always in the crucifixion of the Son of God.

James S. Stewart

Lord Jesus, You were nailed to a cross for me. It is a fact I cannot dispute, for my sin is such that I do not deserve such love. Yet, freely and willingly You gave Your life. Thank You, beloved Savior.

APRIL 14

He is not here: for he is risen, as he said. Matthew 28:6

◆──◆

*T*HE EASTER BELLS PEAL OUT THE MESSAGE of immortality. Death stalks us relentlessly, cutting off people in the prime of life and in the midst of their most exciting work. On everyone's horizon is the shadow of death. But in Easter's message there is hope that those who believe in Him shall someday rise from the dead. To the Christian, death has lost its fear and sting. Because Christ lives, we have the hope that we shall live too.

The message of the Easter bells is one of triumph over human iniquity. The great issues facing the world—human poverty and misery, hunger, hate, terror—are only reflections of individual problems. Dr. Nathan M. Pusey, former president of Harvard University, said, "The whole world is searching for a creed to believe and a song to sing."

Jean Paul Sartre, the French existentialist philosopher, urged people to find a set of values or a standard of some kind and commit themselves to it. Let Jesus Christ be that creed, that standard. Commit yourself to Him. Let His Easter message be the song you sing. When the bells of Easter ring out their message this spring, let Christ be risen in your heart that you may share in bringing His peace to the world.

Billy Graham

The resurrection never becomes a fact of experience until the risen Christ lives in the heart of the believer.   *Peter Marshall*

Savior, the message of that first Easter triumphs over all this world's heartache. May I be used to help bring this glorious news to others.

APRIL 15

...if he is still dead, then all our preaching is useless and your trust in God is empty, worthless, hopeless.... But the fact is that Christ did actually rise from the dead....
I Corinthians 15:14,20 (*TLB*)

*T*HAT THE RESURRECTION HAPPENED, and that in consequence of it Jesus' followers who had been scattered drew together again, resolved to go about their Master's business, seems to me indubitably true. Likewise, Jesus' claim to be the Light of the world, and His related promise that through Him we may be reborn into new men, liberated from servitude to the ego and our appetites into the glorious liberty of the children of God. Compared with these tremendous certainties, dubieties about the precise circumstances of Jesus' birth, ministry, death on the cross and continuing presence in the world seem sterile and unprofitable. Either Jesus never was or He still is. As a typical product of these confused times, with a skeptical mind and a sensual disposition, diffidently and unworthily, but with the utmost certainty, I assert that He still is. If the story of Jesus had ended on Golgotha, it would indeed be of a Man Who Died, but as two thousand years later the Man's promise that *where two or three are gathered together in My name, there am I in the midst of them* manifestly still holds, it is actually the story of a Man Who Lives.   *Malcolm Muggeridge*

It is on the unshakable fact of the resurrection of Christ from the dead that I base my faith in God's utter integrity and faithfulness. He let Jesus die—but only because He would raise Him again. You can count on Him! You can stake your faith on God—the God of Jesus Christ. He will keep His word.   *Leighton Ford*

Lord Jesus, I am so thankful that it was not the end on Golgotha, but You live and are with me today!

...because I live, ye shall live also. John 14:19

I MAGINE THE DESPAIR OF JESUS' DISCIPLES! They had seen their beloved Lord die the most cruel and ignominious death. In almost uncontrollable grief they had gently taken Him down from the cross and placed Him in a tomb carved out of rock. They had watched while a great boulder was rolled across the opening with unrelenting finality—a finality that so many experience when they attend a loved one's funeral.

Fear and despair were their companions. All their hope was shattered; there was nothing for them to live for. The cause of Christianity was dead.

In the Apostles' Creed it says that He "was crucified, dead and buried." Could anything sound more final, more hopeless?

How beautiful are the following words from the same Creed: "The third day He rose again from the dead; He ascended into heaven, and sitteth on the right hand of God the Father Almighty."

The knocking on the door and Mary Magdalene's urgent voice awakened the disciples out of their despair as she told them that she had seen the Lord—that He had risen as He said He would! What joy, doubt, excitement must have crowded into their minds as they ran back to the garden where the tomb was and saw with their own eyes that the stone had been rolled away and that the tomb was empty! No gravestone would ever be inscribed HERE LIES JESUS CHRIST, for He is *alive*! *J.W.B.*

> Afraid? Of what?
> To feel the spirit's glad release?
> To pass from pain to perfect peace?
> The strife and strains of life to cease?
>   Afraid—of that?
>
> Afraid? Of what?
> Afraid to see the Savior's face?
> To hear His welcome, and to trace
> The glory gleam from wounds of grace?
>   Afraid—of that?
>
> *E. H. Hamilton*

Lord Jesus, because of Your victory over death I will not be afraid when my time comes to journey into eternity. You will be there!

I am he that liveth, and was dead; and, behold,
I am alive for evermore, Amen.... Revelation 1:18

*I*N ONE OF MY TOURS TO THE HOLY LAND, I said to our guide that I wanted to go to Emmaus. This is a place that tours do not usually go because it is off the beaten track. But I am so glad that we drove those seven miles that day. For one thing, it brought to mind the story of those two people who were walking back to their home that Sunday on which Jesus rose from the dead. They were sad, saying, "We trusted that it had been he which should have redeemed Israel..." (Luke 24:21). Their trust was in the past tense because they had seen Jesus die. He went into their house with them, and as He broke the bread they recognized Him, and they realized that He was alive again.

It was a wonderful experience for these sad people. Emmaus is a beautiful place. I really think one of the loveliest views in all Israel can be seen when one stands in Emmaus. It was at this place that Henry F. Lyte wrote that lovely song "Abide With Me." As our group stood there, we talked about the experience of Emmaus and then we sang together those words:

> Abide with me—fast falls the eventide;
> The darkness deepens—Lord, with me abide;
> When other helpers fail and comforts flee,
> Help of the helpless, O abide with me!

There are times when all of us feel comfortless and helpless, but there is great strength in remembering the One who abides with us.

Charles L. Allen

For no way can be lonely if it is the way Christ walks...
No way can be lonely if it is the way to which He calls you.

Peter Marshall

Lord Jesus, You abide with me and my life can never be lonely again.

...know assuredly, that God hath made that same Jesus,
whom ye have crucified, both Lord and Christ. Acts 2:36

*T*HE RESURRECTION, THE ASCENSION, and the shedding forth of the Holy Spirit were proof that Jesus was in control at the power center of all reality.

The disciples who prayed in that upper room after Jesus had left were like men huddled in a dark cabin on a stormy night, without lights, because the storm had caused damage at the transformer. They are waiting for one of their number who is stumbling through the black night, the torrents of rain, and the cracking lightning to find his way to the powerhouse and repair the breakdown. For long minutes they wait...and suddenly the lights come flashing on. "He's there! He's made it!" someone cries. That was what happened for the disciples. The Holy Spirit had invaded them. The power was on! The world was illuminated! They knew that Jesus had made it!

Leighton Ford

The miracle of Christ's resurrection: out of the grave into my heart.

David J. Netz

Yes, Lord Jesus, I feel Your presence and delight to know my Redeemer lives!

APRIL 19

...lo, I am with you alway, even unto the end of the world.

Matthew 28:20

---

*F*ELLOWSHIP WITH KINGS IS USUALLY RESERVED for the few. To have audience with a queen has become an act of privilege, and it is always carefully prepared for and rehearsed. In the army it is unusual for a private to have audience with a general, and he is fortunate if he even sees one.

But these privileges are daily practices with the followers of Christ. There is not a day when the Christian cannot have personal audience with Him in prayer—or should have. No man should ever join a church, which is the Army of Christ, without having known Him and met Him personally. More startling still, Christ never sends a man on an errand without the promise of going with him.

Louis H. Evans, Sr.

No distant Lord have I,
  Loving afar to be;
Made flesh for me, He cannot rest
  Until He rests in me.

Brother in joy or pain,
  Bone of my bone was He;
Now—intimacy closer still—
  He dwells Himself in me.

I need not journey far,
    This dearest Friend to see;
Companionship is always mine,
    He makes His home with me.

Malthie Babcock

Lord Jesus, King of kings, wherever You send me to do Your will, I shall remember that You have promised to be with me—always!

APRIL 20

...whether we live, therefore, or die, we are the Lord's. Romans 14:8

F. B. MEYER, in his 80s, sat down to write a letter to a friend. "I have just heard to my surprise," he said, "that I have only a few days to live. It may be before this reaches you, I shall have entered the palace. Don't trouble yourself to write. We shall meet in the morning. With much love. Yours affectionately."

That is triumph. That is no counterfeit comfort. That is reunion with the Father.

John Thornton received word he had only a few days to live. He tells how he sat at his window and looked out at the river before him and the mountains beyond. He looked at the stars shining in the sky. Then he wrote: "I'm going to leave. But river, I'll be alive when every drop in you has dried up. Mountains, I'll be alive when you have disappeared. Stars, I'll be around when your light has burned out. For my spirit goes to God who gave it. I commit myself into the hands of the Father."

John M. Drescher

The stars shine over the mountains,
    the stars shine over the sea,
The stars look up to the mighty God,
    the stars look down on me;
the stars shall last for a million years,
    a million years and a day,
But God and I will live and love
    when the stars have passed away.

Robert Louis Stevenson

Almighty God, in Your hands is my life and I rejoice at the peace this knowledge brings. Whether I am awake or asleep, I am safe in You.

But rejoice, inasmuch as ye are partakers of Christ's sufferings; that, when his glory shall be revealed, ye may be glad also with exceeding joy. I Peter 4:13

PETER, WHO HIMSELF DIED AS A MARTYR, tells us in his letters what it means to be one. Perhaps there have never been so many children of God who died as martyrs as in our day. Probably many more will follow. That is said quite clearly in the Book of Revelation.

I remember as a child saying to my father: "I am afraid that I will never be strong enough to die as a martyr."

But he said: "When you have to go on a journey, when do I give you the money for the fare—two weeks before?"

"No, Daddy, on the day that I am leaving."

"Precisely, and that is what the Savior does also."

He does not give us grace now for something we may have to pass through later on. If He thinks we are worthy to die as a martyr, He gives us the strength for it at that moment.   *Corrie ten Boom*

> God hath not promised
> Skies always blue,
> Flower-strewn pathways
> All our lives through:
> God hath not promised
> Sun without rain,
> Joy without sorrow,
> Peace without pain.
>
> But God hath promised
> Strength for the day,
> Rest for the labor,
> Light for the way,
> Grace for the trials,
> Help from above,
> Unfailing sympathy,
> Undying love.
>
> *Annie Johnson Flint*

(We do not know what we will face in the days ahead. We *do* know our Lord's strength will never fail us.)

Father, constant is Your love and care. My soul is at peace with You.

God commendeth his love toward us, in that,
while we were yet sinners, Christ died for us. Romans 5:8

WHEN CHARLES WESLEY FOUND CHRIST on Whit Sunday, 1738, his experience overflowed into some marvelous verses ("The Wesleys' Conversion Hymn," *Methodist Hymn Book,* 361) in which the transition from slavery to sonship is the main theme.

> Where shall my wondering soul begin?
> How shall I all to heaven aspire?
> A slave redeemed from death and sin,
> A brand plucked from eternal fire,
> How shall I equal triumphs raise,
> Or sing my great Deliverer's praise?
>
> O how shall I the goodness tell,
> Father, which thou to me hast showed?
> That I, a child of wrath and hell,
> I should be called a child of God,
> Should know, should feel my sins forgiven,
> Blest with this antepast of heaven!

Three days later, Charles tells us in his diary, brother John burst in with "a troop of our friends" to announce that he too was now a believer, and "we sang the hymn with great joy." Had you been there, could you sincerely have joined in? Can you make Wesley's words your own? If you are truly a child of God and "the Spirit of His Son" is in you, Wesley's words have already drawn an echo from your heart; and if they have left you cold, I do not know how you can imagine that you are a Christian at all. *J. I. Packer*

The influence of His life, His words, and His death have, from the first, been like leaven cast into the mass of humanity. *Cunningham Geikie*

Father, I praise You for the joy I know as Your child because of my Savior, Your Son, Jesus Christ.

...whosoever shall say unto this mountain, Be thou removed,
and be thou cast into the sea; and shall not doubt in his
heart, but shall believe that those things which he saith
shall come to pass; he shall have whatsoever he saith.
Mark 11:23

C AN WE CONFIDENTLY CLAIM AND EXPECT the conversion of our loved ones? Well, it must be in God's will. "And this is the confidence that we have in him, that, if we ask anything according to his will, he heareth us" (John 5:14). Does He will the conversion of everyone? "The Lord is not willing that any should perish, but that all should come to repentance" (II Peter 3:9).

Then He will remove this mountain, but we must expect the mountain to move. "All things whatsoever ye shall ask in prayer, *believing*, ye shall receive" (Matthew 21:22). And the verse following our text says, "What things soever ye desire, when ye pray, *believe that ye receive them*, and ye shall have them."

We pray *hoping*, but hoping is not faith. Faith takes God's word for the deed and in its geography lists the mountain as "disappeared."

Got any mountains you think are unsinkable?   *Vance Havner*

> I will not doubt, though all my ships at sea
>   Come drifting home with broken masts and sails;
>   I shall believe the Hand which never fails,
> From seeming evil worketh good to me;
>   And, though I weep because those sails are battered,
>   Still will I cry, while my best hopes lie shattered,
>   "I trust in Thee."

Ella Wheeler Wilcox

Lord, at times there are so many seemingly immovable "mountains" in my life, but by faith I believe You will make them "disappear" in Your time.

----------------------- **APRIL 24** ----------------------

And ye are witnesses of these things. Luke 24:48

W E NEED TO BUILD BRIDGES OF FRIENDSHIP, but we also need to cross the bridges and communicate the Gospel to someone. They're not about to come to Christ unless they hear about Him. When we have explained the Gospel, we ask, "Would you like to trust Christ?" or, "Have you ever personally trusted Christ?"

Generally Christians have to build within a situation. It's true there are one-time opportunities where we meet people, go through the steps to salvation, and invite them to Christ. We should be alert to those. But the more natural ongoing type of evangelism is to present the steps of faith and obedience to the persons to whom we're witnessing and help them move down the road a little farther in response to God and the truth. *Paul E. Little*

I remember, when we were in London, they found one old woman who was 85 years old and not a Christian. After the worker had prayed, she made a prayer herself:

"O Lord, I thank Thee for going out of Thy way to find me."
He is all the time going out of His way to find the lost.   *D. L. Moody*

(Is there someone whom you long to win to Christ? Remember, He is with you, waiting to give His wisdom and love.)

Father, You know who is on my heart today, whom I long to see come into the joy of knowing You and Your Son, Jesus Christ. I pray believing, Lord, that _____

will receive You in Your appointed time.

APRIL 25

***Jesus said, "I am come that they might have life,
and that they might have it more abundantly."*** John 10:10

W HEN A PERSON PUTS HIS FAITH IN JESUS CHRIST, he enters into a personal relationship with God Almighty, which results in changes taking place in his life.

Christian conversion is neither self-improvement nor culturally conditioned. There are many who put their faith in Christ and do it against the pressures of friends and family. The Christian's experience ultimately depends on God and His work in the person's life. This must take place. The experience is grounded in this fact, not in the person himself.

Besides the fact that Christian conversion is based upon something objective, the resurrection of Christ, there is also the universality of Christian experience that must be considered. From the time of Jesus until today, people from every conceivable background, culture and intellectual stance have been converted by the Person of Jesus Christ.
Josh McDowell & Don Stewart

You have looked at the windows of a grand church erected at the cost of many thousands of dollars. From the outside they do not seem very beautiful; but get inside, when the rays of sun are striking upon the stained glass, and you begin to understand what others have told you of their magnificence. So it is when you have come into personal contact with Christ. You find Him to be the very Savior and Friend you need. You will see in Him what you have never seen before.

D. L. Moody

Living Savior, whose Spirit changes a life from despair to joy, I praise You for Your presence which brings life abundantly.

APRIL 26

...If a man love me, he will keep my words: and my Father will love him, and we will come unto him, and make our abode with him. John 14:23

---

*F*OR MANY YEARS AFTER I HAD TRUSTED CHRIST as my Savior and had invited Him to come into my heart and life, I did not grasp the simple, stupendous fact that when I received Him, *I* received *Him*—when He came to live in my heart, *He* came to *live* in *me*. The promise of the Word of God is that the sinner who needs Christ and invites Christ to take up residence will receive a *living* Person—Christ. Yet there are many who believe this to be good, sound doctrine and yet live as if they had received a variety of commodities rather than the Person promised.

Christ, who promised Himself to come through the open door of a repentant heart, did not cheat by pushing in a certificate of forgiveness, a cozy "saved" feeling, a ticket to heaven, and reservations for eternity, together with a dose of peace and joy to be taken three times daily or when needed! *He* promised that *He* would come in, and come in *He* did.

D. Stuart Briscoe

> He taught me all the mercy,
> For He show'd me all the sin.
> Now, tho' my lamp was lighted late,
> There's One will let me in.

Alfred Lord Tennyson

Lord Jesus, I praise You for Your Holy Spirit that lives in me. I love You, Lord.

APRIL 27

I have called you friends.... John 15:15

---

*T*HE PECULIARITY OF CHRISTIANITY is the strong personal tie of real love and intimacy which will bind men, to the end of time, to this Man who died nineteen hundred years ago.

We look back into the wastes of antiquity, and mighty names rise there which we reverence; there are great teachers from whom we have learned and to whom, after a fashion, we are grateful. But what a gulf there is between us and the best and noblest of them!

But there is nothing in the whole history of the world in the least like that strange bond which ties you and me to Jesus Christ.

We stretch out our hands across the waste, silent centuries, and there we touch the warm, throbbing heart of our Friend who lives forever and is ever near us.

A perpetual bond unites men with Christ today. And there are no limitations in that friendship, no misconstructions in that heart, no alienations possible, no changes to be feared. There is absolute rest for us there.

Why should I fear if He walks by my side? Why should anything be burdensome if He lays it upon me and helps me to bear it? What is there in life that cannot be faced and borne—aye, and conquered—if we have Him, as we all may have Him, for the Friend and the home of our hearts? *Alexander Maclaren*

No one else holds or has held the place in the heart of the world which Jesus holds. Other gods have been as devoutly worshiped; no other man has been so devoutly loved. *John Knox*

Lord Jesus, to know that You are not only my Savior but my constant Friend calms all my fears and brings everlasting joy!

---------------•---- **APRIL 28** --•------------------------

He that honoreth not the Son honoreth not the Father which hath sent him. John 5:23

◆————————————————————————————————————◆

P. T. FORSYTH ONCE SAID, "You may always measure the value of Christ's cross by your interest in missions. The missionless church betrays that it is a crossless church, and it becomes a faithless church.

"Do you really believe what you say, Chaplain?" asked a condemned prisoner of the minister who was trying to bring him to faith in Christ. "If I believed your Gospel were true, I would crawl across England on broken glass to tell men about it." Surely the urgency of our witness will measure the reality of our beliefs.

Paul also found his evangelistic urgency in the realm of experience— the Christ-filled heart. "With us, therefore, worldly standards have ceased to count in our estimate of men.... When anyone is united to

Christ, there is a new world; the old order has gone, and a new order has already begun" (II Corinthians 5:16a-17, *NEB*). *Leighton Ford*

I used to ask God to help me. Then I asked if I might help Him. I ended up by asking Him to do His work through me. *J. Hudson Taylor*

(Are our lives Christ-filled with a pressing need to witness to those in a dying world?)

Father, fill my life with a burning desire to tell of Your mercy and grace. May the reality of the Gospel be seared into my soul.

───────────────── APRIL 29 ─────────────────

And I will pray the Father, and he shall give you another Comforter, that he may abide with you for ever.... John 14:16

◆──◆

SO YOU REGARD THE HOLY SPIRIT as indeed as real a Person as Jesus Christ, as loving and wise and strong, as worthy of your confidence and love and surrender, as Jesus Christ Himself? The Holy Spirit came into this world to be to the disciples of our Lord, and to us, what Jesus Christ had been to them during the days of His personal companionship with them. Is He that to you? Do you know Him?

When you hear the apostolic benediction, "The grace of the Lord Jesus Christ, and the love of God, and the communion of the Holy Ghost, be with you all," do you take in the significance of it? Do you know the communion of the Holy Ghost? The fellowship of the Holy Ghost? The partnership of the Holy Ghost? The comradeship of the Holy Ghost? The intimate, personal friendship of the Holy Ghost? Herein lies the whole secret of a real Christian life, a life of liberty and joy and power and fullness. To have as one's ever-present Friend, and to be conscious that one has as His ever-present Friend, the Holy Spirit, and to surrender one's life in all its departments entirely to His control, this is true Christian living.

The doctrine of the personality of the Holy Spirit is as distinctive of the religion that Jesus taught as the doctrines of the Deity and the atonement of Jesus Christ Himself. But it is not enough to believe the doctrine—one must know the Holy Spirit Himself. *R. A. Torrey*

(The Holy Spirit waits to enter our lives—lives that are emptied of all selfish desires.)

> *O Holy Spirit of God, abide with us;*
> *inspire all our thoughts;*
> *pervade our imaginations;*

suggest all our decisions;
order all our doings.

Be with us in our silence and in our speech,
in our haste and in our leisure,
in company and in solitude,
in the freshness of the morning and in the
  weariness of the evening;
and give us grace at all times humbly to
  rejoice in Thy mysterious companionship.

John Baillie

APRIL 30

The glory of the Lord shall endure for ever:
the Lord shall rejoice in his works. Psalm 104:31

---

*A*LL OF US ARE TRANSIENTS. The tides, the waves, the wayward winds, the passing storms, the wheeling seabirds, the shifting restless sands, the schools of fish, the short-lived grasses and trees of marsh and dune are here but briefly. Is there no eternal meaning or message here for our questing spirits? Are we all but bare fragments of material, moved and shifted only in response to the physical, chemical, and biological forces around us? Is there no sense, meaning, or purpose for my short sojourn upon this planet that is hurtling through space? Are my years and thoughts and impressions to be carried away like bits of flotsam on the tides of time? Is there no direction to the deep and profound stirring of my spirit as I stroll by the sea?

Yes, there is. Deep does call to deep. There sweeps over my soul again and again the phrase, "Oh, be still, quiet, alone, silent and *know* that I am God."

All about me there may be the ebb and flow, the rise and fall of changing seasons, changing scenes, a changing world. "But You, O my Father, remain ever the same. You, O Lord, are from everlasting to everlasting." *W. Phillip Keller*

Sometimes a light surprises
  The Christian while he sings;
It is the Lord who rises
  With healing in His wings.

God moves in a mysterious way
  His wonders to perform;
He plants His footstep on the sea
  And rides upon the storm.

William Cowper

Father, in a world of continual change I am thankful that I am anchored in Your sure, steadfast love that never fluctuates.

Is not this the carpenter's son? Is not his mother called Mary? And his brethren, James, and Joses, and Simon, and Judas? And his sisters, are they not all with us?... Matthew 13:55-56

*I*T MUST NEVER BE FORGOTTEN that Jesus was brought up in the heart of a big family (Matthew 13:55; Mark 6:3). Joseph seems to have died comparatively early, for his name disappears from the narrative altogether; and no doubt when Jesus grew to manhood it was upon Him, as the eldest brother, that the main responsibility for the support of the home devolved. Sidelights upon the early home-life of the Master may be found in many of the parables. The turning-out of the house to find a coin that has rolled away into a dark corner and disappeared (Luke 15:8); the measuring of the flour and the leaven for the weekly baking (Matthew 13:33); the plight of the householder who, finding his larder empty on the arrival of an untimely guest, wakes up his churlish neighbor at midnight (Luke 11:5); the lighting of the candles at the gloaming hour (Matthew 5:15); the healthy appetites of children home from school and play (Matthew 7:9) — these touches and many others are surely reminiscent of Mary's home, a home from which in days when trade was bad poverty could not be very far away. Certainly there was no affluence about it. "Is not this the carpenter's son?" they said later, and there was no mistaking the sneer (Matthew 13:55). But to Jesus it was home, and love was there and God was there; and by His own devotion to it all those hidden, waiting years, He has hallowed home-life forever.   *James S. Stewart*

It is to Jesus Christ we owe the truth, the tenderness, the purity, the warm affection, the holy aspiration which go together in that endearing word — home.   *James Hamilton*

Lord Jesus, wherever our home is we can rejoice, for You are there and Your presence blesses our lives. Thank You for honoring our home, Lord.

For there is no respect of persons with God. Romans 2:11

*J*ESUS TOOK A LITTLE CHILD and He said, "Suffer the little children to come unto me, and forbid them not; for of such is the kingdom of heaven."

The disciples were young men, but Jesus did not choose them because of their reputation or their education. He chose them because of their individuality and their individual qualities. I have five children, and every one of them is different. It is amazing that my wife and I could have five children and they be so different. Not one of them is superior to the other. Each has his or her own aptitudes and gifts.

The Bible says God is no respecter of persons. In His sight, everybody is of equal value, but everybody is different. *Billy Graham*

There is nothing you can do...
To make God love you more!
There is nothing you can do...
To make God love you less!
His love is...
Unconditional...
Impartial...
Everlasting...
Infinite...
Perfect!
God is love!

Richard C. Halverson

Almighty God, the equality of Your love reaches me in my need and I am amazed by Your mercy and grace.

MAY 3

...I will pour my Spirit upon thy seed, and my blessing upon thine offspring.... Isaiah 44:3

*W*HO KNOWS THE INFLUENCE YOU CAN BE as you affect children and young people who are tomorrow's world? If the child you take under your wing isn't a king, he could still turn out to be kingly. Your giving him time—laughing with him, crying with him, studying with him, playing with him, urging him on to success, and backing him up with your prayers—could shape one of tomorrow's great influences in the world.

Such was the influence a generation ago of Henrietta Mears, a single woman, on young Bill Bright, who is today the founder and international head of Campus Crusade for Christ.

Adopting. Discipling. Nobody who has Christ in his heart is excused from making a mark on the children around him! They're wet cement. They're ready.

> Parent birds
> Feed young nestlings
> What they can.
> Who can tell
> How high some day
> One of them
> May soar?

Anne Ortlund

Pray for the rising generation who are to come after us. Think of the young men and young women and children of this age, and pray for all the agencies at work among them; that in associations and societies and unions, in homes and schools, Christ may be honored, and the Holy Spirit get possession of them. Pray for the young of your own neighborhood.   *Andrew Murray*

Lord Jesus Christ, I see the children living in a world so full of strife. Use me, Lord, to touch their lives and bring them joy and hope.

MAY 4

The Lord is nigh unto all them that call upon him, to all that call upon him in truth. Psalm 145:18

ANY MOTHER WITH A CHILD AWAY FROM HOME knows the longing for a letter, a call, even a card. True, in prayer we are coming to Almighty God, the Creator of the universe, the King of kings and Lord of lords, but He is also our Father. He longs to hear from us, not just when we are asking for things; but also to tell Him we love Him and to talk over the happenings of the day, just to fellowship.

Once when out of the country I called home to check on Mother and Daddy. After talking with Daddy a few minutes, he said, "Here—your mother wants to say something." Since Mother's speech was affected by a stroke a number of years ago, I wondered how she would do. She came on the line, her voice weak, her spirit indomitable. "I just wanted to hear your voice," she said.

I know how it is with me when the children are away. Just the sound of their voices warms and comforts me.

I wonder if God does not long at times just to hear our voices.

Ruth Bell Graham

Speak to Him, thou, for He hears,
    and spirit with Spirit can meet—
Closer is He than breathing,
    and nearer than hands and feet.

Alfred, Lord Tennyson

Father, as Your child I lift my voice to You this day in praise and thanksgiving for the sense of Your love that surrounds me.

MAY 5

...speaking to yourselves in psalms and hymns and spiritual songs, singing and making melody in your heart to the Lord.
Ephesians 5:19

SOME TIME AGO I TOOK LITTLE CHUCKIE, our youngest, to a grocery store with me. We came up to the checkout stand to purchase a few items. For some reason, the store was abnormally quiet. Chuckie, who was sitting in the cart, reached over and grabbed a handful of mints. While he was trying to unwrap one of them he began to sing in a loud voice, "Jesus loves me this I know (everybody kind of stared at him), for the Bible tells me so. Little ones..." He sang softer as he realized a dozen eyes were on him.

"Go ahead—'to Him belong,'" a young woman said to Chuckie. Then she turned to me: "Do you know Christ as your Savior?"

"Why, yes, I do," I answered.

"I've been a Christian for about a year and a-half," she said.

"Isn't that interesting," I said. "My son led us into an opportunity to encourage each other."

I also found out that the checker (who also had stopped to listen) was disturbed with a broken marriage. Chuckie had just come bursting out with a song at precisely the right moment. His happy heart soothed the hurt of another.

Don't stop singing! *Charles R. Swindoll*

The Wesley brothers, Charles and John, together wrote more than 6,000 hymns. Both men were known to say that they made more converts through their hymns than through their preaching.

Lord, thank You for music, for the joy of singing of Your faithfulness and love that will enter a longing heart.

MAY 6

And Jesus, moved with compassion, put forth his hand, and touched him.... Mark 1:41

S OMETIMES WE ARE AFRAID that we do not have enough faith to pray for this child or that marriage. Our fears should be put to rest, for the Bible tells us that great miracles are possible through faith the size of a tiny mustard seed. Usually the courage actually to go and pray for a person is a sign of sufficient faith. Often our lack is not faith but compassion. It seems that genuine empathy between the pray-er and the pray-ee often makes the difference. We are told that Jesus was "moved with compassion" for people. Compassion was an evident feature of every healing in the New Testament. We do not pray for people as "things" but as "persons" whom we love. If we have God-given compassion and concern for others, our faith will grow and strengthen as we pray. In fact, if we genuinely love people, we desire for them far more than it is within our power to give, and that will cause us to pray.

Richard J. Foster

> Love is a feeling to be learned.
> It is tension and fulfillment.
> It is deep longing and hostility.
> It is gladness and it is pain.
> There is not one without the other.
>
> Happiness is only a part of love—this is what has to be learned. Suffering belongs to love also. This is the mystery of love, its beauty and its burden.
>
> Love is a feeling to be learned.

Walter Trobisch

Father, teach me Christlike compassion. In faith I come to You, knowing I cannot give those I love all that they need, yet You can. In suffering in my loving I come a step closer to realizing Jesus' love for me.

MAY 7

Consider it pure joy, my brothers, whenever you face trials of many kinds, because you know that the testing of your faith develops perseverance. James 1:2-3 *(NIV)*

I BELIEVE THERE ARE TIMES in the lives of most believers when confusion and perplexity are rampant. What could Job have felt, for example, when his world began to crack and splinter? His family members became sick and died, his livestock was wiped out, and he was besieged by boils from the top of his head to the bottom of his feet. But most troubling of all was his inability to make spiritual sense of the circumstances. He knew he hadn't sinned, despite the accusations of his "friends," yet God must have seemed a million miles away. He said at one point, "Oh, that I knew where to find God—that I could go to his throne and talk with him there" (Job 23:3, *TLB*). "But I searched in vain. I see him there, and cannot find him there; nor can I find him in the South; there, too, he hides himself" (Job 23:8-9, *TLB*).

Was this experience unique to Job? I don't think so. In my counseling responsibilities with Christian families, I've learned that sincere, dedicated believers go through tunnels and storms, too. We inflict a tremendous disservice on young Christians by making them think only sinners experience confusion and depressing times in their lives. Apparently God permits these difficult moments for our own education.

James Dobson

> He said not,
>   "Thou shalt not be
>   Tempested;
>   Thou shalt not be
>   Travailed;
>   Thou shalt not be
>   Afflicted:
> But he said,
>   "Thou shalt not be
>   Overcome!"

Julian of Norwick, A.D. 1373

Almighty God, from out of the depths of the dark night of my soul I have known the assurance that even when I could not see Your light, You were still there loving me.

MAY 8

In the world ye shall have tribulation: but be of good cheer; I have overcome the world. John 16:33

WITH A HUSBAND AND SIX CHILDREN, I find that I have a household that never stops; and I must admit, there are times that I get a bit discouraged and tired. Not from lack of love and appreciation, but from the fact that every minute is taken and busy. A verse taken from a translation by William F. Beck has blessed me.

> Lord, the rivers make a noise,
>   the rivers make a roaring noise,
>   the rivers make a crashing noise,
>   But, more than the noise is
>   the might of the Lord above.

This thought has blessed me because I can find quiet amid the noise if I remember my resources which are all wrapped up in the Person of Jesus Christ. He can give quiet amid the storm; He can give strength when I feel I am at the end of mine. He never promised to take away all hardship, all sorrow, nor absolve all impossible situations, nor remove all the giants in our lives; but He did and does promise to be with us in and through these times and for all time.   *Gigi Graham Tchividjian*

> There is a place of quiet rest
> Near to the heart of God,
> A place where sin cannot molest,
> Near to the heart of God.
>
> *Cleland B. McAfee*

Lord, there are times when I get so exhausted from the everyday routine. Help me to seek Your peace and make me aware of the renewal of Your touch.

————————————————•— **MAY 9** —•————————————————

Charity suffereth long, and is kind.... I Corinthians 13:4

◆——◆

*I*F YOU ARE A HUSBAND, when was the last time you cared enough to stop and give your wife genuine gratitude for a meal she prepared? If you are a wife, when have you been thoughtful enough to congratulate your husband on putting up with the stresses and strains of his work to provide a home and income for you? When as a parent have you written your child a letter complimenting him/her on their achievements? What thought and appreciation have you shown your parents for all the sacrifice endured to assure your success in life?

All of us take each other too much for granted. It is a deadening, dulling, destructive habit. God calls us to care. He calls us to see with knowing eyes. He calls us to detect with sensitivity the heart needs of those around us. Our response can be one of enormous benefit and blessings, not in some grandiose performance, but in a hundred little helping ways.

We can be salt to our associates. We can bring zest, fun, vitality, love and light to their lives. We can enliven their drab days.   *W. Phillip Keller*

> That best portion of a good man's life—
> His little nameless, unremembered acts
> Of kindness and of love.
>
> *William Wordsworth*

Father, in Your love let me be kind to those around and make me aware of their needs, I pray.

Remember, I beseech thee, the word that thou commandedst thy servant Moses, saying, If ye transgress, I will scatter you abroad among the nations: but if ye turn unto me, and keep my commandments, and do them; though there were of you cast out unto the uttermost part of the heaven, yet will I gather them from thence, and will bring them unto the place I have chosen to set my name there. Nehemiah 1:8-9

*W*HENEVER OUR FAMILIES ARE IN TROUBLE and we need to kneel and pray, we must believe the God we speak with has the *power* to move mountains, men, monarchs, and even mothers-in-law if need be! Just to rest in a God who can motivate the unmotivated and move the immovable will prove to be a heart-releasing experience. We need to practice a continual trust in this "awe-ful" God, especially when we've been waiting for something to give in a certain situation. Perhaps we've even been patient for many years and feel we have grown old with hoping. We must come to understand that delay may be telling us that God is not necessarily saying "not ever," but simply "not now."

Jill Briscoe

The many troubles in your household will tend to your edification, if you strive to bear them all in gentleness, patience, and kindness. Keep this ever before you, and remember constantly that God's loving eyes are upon you amid all these little worries and vexations, watching whether you take them as He would desire. Offer up all such occasions to Him, and if sometimes you are put out, and give way to impatience, do not be discouraged, but make haste to regain your lost composure.

Francis de Sales

Father, I know Your eyes are upon me and those I love, so help me to be patient as I await the answer to my prayers for each one of them.

For whosoever will save his life shall lose it: but whosoever will lose his life for my sake, the same shall save it. Luke 9:24

*Y*OUR PROBLEM COULD BE YOU. It could be a member of your family. It could be that you have no family at all. Whatever it is, He knows about it. Whatever it is, if you have had it awhile and are still troubled by it, you should see by now that you can't cope with it.

But Christ can.

He *is* one and the same with God. Either He is, or He was mistaken about Himself because He said, "I and the Father are one."

Life is never going to be without trouble. "Man is born unto trouble, as the sparks fly upward." Jesus graciously reminded us that if we follow Him we will not be exempt from trouble. "In the world ye shall have tribulation: but be of good cheer; I have overcome the world."

Jesus Christ tells us quite clearly that we are to lose our lives for His sake. To me, this means that my total personality is to be placed into His hands, under His control.

If He is who He claims to be, then day by day I have a right to expect that I will be influenced by Him. I have a right to expect that day by day, as I grow in the knowledge of Him, I will be more able to cope creatively with the various trouble areas in my life.   *Eugenia Price*

Oh, how great peace and quietness would he possess who should cut off all vain anxiety and place all his confidence in God.

Thomas à Kempis

Almighty God, thank You for Your promise of victory over all the trials in my life. May I claim it and keep this knowledge before me—always.

---—•—— **MAY 12** —•————

Judge not, that ye be not judged. Matthew 7:1

•————————————————————————————•

THE CHRISTIAN MUST NEVER BE JUDGMENTAL in his relationship with others. He must be loving in his spirit no matter what kind of person he is dealing with or under what circumstances. We are not talking about compromise but compassion. Jesus was a perfect Person. Yet the sinners felt much more comfortable in His presence than they did with some of His disciples. A classic example is the difference in the attitude of Jesus and that of His disciples toward the Samaritan woman (see John 4). He was comfortable enough with her to discuss both her husbands and His heavenly Father, both water from the well and living water. The disciples had all sorts of hang-ups about her, and their judgmental attitude showed through to her. We must constantly be guarding ourselves against the "holier-than-thou" spirit which is so easy to come by and is so deadly to an effective witness. We should share Jesus Christ in love and in the power of His Spirit and leave the convicting to the Holy Spirit.   *Kenneth L. Chafin*

Everyone is eagle-eyed to see another's faults and deformity.

John Dryden

*Lord Jesus, how easy it is to judge others. May I always remember the
undeserved love and forgiveness You gave to me.*

―――――――――――――――•▸ **MAY 13** ◂•――――――――――――――

...unto thee will I pray. Psalm 5:2

•――――――――――――――――――――――――――――――――――――――•

DO NOT—I REPEAT—*DO NOT* TRY TO CHANGE PEOPLE to fit
your specifications. Don't try to manipulate people, play games,
plan schemes, trick, or deceive them. Instead, tell God on them! You
may have a spouse who is just plain ornery, and you were told this very
morning that he or she does not plan to change! Let God deal with your
mate's stubbornness.

Perhaps you are working with someone who is unfair and unbend-
ing, just plain *unreal.* How are you going to work in this situation?
You've tried every manipulative move in the world without success.
Talk to God about them.

You may know people in business or at school who are impossible
creatures! God says, "Let Me at them. I will change them in ways you
never would believe possible. Now, I'm not going to do it according to
your timetable. I'm going to do it in My time." So between now and
then, just relax.   Dr. Paul Brand and Philip Yancey

I always seek the good that is in people
and leave the bad to Him who made mankind
and knows how to round off the corners.
Goethe's mother

*Dear God, You are the One who can change a person completely. Help
me to keep my hands off and pray, in love, for them.*

―――――――――――――――•▸ **MAY 14** ◂•――――――――――――――

**And to know the love of Christ, which passeth knowledge,
that ye might be filled with all the fullness of God.** Ephesians 3:19

•――――――――――――――――――――――――――――――――――――――•

AS CHRISTIANS, WE AREN'T BOUND to a book of etiquette, but
we do need an example...someone who has both inner and outer
breeding...and we have One in Jesus. There were standards of acceptable behavior in His day—just as there are in ours—but there were
times when He didn't live by them. Jesus did what He felt was right...
He acted out of love...and sometimes that meant that He cut across
the cultural standards of His day. Think of the way He behaved toward the woman who sat at His feet and washed them with her tears...
or the woman taken in adultery...or the Samaritan woman at the well.
If He had done the socially accepted thing, He wouldn't have had any-

thing to do with those women...He wouldn't even have been seen with any of them. They were outcasts, considered sources of uncleanness... the kind of people one would never invite to dinner, ill-bred persons who burst into private little get-togethers and spoke to strangers without a proper introduction. There were others, too—the tax collector, the leper, the beggar, and all the little, forgotten people of the world. Manners, to Jesus, were not meaningless rituals...they were the way in which He reacted to people—all people. His behavior was governed not by propriety, but God's *agapē* love for man.

Colleen Townsend Evans

> There's a wideness in God's mercy
> Like the wideness of the sea;
> There's a kindness in His justice
> Which is more than liberty.
>
> For the love of God is broader
> Than the measure of man's mind,
> And the heart of the Eternal
> Is most wonderfully kind.

F. W. Faber

Lord Jesus, teach me in my relationships with others to be totally reliant on Your example of love.

MAY 15

**The fear of the Lord is clean, enduring for ever:
the judgments of the Lord are true and righteous
altogether. More to be desired are they than gold....**

Psalm 19:9-10

MOTHER HAD THE HABIT of leaving little notes—poems, quotations, essays—around the house for her children to read. Her communiques to me were always left on the piano or on my violin case. One Sunday morning, she placed on the piano a little poem by Rhea F. Miller. Mother thought its message beautiful and I did, too. Instead of practicing the hymn I had intended to play that Sunday in church, I turned to this poem. Melody just seemed to form around the words. When I had played and sung it through for the first time, Mother came from the kitchen where she had overheard. She wrapped both arms around my shoulders and placed her wet cheek next to mine. In church that morning I sang for the first time...

> I'd rather have Jesus than silver or gold,
> I'd rather be His than have riches untold,

I'd rather have Jesus than houses or lands,
I'd rather be led by His nail-pierced hands
Than to be the king of a vast domain,
Or be held in sin's dread sway,
I'd rather have Jesus than anything this world
affords today.

Heavenly Father, thank You for all earthly mothers who guide their children to Your love and for the memory of those who are with You now.

MAY 16

As one whom his mother comforteth, so will I comfort you.... Isaiah 66:13

T HE BIBLE CONTINUALLY HONORS the estate of motherhood. In the Old and New Testaments it is affirmed as we read of dedicated mothers like Hannah, Ruth, Elizabeth, Salome and Eunice.

It was to Mary that the supreme honor fell—to bear the Son of God. At the annunciation she had spoken the self-sacrificial words, "Be it unto me according to thy word" (Luke 1:38). She approached motherhood with a quiet, gentle trust. The birth of Jesus though in a crude, cold stable only brought joy to this young mother.

Mary watched her children grow into adulthood and shared their laughter and tears; the little house in Nazareth must have resounded with the noise made by Jesus and His brothers and sisters. Then one day Jesus left the close-knit family home to begin His ministry and all that faced Him in Jerusalem.

Jesus' mother experienced the inevitable sorrow that all mothers feel when a child grows up and his footsteps take him far away from the old familiar background. There would be the empty chair at mealtimes...the unused bed at night.

The deepest sorrow and loneliness was experienced as Mary faced the torment of Good Friday, seeing her beloved Son crucified—"there stood by the cross of Jesus his mother..." (John 19:25).

As she had comforted Him so often in life, how she must have longed to comfort Him in death.

J.W.B.

Mary's Song

I rocked Him as a Baby
I fed Him as a Child

I heard Him call my name out
    in the night.
I helped Him take His first step
I cried when I heard His first words
I wish they all could see through
    a mother's eyes.

David Mullins

Lord Jesus, for the example of Mary's love we thank You; and for Your love, obedient unto death, we praise You.

MAY 17

...my Father will love him, and we will come unto him, and make our abode with him. John 14:23

*D*URING THE WAR A BOY WAS BROUGHT into the hospital badly wounded. Word was sent to the mother that the boy was dying. She came to the hospital and begged to see him, but the doctors said that he was just hovering between life and death and that the slightest excitement might kill him. Besides, he was unconscious and would not know her. She promised that she would not speak to him or make the slightest noise, but begged to sit by the side of his bed and be with him. The doctor relented and gave permission for her to sit there without a word. She sat by her boy with her heart bursting. His eyes were closed. She gently put her hand upon his brow. Without opening his eyes the boy whispered, "Mother, you have come." The touch of that mother's hand was self-verifying to the boy. He knew it. When Christ puts His hand upon the fevered brow of our souls, we know the meaning of that touch and say from the inmost depths, "My Savior, You have come." E. Stanley Jones

The healing of His seamless dress
Is by our beds of pain;
We touch Him in life's throng and press,
And we are whole again.

John Greenleaf Whittier

Lord Jesus, the comfort of Your healing touch is felt in our times of illness and sorrow. We are loved.

MAY 18

For even the Son of man came not to be ministered unto, but to minister, and to give his life a ransom for many.

Mark 10:45

*T*OO OFTEN WHEN WE THINK OF STEWARDSHIP we have in mind money alone, forgetting that we must serve one another, each with the gift he has received, to the glory of God. A whole Life, the only perfect Life, has been given for us, and we should meet that matchless gift with nothing less than wholehearted service.

The happiest, most joyful, and most useful Christians are those who are giving in substance and service generously proportionate to their receiving. They are channels of blessing. Each blessing received brings a new opportunity to pass on a blessing. As one's contacts with people increase and become more intimate, the opportunities multiply to influence them and help them to live more useful lives and, above all, to point them upward to the Lamb of God who takes away the sins of the world.

Time has been given by God to use as a sacred trust. Each day of our lives is precious with opportunities for speaking a kind word, doing a noble deed, or rendering a Christlike service. Used in winning a soul to Christ and thereby adding a star to the Savior's crown, a few moments of time have a value that eternity alone can reveal. Let us be up and doing while it is day, for "the night cometh, when no man can work" (John 9:4).   *Morrow Coffey Graham*

> I am but one, but I am one; I cannot do
> everything, but I can do something. What I can
> do, by the grace of God, I will do.
>
> *Author unknown*

Lord, may I use every opportunity each day to minister in Your name. May others see Your joy in my life and be drawn into the reality of forgiveness in You, the Lamb of God, my Savior and my Lord.

MAY 19

The Lord is the portion of my inheritance.... Psalm 16:5

I HAVE SOMETHING TO SHARE WITH YOU which has filled my heart since my grandmother, Morrow Coffey Graham, went to be with the Lord Jesus Christ in heaven. In the months before she died, she had one aim, one burden, and that was to be assured that each member of her family—her children, her grandchildren and her great-grandchildren—would personally commit his life to the Lord Jesus Christ. As far as I know, each one has. The week before my grandmother died, my aunt went to visit her, and she put her arms around my aunt's neck and said, "Pass it on"—meaning, of course, her faith.

One of the reasons I'm willing to share my faith with you is in deference to my grandmother's wishes. I come from a Christian family. My parents are Christians, and my grandparents on both sides were Christians. My great-grandparents were committed Christians. As far back as I know, each person in my family has had a personal commitment to the Lord Jesus Christ.

I can say with King David, "The lines are fallen unto me in pleasant places; yea, I have a goodly heritage" (Psalm 16:6). Yet my "goodly heritage" would amount to nothing in God's sight if I had not made the choice to open my heart and receive Jesus Christ as Savior and commit my life to Him as Lord. I made that choice when I was very young and have reconfirmed that choice many times since.

So I am standing not on my grandmother's faith or on my father's faith; I stand squarely on my own faith in Jesus Christ, knowing that in God's sight I belong to Him because of the transaction that I have made with His Son at the cross. I love the Lord Jesus with my whole heart.

I would challenge you, even if you are from a Christian home or have a church background, to examine your heart and see if in God's sight you belong to Him. You have to come to Him yourself, open your heart and receive His Son as your Savior and commit your life to Him as Lord. You have to make that personal transaction because God has no grandchildren. *Anne Graham Lotz*

Jesus Christ will be Lord of all or He will not be Lord at all.
Augustine

Father, for the rebirth through Your Son that has brought a newness and purpose to my life, I thank You.

---————•———— **MAY 20** —•————————————

Then shall the righteous answer him, saying, Lord, when saw we thee an hungered, and fed thee? or thirsty, and gave thee drink?... And the King shall answer and say unto them, Verily I say unto you, Inasmuch as ye have done it unto one of the least of these my brethren, ye have done it unto me. Matthew 25:37,40

*I*T IS WELL TO REMEMBER that when we do something for another person with love, and for the Lord, it is inevitably connected with doing it for someone who *would not normally be cared for in that way.* I really do not think that it means providing a big steak dinner for your husband's employer, or for some important client, or for someone you want to impress, or for someone who has entertained you and to whom you are returning the favor. I do not think when we are told to be "given to hospitality" it means that we are to be hospitable only to old friends. After all, we are told that if we are hospitable, in this special way, we *may* sometimes entertain "angels unawares." To do that we should have to be doing something special for a *stranger*. In any case, to do something directly for Him we would have to be doing it for "one of the least of these."

Edith Schaeffer

> Lo! I come with joy to do
>   The Father's blessed will;
> Him in outward works pursue,
>   And serve His pleasure still.
> Faithful to my Lord's commands,
>   I still would choose the better part;
> Serve with careful Martha's hands,
>   And loving Mary's heart.

Charles Wesley

(Remember, we may be serving in Jesus' name an "angel unaware.")

Father, grant to me the spirit of true hospitality when serving any of Your children, rich or poor, lovely or unlovely.

MAY 21

Be not forgetful to entertain strangers.... Hebrews 13:2

---

*I*N A WORLD THAT HAS LOST THE DIMENSION of personal involvement in the concern of others, it is refreshing to know that Christian hospitality specializes in thoughtfulness toward others. The test of that thoughtfulness is an interest in and concern for those who are strangers to us.

It requires no exercise of love to show ourselves friendly to those who are our friends. The grace of God calls us to go out of our way to show compassion to those who are complete strangers to us. This is the essence of hospitality. With this friendliness there must be helpfulness toward our guests. In ancient times, such friendliness involved washing the feet of a guest, anointing the head with oil, providing a change of raiment, and food and sleeping accommodations. Hospitality was judged by the measure in which these services were effectively rendered.

Stephen F. Olford

(Let us ask our Lord to help us be gracious hosts and hostesses, more conscious of another's need than our own.)

> *O Keeper of our hearth,*
> *Master of our home,*
> *Seeker of wayward souls,*
> *One prayer we ask of thee:*
> *Take our hesitating hearts*
> *And give us eyes to see*
> *and tongues to say Your "Welcome,"*
> *Give willingness*
> *to open doors or roofs*
> *to chilly winds that blow,*
> *That by our hearths*
> *the lame may walk,*
> *the weary rest,*
> *the loveless and unknown*
> *find in Thee a warm embrace,*
> *an everlasting home.*
>
> *Bonnie Barrows Thomas*

MAY 22

There came unto him a woman having an alabaster box of very precious ointment.... Matthew 26:7

MARY IS AT A LOVELY SOCIAL FUNCTION at the house of one Simon. There she is, circulating among the friends and guests, but her Lord is all-important to her. "There came unto him a woman." And as a present she brings from her possessions the only treasure she has. It is an alabaster box of ointment, perfectly blended, so that its delightful aroma fills the room. This is what she poured on her Lord. It was the best that she had, and she gave Him the best.

I am very conscious of the fact that I am personally prone to give the Lord the leftovers in my life—the leftovers of my time, my talent, my day, my week. Not the choicest, nor the best. Meister Eckhart once said that people would give to God their possessions, their money, their land, even their children, but they did not want to part with themselves. The self is the treasure. Have you parted with your treasure? Have you given yourself to Him in complete commitment?

Christ demands the best in our lives.   *Millie Dienert*

Accept His will entirely, and never suppose that you could serve Him better in any other way. You can never serve Him well, save in the way He chooses.   *Francis de Sales*

Lord, forgive the times I give You the leftovers. I would surrender myself completely and give You all the power of choice in my life.

MAY 23

We then that are strong ought to bear the infirmities of the weak, and not to please ourselves. Romans 15:1

A YOUNG DOCTOR WAS TURNING THE LIGHTS OUT in a mission hall, where he had been working in the East End of London, when he found a small, dirty little boy. The lad begged the doctor to let him sleep there as he had nowhere else to go. The boy told him that he had been living in a coal bunker with some other boys. As the doctor won the confidence of the child, he persuaded him to show him where the place was. After going through many dark alleys, they came to a hole in a wall that was part of a factory. Crawling through, the doctor found 13 boys huddled under rags to keep warm. All were asleep.

Because of this experience the doctor's heart was burdened by the Lord to start a home in London for abandoned children. When he died, Dr. Thomas J. Barnardo had founded homes for over 80,000 homeless boys and girls. This work started when he saw one small child without a place to sleep. In each town or city where we live there is still a need that Christ wants *us* to reach out and touch in His name. Are we willing to open our hearts?   *J.W.B.*

> Love has a hem to her garment
>   That trails in the very dust;
> It can reach the stains of the streets and lanes,
>   And because it can, it *must.*
>
> *Author unknown*

Lord Jesus, burden my heart and let me be willing to love in Your name, even though it may cause me to abandon desires I have felt so important.

MAY 24

For our gospel came not unto you in word only, but also in power, and in the Holy Ghost, and in much assurance.... I Thessalonians 1:5

I THINK IT WAS ABOUT FIVE THIS MORNING that I opened my Testament on the words, "(There) are given unto us exceeding great and precious promises: that by these ye might be partakers of the divine nature" (II Peter 1:4). Just as I went out, I opened it again on those words, "Thou art not far from the kingdom of God" (Mark 12:34).

In the evening I went very unwillingly to a society in Aldersgate Street, where one was reading Luther's preface to the Epistle to the Romans. About a quarter before nine, while he was describing the change which God works in the heart through faith in Christ, I felt my heart strangely warmed. I felt I did trust in Christ, Christ alone, for salvation; and an assurance was given me that he had taken away my sins, even mine, and saved me from the law of sin and death.
John Wesley's Journal, May 24, 1738

There is but one way to tranquility of mind and happiness, and that is to account no external things thine own but to commit all to God.
Epictetus

Almighty God, as I commit all I am to You, Your peace and joy flow into my being and I am at one with You, my Creator.

MAY 25

Come unto me, all ye that labor and are heavy laden, and I will give you rest. Matthew 11:28

A MISSIONARY FRIEND TOLD ME of a time of great crisis in her life. They were stationed in a primitive area, and her husband had to go on an extended trip into "the bush." He had scarcely left when one of the children contracted polio. Soon the others developed a minor malady with alarmingly similar symptoms. My friend felt desperate. How could she bear the responsibilities—day and night nursing, the anxiety at home as well as concern for her husband who was venturing into unknown territory?

Eventually the episode had a happy ending. The children recovered; the mother lived through a very difficult time; and the father returned safely, rejoicing because of souls who came to know Christ because he had gone to them with the Gospel message.

Our conversation had started because she was comforting me during a period in which my tribulations loomed large. But as she talked they seemed small compared to some of her experiences.

"How did you survive?" I asked her. "Of course I know you must have prayed and prayed and prayed!"

"Actually, I didn't," she confessed. "I was too exhausted to formulate the words. I moved like an automaton from one task to the next one. God understood, and I felt His presence. Also, He gave me a simple sentence that kept me going day and night. I want to share it with you. Try it; it will sustain you through anything: I've proven its worth. I just affirmed: 'For this, I have Jesus.'"   *Winola Wells Wirt*

The moment I awaked, "Jesus, Master," was in my heart and in my mouth; and I found all my strength lay in keeping my eye fixed upon Him, and my soul waiting on Him continually.
John Wesley's Journal, May 25, 1738

Lord, when problems weigh heavily upon my heart it is more than enough for me to say, "Jesus," for I know You hear and are with me.

MAY 26

Behold, what manner of love the Father hath bestowed upon us, that we should be called the sons of God.... I John 3:1

---

*A*LL OF US HAVE THE NEED TO BELONG. Ultimately, that need is for more than natural or adoptive parents. It is a need to be able to say to God, "My Father." I have read someplace that Anna Marx, the daughter of Karl Marx, the father of Communism, told a friend that she had come across an old prayer which began, "Our Father, who art in heaven." With her secular upbringing she did not recognize the Lord's Prayer, but she told her friend wistfully, "If there really was a God like the One described in that prayer, I could believe in Him."

As an adopted son of the heavenly Father I would like to say, "Anna, He is real. He is a home for all your longings. Believe in Him."

Being adopted by God brings great privileges but also great responsibilities. He has chosen us to bear "the family likeness." He expects us not to dishonor the family name, but to live a life worthy of being God's child.

The Apostle John puts the privilege and responsibility into perspective: "See how very much our heavenly Father loves us, for he allows us to be called his children—think of it—and we really are! But since most people don't know God, naturally they don't understand that we are his children. Yes, dear friends, we are already God's children, right now, and we can't even imagine what it is going to be like later on. But we do know this, that when he comes we will be like him, as a result of seeing him as he really is. And everyone who really believes this will try to stay pure because Christ is pure."   *Leighton Ford*

By a Carpenter mankind was made, and only by that Carpenter can mankind be remade.   *Erasmus*

Father, thank You for the assurance that I belong to You and that You love me.

———————————————•— **MAY 27** —•———————————————

That their hearts might be comforted, being knit together in love, and unto all riches of the full assurance of understanding.... Colossians 2:2

◆——◆

ON MY FIRST VISIT TO THE CHURCHES OF NORWAY I felt very much alone, far from home and family. Everything around me seemed strange. I was deeply concerned about my witness of the Gospel. Would the people understand it? Would they accept my preaching and the ideas about evangelism that I was seeking to share?

The morning after arriving in Oslo I was dressing in my room and discovered a Scripture verse in my shirt pocket. My shaving kit had another one. My Bible had several new bookmarkers of Bible verses written out in longhand. My coat pockets had several more little slips of paper with Bible passages on them. Almost every day I discovered one of these slips of paper in the most unusual places. My wife had selected the Bible passages, and my daughter had written them out and had hidden them in my belongings.

One verse after another assured me that I had been commended to God and to the Word of His grace. I was assured of family prayers daily on my behalf. These helped me enormously as I went through the day, giving me confidence in what I was doing. I knew I was not alone. God was with me like a pillar of cloud by day and a fire at night.   *Conrad M. Thompson*

Shall I tell you what supported me through all these years of exile among a people whose language I could not understand, and whose attitude toward me was always uncertain and often hostile? It was this, "Lo, I am with you alway even unto the end of the world."
David Livingstone

Almighty God, for the confidence of Your presence and loving care for us wherever we may be, we praise and magnify Your name.

———————————————•— **MAY 28** —•———————————————

Commit thy way unto the Lord; trust also in him; and he shall bring it to pass. Psalm 37:5

*T*HE LORD JESUS CHRIST TELLS US if we close our hot little fists over anything we are going to lose it. Our Lord teaches that we are simply stewards of what He gives—health, intellect, family, friends, material possessions and the time allotted to us in this life. We save and lose; we lose and save.

One of our young people made a trip to a missionary station where he met a fine young girl for whom he felt a strong attachment. When he left, the girl gave him a rose as a reminder of their friendship. He was in love, and he carried this beautiful flower in his left fist for the whole 36-hour return trip to Boston. Upon his arrival he told Marian and me of all that had happened and of the beautiful flower he had been given. He then opened his hand and to his horror the flower was now something to be disposed of quickly. We see children held too tightly by parents. We see possessions strangling the possessor.

Son Allan explained to us, as he viewed his own life in the light of Galatians 2:20. "For one who is crucified with Christ, hanging on a cross, there is no comfortable future, no career plan. There is the freedom of being with Christ, sharing His cross, and the joy of facing an eternity with Him."

We each have our own ways to abandon ship. God speaks to us in different ways to surrender different things to make us free. To a seaman the text is simple enough. It is the solemn, urgent command— "Now hear this: Abandon Ship, All Hands!"   *Allan C. Emery*

I have held many things in my hands and lost them all; but whatever I have placed in God's hands, that I still possess.   *Martin Luther*

Father, all that I possess is Yours. My trust is in Your loving power and grace.

--------------------------- **MAY 29** ------------------

...God the Judge of all.... Hebrews 12:23

*S*OME YEARS AGO A VETERAN MISSIONARY WAS STAYING in my home. During his stay, a particularly precocious young student in a nearby Bible school asked to speak to my friend. He delivered a long lecture to the missionary on the subject of his own attributes and excellences and came to a crashing climax with the immortal words, "My father thinks that for me to serve God as a missionary would be a total waste." The veteran looked up slowly and with a steady, quiet voice said, "So much for your father's view of God. Now let me tell you God's view of your father." It is God's view of man that is so largely misunderstood, because man likes to spend time expressing his view of God instead of taking time to learn God's view of man. To be reminded that "The eyes of the Lord are everywhere, keeping watch on the wicked and the good" (Proverbs 15:3) is to be alerted to the possibility of His watching us.   *D. Stuart Briscoe*

The one thing we need is to know God better.   *J. Hudson Taylor*

Almighty and everlasting God, I would take more time to discover the wonder and glory of You, my Creator.

<hr>

MAY 30

...the one who is the true Light arrived to shine on everyone coming into the world. John 1:9 *(TLB)*

<hr>

*T*HE FIRST SPRING WE LIVED IN OUR HOUSE IN ST. PAUL, I came down to the dining room one morning to see it alive with brilliant color. The whole room was aglow with little rainbows all over the walls, ceiling and furniture. The rising sun had come far enough north to be directly in line with my small kitchen window, the dining room door and then our crystal chandelier. And the piercing white light of that morning sun was producing hundreds of rainbows by diffusing through all of the crystals every color of the spectrum. I swung the chandelier ever so slightly, and the colors danced and flashed around the room. I stood spellbound at the spectacular sight.

How similar that is to God's penetration of my life. Webster's *New World Dictionary* defines *white* as "the color of radiated, transmitted, or reflected light containing all of the visible rays of the spectrum." And God, too, is the sum total of all that exists. He is infinite. One of His attributes is infinity—that quality of being limitless, to which nothing can be added. And He enters me as pure white piercing light. God in me, my Source of change, wanting to *radiate* through me all the visible rays of the sum total of all that He is. God's acceptable will for me is that I will let Him change me until I sparkle and glow and radiate Him into my whole environment.

Evelyn Christenson

God is the presence, warm, all-enfolding,
   touching the drab world into brilliance, lifting

the sad heart into song, indescribable, beyond understanding,
yet by a bird's note, a chord of music,
a light at sunset, a sudden movement of rapt insight,
a touch of love, making the whole universe
a safe home for the soul.

An early Christian

Almighty God, the luster of Your love brings radiance to my days.
May my life be luminous, Lord, for You.

MAY 31

I go to prepare a place for you. John 14:2

◆   ◆

*W*ONDERFUL AS OUR HOMES AND FAMILIES MAY BE, they are not permanent. Sometimes I look at my own children and can hardly believe they are all grown and on their own—and have made me a grandfather many times over. My wife and I are alone in an empty house that once rang with the laughter of five children.

When Jesus said, "In my Father's house are many mansions," we find a very interesting meaning for the word *mansion.* The Greek word used does not mean an imposing house but a resting place. The expression is translated in the margin of the *American Standard Version* as "abiding places." This comes from the same stem as the English word *remain.*

During Christ's ministry on earth He had no home. He once said, "Foxes have holes and birds of the air have nests, but the Son of man has no place to lay his head" (Matthew 8:20).

His home in heaven is not transitory, however, but permanent.

The early disciples who for Christ's sake had given up houses and lands and loved ones knew little of home life or home joys. Christian pilgrims suffered in many ways, and Jesus knew it—for He suffered more severely than any of His followers. It was as if Jesus had said to them: "We have no lasting home here on earth, but My Father's house is a home where we will be together for all eternity."

Billy Graham

(We as Christians have so much to look forward to. The last journey is not the one to fear but to anticipate with joy!)

When outward bound we boldly sail
And leave the friendly shore,
Let not our hearts of courage fail
Before the voyage is o'er.
We trust in Thee, whate'er befall;

Thy sea is great, our boats are small.

When homeward bound we gladly turn,
O bring us safely there,
Where harbor lights of friendship burn
And peace is in the air.
We trust in Thee, whate'er befall;
Thy sea is great, our boats are small.

Henry Van Dyke

JUNE 1

It is of the Lord's mercies that we are not consumed, because his compassions fail not. They are new every morning: great is thy faithfulness. Lamentations 3:22-23

◆ ―――――――――――――――――――――――――――――――――――― ◆

GREAT IS THY FAITHFULNESS, O God my Father!
There is no shadow of turning with Thee;
Thou changest not, Thy compassions, they fail not:
As Thou hast been Thou forever wilt be.
Great is Thy faithfulness,
Great is Thy faithfulness,
Morning by morning new mercies I see;
All I have needed Thy hand hath provided—
Great is Thy faithfulness, Lord, unto me!

Thomas O. Chisholm

Next time you lustily sing this hymn in church or conference...remember that it was what Jeremiah said to the Lord, right after he had been expressing his despair and depression, and while he was still in the same unchanging affliction. We are apt to sing that hymn and think of fresh dew on the morning grass or rose garden (or even of beautiful food spread on a snowy-white linen cloth), without remembering that Jeremiah gave the Lord this praise after he had just been talking about being desolate and being the laughingstock of the people as they tortured him. It was both the memory of the past and the hope for the future that made Jeremiah able to say those lilting words of praise to the Lord. It was trust in the Lord, kindled by rethinking who He is, and faith in the ultimate victory of the Lord that enabled Jeremiah to break out into song. *Edith Schaeffer*

Lord God, I will remember and praise You for all Your faithfulness to me each day, even when those days are dark.

The Lord thy God in the midst of thee is mighty....

Zephaniah 3:17

*W*HETHER YOU ARE SOLOING OR DUETTING at this moment, don't ever listen or take to heart the voices around you that would shout: "God doesn't care about you. Who are you to Him? How can He be involved in the tiny details of your life when He has billions of people to look after?"

We have, carefully preserved, for *all* of us, the marvelous words of Psalm 121. Read these words slowly and inject them into the bloodstream of mind, body and soul: "He will never let me stumble, slip or fall. For he is always watching, never sleeping.... He keeps his eye upon you as you come and go, and always guards you" (Psalm 121:3-4,8, *TLB*).

Our God never sleeps, and His eyes are always watching and guarding us. Astounding!

Joyce Landorf

A mighty fortress is our God,
A bulwark never failing;
Our helper He amid the flood
Of mortal ills prevailing.
For still our ancient foe
Doth seek to work us woe—
His craft and power are great,
And armed with cruel hate.
On earth is not His equal.

Did we in our own strength confide,
Our striving would be losing,
Were not the right man on our side,
The man of God's own choosing.
Dost ask who that may be?
Christ Jesus, it is He—
Lord Sabaoth His name,
From age to age the same,
And He must win the battle.

Martin Luther

Lord God, how comforting it is to know that You are interested in every detail of my life. Thank You for Your vigilant care.

*...thou hast made the heaven and the earth
by thy great power and stretched out arm,
and there is nothing too hard for thee....* Jeremiah 32:17

THE PURSUITS OF LIFE ILLUSTRATE FAITH in many ways. The farmer buries good seed in the earth and expects it not only to live but to be multiplied. He has faith in the covenant arrangement that "seed-time and harvest shall not cease," and he is rewarded for his faith.

The merchant places his money in the care of a banker and trusts completely the honesty and soundness of the bank. He entrusts his capital to another's hands and feels far more at ease than if he had the solid gold locked up in an iron safe.

The sailor trusts himself to the sea. When he swims he takes his foot from the bottom and rests upon the buoyant ocean. He could not swim if he did not wholly cast himself upon the water.

The goldsmith puts precious metal into the fire which seems eager to consume it, but he receives it back again from the furnace purified by the heat.

You cannot turn anywhere in life without seeing faith in operation between man and man or between man and natural law. Now, just as we trust in daily life, even so are we to trust in God as He is revealed in Christ Jesus. *Charles H. Spurgeon*

Turn to the New Testament, and...all is freshness and wonder, and a strange eager tension of expectancy, and the continual surprise of discovery. It is this that differentiates a dynamic and infectious faith from the dull tedium of conventional religion. And it is this that differentiates a living church from a dead ecclesiastical machine—this tension of expectancy, this urgent waiting upon God, this wondering what God will do next. "I have both glorified (My name), and will glorify it again." And if you will receive it, this is the word of the Lord for you. Expect great things from God! *James S. Stewart*

O God, my soul is waiting for Your next communique!

Fight the good fight of faith.... I Timothy 6:12

*W*HEN SATAN WANTS TO GAIN VICTORY OVER A MAN and keep him from fighting the good fight of faith, he does not have to throw an unconquerable foe against that individual. All he has to do is change the person's attitude toward victory, for when that man is convinced that victory is no longer possible, he is already defeated. Satan does not enjoy bringing God's children into an arena for a contest for supremacy. He delights in keeping the child of God from ever entering the arena by discouraging him before he begins. Day by day we have to fight the battle of discouragement and faintheartedness in the fight of faith. Discouragement is principally self-preoccupation. A man is discouraged because he has turned his eyes inward upon himself and he evaluates all things in terms of himself. He sees every situation in its effect upon him personally and, being totally occupied with himself, he is easily discouraged because he knows he is inadequate for any situation. While it is true that the believer can do all things through Christ who strengthens him, it is also true that by himself the child of God can do nothing; and as soon as he is no longer occupied with Jesus Christ but becomes occupied with himself, he is ready prey to discouragement.   *J. Dwight Pentecost*

The first step to victory is to recognize the enemy.
                                                          Corrie ten Boom
Lord, when I get discouraged keep me constantly aware of the source, and in Your name I will claim victory over Satan's power.

JUNE 5

...Have faith in God. Mark 11:22

---

*T*HE ALMIGHTY IS NEVER TAKEN BY SURPRISE. His wisdom and knowledge are infinite and complete. He knows the end from the beginning, a truth we recognize but little comprehend. Often in the Bible we are reminded that the Lord is good and that He has the deepest interest in our highest welfare. In Jeremiah 29:11 He assures us of that, saying, "For I know the thoughts that I think toward you...thoughts of peace, and not of evil, to give you an expected end." He has a plan and purpose for us. He has unfailing provision with which to furnish His table. He unfolds His plan and makes available His provision for us as He sees best, sometimes far in advance, sometimes a day at a time, almost moment by moment. The trusting heart does not tremble at the apparent lack of plan or provision, for he knows that the Shepherd has already made full preparation. Our part is to enter by faith into God's plan for our life and to take from His hand the provision He has prepared for us. The Lord makes life an adventure for those who truly love and trust Him.

V. Raymond Edman

(How many times we run ahead of our Lord, failing to wait on Him in every circumstance in our life. Let us *really* trust Him.)

Take away anything I have, but do not take away the sweetness of walking and talking with the King of Glory! It is good to let our thoughts run away with us sometimes, concerning the greatness of our God and His marvelous kindness to us. As we look back, what wonderful leadings and providences we see; what encouragement we find for the future. *John Stam*

Lord Jesus, how lovingly You have led me through all my days. The memories give me courage to face each day, knowing in You is victory.

JUNE 6

Blessed are they that do his commandments.... Revelation 22:14

*F*AITH IS THE ROOT OF OBEDIENCE, and this may be clearly seen in the affairs of life. When a captain trusts a pilot to steer his vessel into port, he manages the vessel according to his direction. When a traveler trusts a guide to conduct him over a difficult pass, he follows the track which his guide points out. When a patient believes in a physician, he carefully follows his prescriptions and directions. Faith which refuses to obey the commands of the Savior is a mere pretence and will never save the soul. We trust Jesus to save us. He gives us directions as to the way of salvation; we follow those directions and are saved. Do not forget this. Trust Jesus and prove your trust by doing whatever He bids you. *Charles H. Spurgeon*

> He leadeth me, O blessed thought!
> O words with heav'nly comfort fraught!
> Whate'er I do, where'er I be,
> Still 'tis God's hand that leadeth me.
>
> > He leadeth me, He leadeth me,
> > By His own hand He leadeth me;
> > His faithful follower I would be,
> > For by His hand He leadeth me.

And when my task on earth is done,
When by Thy grace the victory's won,
E'en death's cold wave I will not flee,
Since God thru Jordan leadeth me.

Joseph H. Gilmore

Lord Jesus, whatever You ask me to do, may my spirit be one of love and utter obedience to You.

...if thou shalt confess with thy mouth the Lord Jesus, and shalt believe in thine heart that God hath raised him from the dead, thou shalt be saved. Romans 10:9

◆ ── ◆

G RACE IS GOD COMING DOWN TO US. Initiated by His love, grace is the spiritual force that invades our lives. Indeed, it is God Himself offering us His spiritual favor. He meets us where we are—while we are yet sinners. Salvation is beneficent on His part, unmerited on ours. It is totally God's work, and in love He bestows it on us.

Now for our part: Faith is our response to God, involving our minds, our hearts, and our wills. It includes, but is much more than, mental assent to a propositional statement.

Faith, in the biblical sense, means turning to God in our need and helplessness, and responding by accepting the gifts He offers. This is more than an abstraction. It means we receive, or trust in, the Lord Himself.

Russell T. Hitt

Many, who often hear the Gospel of Christ, are yet but little affected, because they are void of the Spirit of Christ.

But whosoever would fully and feelingly understand the words of Christ must endeavor to make all his life like in its beauty unto His.

What will it avail thee to dispute profoundly of the Trinity if thou be void of humility and art thereby displeasuring to the Trinity?

Surely, high words do not make a man holy and just, but a virtuous life maketh him dear to God.

I had rather feel compunction than understand the definition thereof.

If thou didst know the whole Bible by heart, and the sayings of all the philosophers, what would all that profit thee without the love of God and without grace?

Thomas à Kempis

Father, bestow upon me a full realization of Your grace so that I will know completely the joy of my salvation and share it with others.

***Beloved, if God so loved us, we ought also
to love one another.*** I John 4:11

*W*HEN THE NOTED THEOLOGIAN KARL BARTH was speaking in America, a group of theologians asked him what was the most significant theological discovery of his life. Expecting to hear a complicated answer, they were surprised when he said, "The most important truth I've learned is, Jesus loves me this I know, for the Bible tells me so."

If there's one statement of affirmation I would want you to retain, it's this: God loves you. Jesus came to earth to prove it and to clear sin out of the way so that we could experience God's highest desire for us —an abundant and ultimately fulfilling life. He wants us to personally know His love daily—to enjoy and share it with others. And He wants us to mature in the way He originally intended us to grow up. He has communicated to us His principles of conduct to protect and provide for our welfare.

He has even gone so far as to take care of our failures when we confess them and accept His forgiveness. Through a personal relationship to Jesus Christ, we become transformed. Our minds are renewed. We are changed. We no longer have to be dumb or deliberate or distracted or destitute of discipline. We are set free to love and serve and live an unparalleled life, whether it's in the bedroom or any other room of life.

That's the secret of loving. There is no other.

Don't miss out. I challenge you

...GO FOR IT!

Josh McDowell & Paul Lewis

> *Immortal Love, forever full.*
> *Forever flowing free,*
> *Forever shared, forever whole*
> *A never-ebbing sea.*

John Greenleaf Whittier

Charity never faileth.... I Corinthians 13:8

*L*OVE IS SUCCESS. Love is happiness, love is life.
"Love, I say," with Browning, "is energy of life.
For life, with all it yields of joy and woe

And hope and fear,
Is just our chance o' the prize of learning love—
How love might be, hath been indeed, and is."

Where Love is, God is. He that dwelleth in Love dwelleth in God. God is Love. Therefore *love*. Without distinction, without calculation, without procrastination, love. Lavish it upon the poor, where it is very easy; especially upon the rich, who often need it most; most of all upon our equals, where it is very difficult, and for whom perhaps we each do least of it. There is a difference between *trying to please* and *giving to pleasure*. Give pleasure. Lose no chance of giving pleasure. For that is the ceaseless and anonymous triumph of a truly loving spirit. "I shall pass through this world but once. Any good thing therefore that I can do, or any kindness that I can show to any human being, let me do it now. Let me not defer it or neglect it, for I shall not pass this way again." *Henry Drummond*

If I had only one day to see people for what they really are, I would want to look beyond all the things that are so obvious to my eyes... all the imperfections and even the glaring mistakes in their lives. I would want to look at the inner person, not at the outer garments.... I hope I would get down to basics and look for the good in each man and woman, because that's what really counts. I hope I would see each one as God sees him...for though we may say *no* to God—God never rejects anyone. I guess what I'm really saying is that I hope I would *hope*—because that's the best way I can say, "I love you." *Colleen Townsend Evans*

Our Father, let me look beyond the faults and failures of others and see a soul You love.

―――――――――――――――― • **JUNE 10** • ――――――――――――――――

...let us stop just saying we love people; let us really love them, and show it by our actions. I John 3:18 *(TLB)*

◆―――◆

*H*OW CAN WE TELL THAT WE ARE TRULY BOUND IN LOVE to other Christians? For one thing, we are concerned about them. The believers at Philippi were concerned about Paul and sent Epaphroditus to minister to him. Paul was also greatly concerned about his friends at Philippi, especially when Epaphroditus became ill and did not return right away (Philippians 2:25-28). "My little children, let us not love in word, neither in tongue, but in deed and in truth" (I John 3:18).

Another evidence of Christian love is a willingness to forgive one another. "And above all things have fervent charity (love) among yourselves: for charity (love) shall cover the multitude of sins" (I Peter 4:8).

"Tell us some of the blunders your wife has made," a radio quizmaster asked a contestant.

"I can't remember any," the man replied.

"Oh, surely you can remember something!" the announcer said.

"No, I really can't," said the contestant. "I love my wife very much, and I just don't remember things like that." First Corinthians 13:5 states that "love keeps no record of wrongs" (*NIV*).

Christians who practice love always experience joy; both come as a result of the presence of the same Holy Spirit. "The fruit of the Spirit is love, joy..." (Galatians 5:22). *Warren B. Wiersbe*

The love that we need is God Himself coming into our hearts. When the soul is perfected in love, it has such a sense of that love that it can rest in it for eternity, and though it has as much as it can contain for the time being, it can always receive more. *Andrew Murray*

Gracious God, because of the gift of Your love may others see a loving and forgiving spirit within me.

JUNE 11

...love...thy neighbor as thyself. Luke 10:27

---

*I*F YOU ARE GOING TO BE ABLE TO VALUE OTHERS, you must first be able to see something of value in yourself. If you do not love (in the truest sense of the word) and value yourself, you will be unable to value others.

Some Christian writers have questioned whether self-love is biblical. Did Jesus really mean that we should love our neighbor as ourselves *as a command*, or was He merely saying in effect, "You already love yourself too much and you should therefore love your neighbor just as much"? In other words, is Jesus presupposing self-love—or is He commanding it? There is no doubt in my mind that Jesus is addressing Himself primarily to the error of misunderstanding the term *neighbor* and that He presupposes self-love. Paul does the same in Ephesians 5:28 when he tells us to love our wives as our own bodies. In neither case is self-love condemned, however, and the difficulty we have with understanding it today is more a problem with what it means to *love* than anything else. *Archibald D. Hart*

Instead of allowing yourself to be unhappy, just let your love grow as God wants it to grow. Seek goodness in others. Love more persons more. Love them more impersonally, more unselfishly, without thought of return. The return, never fear, will take care of itself.

Henry Drummond

Lord Jesus, teach me to love—in the right way—myself, so in turn I may love my neighbor.

 JUNE 12

A new commandment I give unto you, That ye love one another; as I have loved you, that ye also love one another. By this shall all men know that ye are my disciples, if ye have love one to another. John 13:34-35

...that they all may be one; as thou, Father, art in me, and I in thee, that they also may be one in us: that the world may believe that thou hast sent me. John 17:21

●——●

*W*HAT THEN SHALL WE CONCLUDE but that as the Samaritan loved the wounded man, we as Christians are called upon to love *all* men as neighbors, loving them as ourselves. Second, that we are to love all true Christian brothers in a way that the world may observe. This means showing love to our brothers in the midst of our differences—great or small—loving our brothers when it costs us something, loving them even under times of tremendous emotional tension, loving them in a way the world can see. In short, we are to practice and exhibit the holiness of God and the love of God, for without this we grieve the Holy Spirit.

Love—and the unity it attests to—is the mark Christ gave Christians to *wear* before the world. Only with this mark may the world know that Christians are indeed Christians and that Jesus was sent by the Father.

Francis A. Schaeffer

Believers are one in Christ, as He is one with the Father. The love of God rests on them, and can dwell in them. Pray that the power of the Holy Ghost may so work this love in believers that the world may see and know God's love in them. Pray much for this.

Andrew Murray

Lord Jesus, amid any times of differences I would ask for Your grace to deal, in love, with my neighbors and fellow Christians.

...lovers of their own selves.... II Timothy 3:2

S ELF-LOVE TAKES MANY FORMS. Not only pride and vanity and worldly ambition, but a sickly preoccupation with one's own troubles, physical or otherwise. Such self-centered, ingrown souls make themselves the center of their universe. Self thrives on attention. It grows as it is petted and coddled, until it becomes a colossus dominating one's life and all others it can by making friends and loved ones the slaves of such self-worship.

The best treatment is neglect by becoming preoccupied with something or someone else. Such ailments disappear when ignored. The supreme preoccupation is not a mere person or cause but Christ Himself. That is why He asked us to deny self, take up the cross, and follow Him. That is why He bade us lose our lives to find them. When He fills our minds and hearts and lives, other gods vanish. And no god is harder to topple from its shrine than self. It will gladly give up all lesser idols if only it be allowed to retain the throne.

Vance Havner

The sin of pride particularly has caused the downfall of many men. If pride could bring about the downfall of Lucifer in heaven, most certainly it can bring mortal man down too. We must be on guard against pride, or we are headed for a fall patterned after the fall of Lucifer and his angels, who turned into demons.

Billy Graham

Lord, open my mind so that I may see any pride or vanity that keeps me from being in the center of Your will.

But I am poor and needy; yet the Lord thinketh upon me.... Psalm 40:17

S EED-LOVE CRIES TO GOD from our poverty; Gift-love longs to serve, or even to suffer for, God; Appreciative love says: "We give thanks to Thee for Thy great glory." Need-love says of a woman "I cannot live without her"; Gift-love longs to give her happiness, comfort, protection—if possible, wealth; Appreciative love gazes and holds its breath and is silent, rejoices that such a wonder should exist even if not for him, will not be wholly dejected by losing her, would rather have it so than never to have seen her at all.

We murder to dissect. In actual life, thank God, the three elements of love mix and succeed one another, moment by moment. Perhaps none of them except Need-love ever exists alone, in "chemical" purity, for more than a few seconds. And perhaps that is because nothing about us except our neediness is, in this life, permanent.

C. S. Lewis

How wonderful to know you are loved. You can face all the trials, the disappointments, the rejections of others, if you know that you as a person are *loved.*

It is hard perhaps to realize that God, who created this vast universe, could possibly care for the individual. For me, it has always been necessary to imagine an immense family—the Father caring for each of His children as an earthly father does. He does not love the family in a general way, He loves each individual in a very special way.

J.W.B.

Yes, Lord, my need for Your eternal love in my life is permanent. Thank You for loving me.

JUNE 15

Even as the Son of man came not to be ministered unto, but to minister, and to give his life a ransom for many.

Matthew 20:28

O UR SON, FRANKLIN, SPENT SOME DAYS ON A BOAT in the South China Seas searching for boat people fleeing the oppressive regime in Vietnam. On board, Ha Jimmy, the first mate, told him how the week before they had rescued such a boat. It had been boarded by pirates, the passengers robbed, women raped, others wounded. The pirate ship was ramming the smaller boat to destroy all evidence when the rescue ship appeared and they fled.

First the wounded had to be tended to. Then the rescued needed to be fed, bathed, and allowed to rest. Later they were told of Jesus and His love.

One mother on board with several small children saw her baby die. There was nothing to do but put the tiny body overboard and watch it float away. A few days later the next child died. Once more the mother had to watch the little body floating away into the sea.

Ha Jimmy looked at Franklin, his eyes dark with fatigue, and asked, "Franklin, after all she had been through, if I hadn't given her Jesus, what had I really done for her?"

God can use a sensitive Christian to be a rich blessing in the life of one who knows pain and sorrow. Scripture provides guidelines for those who are in a position to help someone suffering.

Billy Graham

Tell me how much you know of the sufferings of your fellowman and I will tell you how much you have loved them.   *Helmut Thielicke*

Father, I would be involved with the world's suffering. So many are in pain both mentally and physically. Bless them, Lord, and make my heart tender.

JUNE 16

Jesus said, "...the kingdom of God is within you." Luke 17:21

WHEN HE REIGNS SUPREME IN OUR HEARTS we can pray, "Thy Kingdom come, Thy will be done on earth as it is in heaven." That means that His will becomes the passionate purpose of our lives. All our worthy ambitions must become secondary to our ultimate purpose. The lesser pearls of our pleasures, plans, priorities, and popularity must be surrendered to claim the pearl of the absolute rule of God in all of life's relationships and responsibilities.

The great need of our time is for Christians to live out the implications of the Kingdom of God. That requires study, prayer, imagination, and commitment. The more we come to know Christ and spend prolonged periods in prayer with Him, the more aware we will be of His guidance and direction. We will be able to imagine what our life could be if it was filled with Him and motivated by His love. If we ask Him, He will reveal what we are to do and say to *be* His love to others. He will expose the contradictions in our personal and interpersonal lives. The needs in our society that break His heart will break us open to specific caring. Get close to Christ and injustice will disturb us out of bland inactivity.   *Lloyd John Ogilvie*

Dare to look up to God and say, "Make use of me for the future as Thou wilt. I am of the same mind; I am one with Thee. I refuse nothing which seems good to Thee. Lead me whither Thou wilt, clothe me in whatever dress Thou wilt. Is it Thy will that I should be in a public or a private condition, dwell here, or be banished, be poor or rich? Under all these circumstances I will testify unto Thee before men.   *Epictetus*

Almighty God, motivate me with Your love, I pray, and use this life of mine to hasten Your Kingdom.

Now unto the King eternal, immortal, invisible,
the only wise God, be honor and glory for ever and ever.
Amen. I Timothy 1:17

*T*HEY WERE WASHING THEIR NETS after a long night of fishing. There was very little to wash out of their nets because they hadn't caught anything in them!

I can imagine that Peter did not enjoy the fact of his failure. He was a successful man. He was a man of some financial standing. He was not a novice fisherman. He was adept at his work, but he had failed that night.

Christ got into Peter's boat and asked to be taken a little way out from land so He could speak to the crowd that had "...pressed upon him to hear the word of God..." (Luke 5:1).

What could He teach from the boat of a fisherman who had failed to catch fish? We think success is the only podium. I have tried to bargain with Him by saying, "Promote me, Lord, and I'll glorify You from the pinnacle." He has replied, "Glorify Me where you are, or you'll never glorify Me at all."   *Jeannette Clift*

It is not the possession of extraordinary gifts that makes extraordinary usefulness, but the dedication of what we have to the service of God.   *F. W. Robertson*

Lord, You know when this ego pushes ahead and wants to serve You, but with self-glorification. Forgive me and make me more dedicated to glorifying You, I pray.

The Lord's blessing is our greatest wealth.
All our work adds nothing to it! Proverbs 10:22 (*TLB*)

I ONCE KNEW A VERY WISE MAN who understood that lesson very well. He and his wife once listened to a very rich and successful banker speak at a convention banquet. As they applauded the speaker when he had finished, the wife gently patted her husband's hand. "That's all right, honey," she said reassuringly. "Someday we'll be every bit as rich as he is."

Her husband turned to her, smiling, "We're rich now," he said quietly. "And someday we'll have money."

Jesus reminds us that the quality of a man's life does not consist in the abundance of the things which he possesses. Scriptures remind us again and again of the folly of putting our confidence in material wealth. On the other hand, we are exhorted to lay up for ourselves treasures in heaven—treasures that cannot rot or decay or be stolen from us. God reminds us that where our treasure is, there our hearts will be. And He wants us to be sure that our hearts are in a safe place where we cannot be hurt or disappointed.

> If you work for the things you believe in
>   You are *rich*, though the way is rough—
> If you work only for money
>   You can never make quite enough.
>
> Mary C. Crowley

(We are rich indeed with the blessings of God, for He is *always* generous.)

O Lord, Thou knowest that which is best for us. Let this or that be done, as Thou shalt please. Give what Thou wilt, how much Thou wilt, and when Thou wilt.   Thomas à Kempis

------------------------- • **JUNE 19** • -------------------------

Christ taught you! If you have really heard his voice... then throw off your old evil nature—the old you that was a partner in your evil ways.... Ephesians 4:20-22 (TLB)

◆————————————————————————————◆

THERE ARE TWO POWERS PRESENT IN OUR LIVES as Christians. There are our own personalities with our plans and purposes, and there is the Spirit of Christ. It is at this point that the secret of being a saint becomes clear. If we want to be a Christian with a true, lovely character, then we must know and experience a real change of heart. Here is the basic rule: The secret of a changed life is an exchanged life. John became a Christlike man because Christ was living in him in such a wonderful way that men could see only Christ.

This brings to us new hope in our daily living. If John had been born sweet and saintly, we would find not encouragement in his story, but rather a standard which condemned us, without giving us the hope of escaping from it. But John wasn't always sweet and saintly; he was like many Christians today—awkward, unlovely, quick-tempered and difficult to get along with.

John's willingness to know a changed life through an exchanged life brings to each of us the chance to open our hearts and lives to the overruling presence and power of the indwelling Spirit of Christ.

John E. Hunter

What you need to do is to put your will over completely into the hands of your Lord, surrendering to Him the entire control of it. Say, "Yes, Lord, yes!" to everything, and trust Him so to work in you as to bring your whole wishes and affections into conformity with His own sweet and lovable and most lovely will. It is wonderful what miracles God works in wills that are utterly surrendered to Him. He turns hard things into easy and bitter things into sweet. It is not that He puts easy things into the place of the hard, but He actually changes the hard thing into an easy one. *Hannah Whitall Smith*

Lord Jesus, change my heart into one that delights completely to do Your will.

---------•- **JUNE 20** -•---------

When pride cometh, then cometh shame: but with the lowly is wisdom. Proverbs 11:2

♦————————————————————————♦

*W*HAT *IS* THE BIBLICAL MEANING OF PRIDE? I believe sinful pride occurs when our arrogant self-sufficiency leads us to violate the two most basic commandments of Jesus: first, to love God with all our heart, mind and strength; and second, to love our neighbor as ourselves. A proud person is too pompous and haughty to bow humbly before his Maker, confessing his sins and submitting himself to a life of service to God; or he is hateful to his fellowmen, disregarding the feelings and needs of others. And as such, most of the ills of the world, including war and crime, can be laid at its door. That's why the writer of Proverbs put "a proud look" above all other evils, for that is where it belongs. *James Dobson*

> He that is down needs fear no fall,
>   He that is low, no pride;
> He that is humble ever shall
>   Have God to be his Guide.
>
> I am content with what I have,
>   Little be it, or much:
> And, Lord, contentment still I crave,
>   Because Thou savest such.
>
> Fullness to such a burden is
>   That go on pilgrimage;

Here little, and hereafter bliss,
Is best from age to age.

John Bunyan

Almighty God, who is always waiting to hear our prayers, create in me a humble and content heart, I pray.

JUNE 21

I have blotted out, as a thick cloud, thy transgressions, and, as a cloud, thy sins: return unto me; for I have redeemed thee. Isaiah 44:22

---

*I*N ONE OF THE GREAT CATHEDRALS OF ENGLAND is a beautiful stained-glass window through which the sunlight streams. It displays the personalities of the Old and New Testaments and the glorious truths and doctrines of the Christian faith. This window was fabricated by the artist out of broken bits of glass that another artist had discarded. No matter how broken or ugly our past, Christ has promised to make it into a thing of beauty if we will but turn our life over to Him. That is why the Apostle Paul could say, "Forgetting those things which are behind...I press toward the mark for the prize of the high calling of God in Christ Jesus."

Can you forget those things which are behind? Too many of us are like the man who paid $3,000 to have his family tree looked up and then $5,000 to have it hushed up. We have all kinds of things that we push back into the closets of our lives where they become skeletons that rattle and haunt us and give us nightmares.

Jesus Christ says that you can empty the closets and let the light in. Let the fresh air in. Take the skeletons out. He'll forgive your sins and take all of your failures and disappointments and frustrations and fit them into a pattern for your good and for the glory of God.

B. Clayton Bell

Between us and Thyself remove
Whatever hindrances may be,
That so our inmost heart may prove
A holy temple, meet for Thee.

From the Latin (15th century)

Lord, open the closet of my soul and let the cleansing light of Your Holy Spirit permeate every corner.

Moreover if thy brother shall trespass against thee,
go and tell him his fault between thee and him alone:
if he shall hear thee, thou hast gained a brother. Matthew 18:15

*W*HEN THE HOLY SPIRIT APPROACHES US about our need to forgive someone who has sinned against us, we are usually more concerned about our feelings. We tend to focus on *our* need to forgive, on overcoming *our* bitterness and anger. The whole exercise and experience of forgiving someone else is designed, we are convinced, solely to help us feel better.

But by implication, Jesus in Matthew 18:15 taught that this focus on our feelings is wrong. The goal is not to get us straightened out; it is to restore the brother or sister to fellowship. We are not to be so much concerned about our clear conscience as we are about the restoration into fellowship of the person who has sinned against us. In other words, the goal of forgiveness is restoration.   *Erwin Lutzer*

In this life, if you have anything to pardon, pardon quickly. Slow forgiveness is little better than no forgiveness.   *Arthur W. Pinero*

Lord Jesus, forgive me when I harbor feelings of bitterness toward another. Restore love and forgiveness in me.

Just as each of us now has a body like Adam's,
so we shall some day have a body like Christ's.

I Corinthians 15:49 *(TLB)*

*J*ESUS CHRIST LOOKED AT THE PEOPLE the way the famous horticulturist Luther Burbank looked at plants. Burbank is said to have viewed every weed as a potential plant.

Take Simon Peter. Others saw a blundering, awkward, unstable fisherman who couldn't be depended on because he was up one moment and down the next. But Jesus changed his name from *Simon*, meaning "reed," to *Cephas*—Peter—meaning "rock." He knew Peter was weak and unstable, but He also recognized what Peter could be (John 1:42).

Or think of the woman caught in the act of adultery. Others said she was a worthless sinner and wanted to stone her. But Jesus said,

"I know what you are. I don't condemn you, I know what you can be. Go, and sin no more."

Or think of Zacchaeus. Others avoided him because they saw a little, dried-up tax collector who defrauded his people and worked with the Romans. But when Jesus saw him in the tree, He called him by name, recognizing his reputation, but also knowing that he could be a great example of Jesus' power to change people. "Come down immediately. I must stay at your house today," Jesus said (Luke 19:5).

We Christians stereotype too easily. It is important to link the biblical teaching about people being sinners with the biblical fact that all are made in the image of God, with the potential of being remade.   *Leighton Ford*

When I came to believe in Christ's teaching, I ceased desiring what I had wished for before. The direction of my life, my desires, became different. What was good and bad changed places.   *Leo Tolstoy*

Lord, forgive me when I start to categorize certain people when all the time they are potential for being remade by Your transforming power.

———————————•— **JUNE 24** —•———————————

...they that wait upon the Lord
shall renew their strength. Isaiah 40:31 (TLB)

◆————————————————————————————————————◆

*I*N THIS INSTANCE THE WORD *WAIT* MEANS "TO TWIST or to stretch in order to become strong." In noun form it means "a line" or "a rope." In other words, it's the idea of stretching or twisting strands of hemp so that, in the process, far greater strength comes.

Someone has called this "the exchanged life," where we trade in our weakness for God's strength. I take my strand (like that of a little spider web) and wrap it around a steel cable of His character (via the waiting process), and then my strand is as strong as His character. I exchange my weakness for His cable-like strength. It never gives way in the heart of the fight; it holds firm.

Those who wait (those who exchange their weakness for His strength) upon the Lord will gain new strength. But remember: The key to the Lord's strength is *waiting*.

Look at the three things the prophet Isaiah says will happen.

...They will mount up with wings like eagles,
They will run and not get tired.
They will walk and not become weary (Isaiah 40:31).

The Hebrew meaning is "They will sprout wings like eagles." Isn't that interesting? What do you think of when you picture a soaring eagle? I think of freedom and strength. I think of dependability of flight. Wouldn't it be great to be able to fly? Those who wait upon the Lord somehow have that option open to them. There is the freedom of flight from life's pressures. And this freedom will be accompanied by inner peace. *Charles R. Swindoll*

We find freedom when we find God; we lose it when we lose Him.
Paul E. Scherer

Lord, I praise You that Your strength brings peace and enables me to soar above my problems.

———————————— **JUNE 25** ————————————

A soft answer turneth away wrath: but grievous words stir up anger. Proverbs 15:1

◆————————————————————————————————◆

*I*N OUR HUMAN RELATIONSHIPS, when we love someone, we know it and they know it. When we are angry with them, they know that too. Anger and love are really two extremes of the same emotion.

Settle your differences with God. Get them out where you can deal with them. Jesus said, "I have called you friends" (John 15:15). If two friends can't talk about what has come between them, something is wrong.

Anger that is brought out into the open can lead to reconciliation and restored harmony. Two people who argue and then settle the argument will often be closer than before because neither is harboring hate.

This is just as true with God as it is with the people we love. But for reconciliation I have to be honest enough to say what is bothering me. Refusing to articulate anger is like saying loud and clear: "I don't want it cleared up. I like the wall of separation between us."

That can't be if I love a person, and it can't be if I love God.
Roger C. Palms

The exercise of patience involves a continual practice of the presence of God; for we may be come upon at any moment for an almost heroic display of good temper, and it is a short road to unselfishness, for nothing is left to self; all that seems to belong most intimately to self, to be self's property, such as time, home, and rest, are invaded by these continual trials of patience. The family is full of such opportunities.

F. W. Faber

Father, it is so easy to become angry with those closest to us. Give me the gift of patience to help me live lovingly and honestly each day.

JUNE 26

...above all things have fervent charity among yourselves: for charity shall cover the multitude of sins. I Peter 4:8

---

*T*HE COMMAND THAT WAS PRINTED ON THE WALL of Augustine's dining room might seem out of keeping but often warranted in today's world. It read, "He who speaks an evil word of an absent man or woman is not welcome at this table." I am sure many dinner parties would run out of conversation long before dessert was served!

How easy it is for us to delight when we hear of another's failings. We look down on them and, with a holier-than-thou attitude, survey their less-than-perfect lives.

In the urge to tell another, we use the excuse, "Just so you can pray about it." We rationalize that finding a willing listener justifies our spreading the gossip.

How important it is to examine our motives before spreading malicious news of another.

It is only when we look at the sinless perfection of Jesus that we are able to see the many flaws in our own lives. Then from an equal need of forgiveness we can reach out in prayer for the one about whom we gossiped.

J.W.B.

Lord, make me an instrument of Thy peace.

Where there is hatred, let me sow love;
Where there is injury, pardon;
Where there is doubt, faith;
Where there is despair, hope;
Where there is darkness, light;
Where there is sadness, joy.

O divine Master, grant that I may not so much seek
*   to be consoled, as to console;*
*   to be understood, as to understand;*
*   to be loved, as to love.*

For it is in giving that we receive,
  it is in pardoning that we are pardoned,
  and it is in dying that we are born to eternal life.

JUNE 27

In your patience possess ye your souls. Luke 21:19

*B*E PATIENT WITH OTHER PEOPLE even when they continue to do the things they promised not to do. There is a reason for it; so many problems between people rise out of characteristics that persist. It is probably because of a distortion somewhere along the line, an evidence of insecurity or something else. Talking it over doesn't mean that it is suddenly going to disappear. There is often a time difference, a cultural lag, between deciding what we are going to do and actually getting it done.

People have said to me, "I have given that person chance after chance. Now I'm finished." I remind them of what Peter asked Jesus: "Lord, how many times do You forgive a person?" He thought seven times was very generous indeed. But our Lord told him, "Not seven times, Peter, but 70 times seven." I am so glad that God is patient with me. *Louis H. Evans, Jr.*

Endeavor to be patient in bearing with the defects and infirmities of others, of what sort soever they be; for that thyself also hast many failings which must be borne with by others. If thou canst not make thyself such an one as thou wouldest, how canst thou expect to have another in all things to thy liking? *Thomas à Kempis*

Lord Jesus, thank You that You do not run out of patience with me. Let me be forever conscious of my own faults when dealing with another.

JUNE 28

Peace I leave with you, my peace I give unto you: not as the world giveth, give I unto you. Let not your heart be troubled, neither let it be afraid.

John 14:27

*W*HEN I AM EMOTIONALLY EMBITTERED or discouraged, when I experience that dull ache of loneliness, or I am saddened in the trough of some criticism or failure, He comes to comfort me. It is as though His healing power is extended to my neurotic feelings.

If He can make a leper clean, He can make a neurotic normal. Often I ask Jesus to raise the hand which calmed the winds and waves of Gennesaret over my turbulent soul. Make me calm and tranquil, too. However, I firmly believe that God comes not only to comfort the afflicted, but also to afflict the comfortable.

There are times when He comes not to trouble me, but only to re-arrange my values or make me aware of someone in need; and always to challenge me to grow. I have never asked Him for a problemless life or a plastic tranquillity. I ask only for that peace which knows what is important and what is unimportant, only for that serenity which knows that I have been loved and that I am called to love.

John Powell

(Our Lord's comfort will come to us as He has promised. We must be still and let the balm of His peace restore our troubled hearts.)

> *Drop Thy still dews of quietness,*
> *Till all our strivings cease;*
> *Take from our souls the strain and stress,*
> *And let our ordered lives confess*
> *The beauty of Thy peace.*

John Greenleaf Whittier

JUNE 29

Follow me. John 21:19

*I*F THERE SHOULD SUDDENLY COME TO YOU this clarion query, "For what are you living—what comes first with you?" would you have a quick, crisp, and decisive answer? What is the fundamental strategy underlying your days—your life?

Someone has said that in war, mistakes in tactics, a bad carrying out of detailed plans, may be forgiven, but that no commanding officer is forgiven if he makes a mistake in strategy, the general plan of large-scale action. In this battle of life you and I may make individual mistakes, but we must not make mistakes in strategy, in the general plan of our days.

In football a man may fumble a ball, even be tackled for a loss, but there is no excuse for a man's not knowing where the goal is or knowing what it is to score.

God, through His Son, Jesus Christ, has given us life's supreme purpose. It is found in Matthew 6:33: "Seek ye first the kingdom of God, and his righteousness; and all these things shall be added unto you"—shall be as additions, as of secondary importance to you—but this is supreme!

Louis H. Evans, Sr.

Whenever you look into your own heart, you will find His
    haunting Presence.
He will show you a love that will never let you go.
"Come after Me," He still calls, asking for recruits
                                    for disciples.
Are you ready to answer Him, John Doe?
Are you ready to be—John Doe, Disciple?

Peter Marshall

Lord, I will follow You wherever You lead.

JUNE 30

**...wrath killeth the foolish man,
and envy slayeth the silly one.** Job 5:2

---

*A*LEXANDER MACLAREN, a distinguished Manchester preacher
(1826-1910), wrote, "What disturbs us in this world is not
trouble, but our opposition to trouble. The true source of all that
frets and irritates and wears away our lives is not in external things
but in the resistance of our wills to the will of God expressed by eternal things."

To resent and resist God's disciplining hand is to miss one of the
greatest spiritual blessings we Christians can enjoy this side of
heaven.

Whatever it is—aggravations, trouble, adversity, irritations,
opposition—we haven't "learned Christ" until we have discovered
that God's grace is sufficient for every test. Some unknown poet asks:

If all my years were summer, could I know
    what my Lord means by His "made white as snow"?
If all my days were sunny, could I say,
    "In His fair land He wipes all tears away"?
If I were never weary, could I keep
    close to my heart, "He gives His loved one sleep"?
Were no griefs mine, might I not come to deem
    the eternal life but a baseless dream?
My winter, and my tears, and my weariness,
    even my griefs may be His way to bless.
I call them ills, yet they can surely be
    nothing but love that shows my Lord to me.

Billy Graham

(In the depths of our adversities, we can experience in a new and
glorious way the grace that God will impart—if only we will ask.)

Father, I need Your grace to come into this weary soul of mine and give me hope. Forgive the resentments and the times I resist Your perfect will for me.

JULY 1

...all the earth shall be filled with the glory of the Lord. Numbers 14:21

---

*I*F WE WILL OBEY AND BELIEVE, we can go on pushing back the narrow borders of our spiritual world until it takes in the whole creation of God. And it is all ours, we are Christ's, and Christ is God's.

Two men stood on the shore watching the sun come up out of the sea. One was a merchant from London, the other was the poet, William Blake. As the bright yellow disk of the sun emerged into view, gilding the water and painting the sky with a thousand colors, the poet turned to the merchant and asked, "What do you see?"

"Ah! I see gold," replied the merchant. "The sun looks like a great gold piece. What do you see?"

"I see the glory of God," Blake answered, "and I hear a multitude of the heavenly host crying, 'Holy, holy, holy is the Lord God almighty. The whole earth is full of His glory.'" *A. W. Tozer*

> This is my Father's world;
> And to my listening ears
> All nature sings, and 'round me rings
> The music of the spheres.
>
> This is my Father's world;
> I rest me in the thought
> Of rocks and trees, of skies and seas,
> His hand the wonders wrought.

Malthie D. Babcock

Our Father, we praise You for the beauty of Your creation.

JULY 2

Exalt ye the Lord our God, and worship at his footstool; for he is holy. Psalm 99:5

---

*S*OMETIMES, WHEN I'VE READ A BOOK that has really touched me, or seen a picture that has shown some fresh beauty to me, I've felt I'd give a lot to meet the author or the painter and say a personal "thank you." I'm pretty sure you often feel the same.

The other day, looking at some white lilac and thinking what a miracle of beauty it is, I said to myself, "I wish I could meet the one who designed that..." and then, quite suddenly, I realized what I was saying! *It was God, my Father and your Father!* And I don't mind telling that I worshiped the Supreme Artist who designed and made white lilac.

That's the sort of thing I mean. Once you accept Christ's teaching that God is our Father, hundreds of lovely and "wonderful" things in everyday life make you want to say how thrilled and grateful you are. You'll want to *worship.*   *J. B. Phillips*

> All things bright and beautiful,
> All creatures great and small,
> All things wise and wonderful,
> The Lord God made them all.
>
> *Cecil Frances Alexander*

Almighty God, I worship You as I see the glory of Your handiwork. It is all around me, reminding me of Your greatness—in the smallest flower and the spectacular, majestic mountains.

JULY 3

I beseech you therefore, brethren, by the mercies of God, that ye present your bodies a living sacrifice, holy, acceptable unto God, which is your reasonable service. Romans 12:1

OVER 100 YEARS AGO, TWO YOUNG MEN WERE TALKING in Ireland. One said, "The world has yet to see what God will do with a man fully consecrated to Him." The other man meditated on that thought for weeks. It so gripped him that one day he exclaimed, "By the Holy Spirit in me I'll be that man." Historians now say that he touched two continents for Christ. His name was Dwight L. Moody.

This can happen again as we open our lives to the recreating power of the Holy Spirit. No person can seek sincerely the cleansing and blessing of the Holy Spirit and remain the same afterward. No nation can experience the touch of awakening in its midst and remain the same afterward.   *Billy Graham*

With malice toward none;
With charity for all;

With firmness in the right, as God gives us to see the right,
Let us strive on to finish the work we are in;
To bind up the nation's wounds;
To care for him who shall have borne the battle,
And for his widow,
And his orphan—
To do all which may achieve and cherish a just and lasting peace
among ourselves,
And with all nations.

Abraham Lincoln

Father, I come to You seeking the cleansing of Your Holy Spirit in my life. May I be completely consecrated, worthy to work in this needy world for You.

JULY 4

Yea, the Lord shall give that which is good; and our land shall yield her increase. Psalm 85:12

WHY ARE SO MANY CHRISTIANS RELUCTANT to move into a deeper relationship with Christ? Because the way to deepening in Christ is the way of the cross: the way of self-denial—*of unconditional surrender of one's own will to God's will, and of true covenant commitment to one another.* This is the way to which He has called all serious Christians ("If any man would come after me, let him deny himself and take up his cross daily and follow me"—Luke 9:23), and from all that our Christian experience shows us, it is the *only* way to spiritual maturity.

It also is the only way that we Christians can yet fulfill our nation's call. Individually—and corporately—we need to re-enter the covenant relationship which our forefathers had with God and with one another.

Peter Marshall / David Manuel

God grant that not only the love of liberty but a thorough knowledge of the rights of man may pervade all the nations of the earth, so that a philosopher may set his foot anywhere on its surface and say: "This is my country!"

Benjamin Franklin

Almighty God, for the gift of liberty in Jesus Christ and the privilege of living in a free country—we praise You. May our lives deserve such awesome gifts. Bless those, Father, who live in spiritual bondage; may their eyes be opened to the liberating way of Your Son. To those who live under oppression we ask that they might know the comfort of Your presence.

Now therefore ye are no more strangers and foreigners, but fellow citizens with the saints, and of the household of God. Ephesians 2:19

C ITIZENSHIP IS IMPORTANT. When you travel to another country, it is essential that you have a passport that proves your citizenship. None of us wants to suffer the fate of Philip Nolan in the classic tale *The Man Without a Country.* Because he cursed the name of his country, Nolan was sentenced to live aboard ship and never again see his native land or even hear its name or news about its progress. For 56 years he was on an endless journey from ship to ship and sea to sea, and finally was buried at sea. He was a "man without a country."

The Christian's name is written in "the book of life," and this is what determines his final entrance into the heavenly country (Revelation 20:15). When you confess Christ on earth, He confesses your name in heaven (Matthew 10:32-33). Your name is written down in heaven (Luke 10:20), and it stands written forever. (The Greek verb *written* in Luke 10:20 is in the perfect tense: "It is once-for-all written and stands written.")

Warren Wiersbe

I have a spiritual suitcase, and I know where I'm going.

Ethel Waters

Lord Jesus, in accepting Your gift of eternal life I no longer fear the future. I know I belong to You and heaven is my destination.

They shall beat their swords into plowshares, and their spears into pruning hooks: nation shall not lift up sword against nation, neither shall they learn war any more. Isaiah 2:4

S TUDENTS OF SCRIPTURE MAY OFTEN DISAGREE about the exact time and order of the events of the great day, but all agree that we may anticipate a coming time when a new structure of life will be pressed into history. God's faithful ones will be vindicated; justice will be fulfilled and the potential of creation will be realized to proclaim the glory of God. Heaven's enemies will be pacified and all will call Israel's God, Lord.

To this day many of us yearn for Isaiah's comforting dream. As those who contemplate the nature and work of God, we too ask, "Lord, how long? When shall these things be? When shall the leaders of the earth finally come to grips with the insanity of brutality and hostility? When shall the refugees be permitted to go home, those unjustly in prison released to families, the child able to eat?" So inept is the human race to bring such things about under its own power, we must pray that the great day will be hastened along by a God who one day will ultimately bring a change that will last for eternity. Already in his time Isaiah contemplated and expected that to happen.

I fully believe that until that day arrives, it is the responsibility of the community of Christ, the great Church of our generation, to pursue that dream and the power of God's Holy Spirit. *Gordon MacDonald*

If I did not see that the Lord kept watch over the ship, I should long since have abandoned the helm. But I see Him! through the storm, strengthening the tackling, handling the yards, spreading the sails—aye more, commanding the very winds! Should *I* not be a coward if I abandoned *my* post? Let Him govern, let Him carry us forward, let Him hasten or delay, *we will fear nothing!* *Martin Luther*

Lord, may my eyes be ever on You, and may my prayer continually be for Your peace in this troubled world. Use me, Savior, to hasten the day of Your return.

---————————• **JULY 7** •——————————---

There is salvation in no one else! Under all heaven there is no other name for men to call upon to save them. Acts 4:12 (*TLB*)

◆——◆

*W*E MUST NEVER FORGET that the great enemy who is coming is the anti-Christ. He is not anti-non Christ. He is anti-Christ. Increasingly over the last few years the word *Jesus*, separated from the content of the Scriptures, has become the enemy of the Jesus of history, the Jesus who died and rose and who is coming again and who is the eternal Son of God. So let us take care. If evangelical Christians begin to slip into a dichotomy, to separate an encounter with Jesus from the content of the Scriptures (including the discussable and the verifiable), we shall, without intending to, be throwing ourselves and the next generation into the millstream of the modern system. This system surrounds us as an almost monolithic consensus.

Francis A. Schaeffer

All hail the power of Jesus' name!
Let angels prostrate fall;
Bring forth the royal diadem
And crown Him Lord of all!
Bring forth the royal diadem
and crown Him Lord of all!

Let every kindred, every tribe
on this terrestrial ball
To Him all majesty ascribe
And crown Him Lord of all!
To Him all majesty ascribe
And crown Him Lord of all!

Oh, that with yonder sacred throng
We at His feet may fall,
Join in the everlasting song
And crown Him Lord of all!
Join in the everlasting song
And crown Him Lord of all!

Edward Perronet

*Father, give me discernment and a steadfast faith as I look for that
glorious day when Jesus, who is Lord of all, shall return.*

------------------------- **JULY 8** -------------------------

***...when these things begin to come to pass,
then look up, and lift up your heads; for your
redemption draweth nigh.*** Luke 21:28

◆ ─── ◆

*A*T THE CORONATION OF KING GEORGE AND HIS QUEEN,
many Americans and Canadians came over to London to see
the great event. Their tickets included a seat to view the coronation
procession. They were, however, greatly disappointed to discover
that the seats allocated to them were on a barge on the banks of the
Thames facing the embankment wall over which they could see
nothing. Many voices protested, but the people were told to take re-
freshments in the rooms below and to wait patiently and all would
be well. Meanwhile, silently but surely the tide was coming in and
when ultimately the king drove past, the barge was high above the
wall and every eye could behold the royal procession. We wait patiently for the coming of our King. We see Him not yet, but the tide is
coming in and the waters are rising, and we are lifting up our eyes in

happy expectation. The signs our Lord told us to look for are being fulfilled in our midst and "at any moment." *A. Lindsay Glegg*

There is coming a day that will be called the Day of the Lord. In the midst of hopelessness there is hope! And that hope is centered in the God-man, the Lord Jesus Christ. *Billy Graham*

Lord Jesus, the certainty of Your return brings hope to our hearts. When I contemplate that today could be the very day all eyes will see You, I am filled with joyous expectancy!

JULY 9

...we know that, when he shall appear, we shall be like him; for we shall see him as he is. I John 3:2

*W*HEN CHRIST COMES AGAIN, the first thing He will do is issue us glorified bodies like His. The Apostle Paul taught, "Our citizenship is in heaven. And we eagerly await a Savior from there, the Lord Jesus Christ, who, by the power that enables Him to bring everything under his control, will transform our lowly bodies so that they will be like his glorious body" (Philippians 3:20-21). In I Corinthians 15:50-54, a favorite passage of Winston Churchill, Paul explained that this was "a mystery"; that is, it would take a special miracle: "We shall all be changed—in a flash, in the twinkling of an eye." This would be necessary because "flesh and blood cannot inherit the kingdom of God, nor does the perishable inherit the imperishable." So God performs this necessary miracle and "when the perishable has been clothed with the imperishable, and the mortal with immortality, then the saying that is written will come true: 'Death has been swallowed up in victory.'" *John Wesley White*

Have we not seen Thy shining garment's hem
Floating at dawn across the golden skies,
Through thin blue veils at noon, bright majesties,
Seen starry hosts delight to gem
The splendor that shall be Thy diadem?

O Immanence, that knows nor far nor near,
But as the air we breathe is with us here,
Our Breath of Life, O Lord, we worship Thee.

Worship and laud and praise Thee evermore,
Look up in wonder, and behold a door
Opened in heaven, and One set on a throne;

Stretch out a hand, and touch Thine own,
O Christ, our King, our Lord whom we adore.

Amy Carmichael

Lord Jesus, my life and all my love is surrendered to You. I praise You for the victory over death that brings me peace as I trust in You completely.

JULY 10

...a chariot of fire... II Kings 2:11

◆──◆

THERE WAS ONCE A PROPHET NAMED ELISHA, who had a supernatural gift of insight. Elisha had incurred the fury of the king of Syria, who was at war with Israel, by repeatedly telling his own monarch the enemy's plans. Elisha's servant rose early one day and, going up to the top of the house, saw a great host of soldiers that had been sent to end his master's interference. "Oh, my lord, what shall we do?" the servant cried, for the soldiers were surrounding the city. He couldn't understand how Elisha could be so cool, calm, and collected about it all. Seeing the young man's distress, the prophet asked the Captain of the hosts of heaven to open the frightened man's spiritual eyes so he could see what he himself had been able to see all the time. God answered that prayer, and the astonished servant saw the armies of heaven and their fiery chariots all around them. "Don't be afraid," said Elisha. "Those who are with us are more than those who are with them."

The battle for the boundaries *is* raging, but the battle is the Lord's, and those who are with us are more than those who are with them. So take courage. We *are* on the winning side!

Jill Briscoe

Do not look forward to the changes and chances of this life in fear; rather look to them with full hope that, as they arise, God, whose you are, will deliver you out of them. He is your Keeper. He has kept you hitherto. Do you but hold fast to His dear hand, and He will lead you safely through all things; and, when you cannot stand, He will bear you in His arms. Do not look forward to what may happen tomorrow. Our Father will either shield you from suffering, or He will give you strength to bear it.

Francis de Sales

Almighty God, the power of Your heavenly armies that You gave to Elisha is ours. With this assurance we will not fear what man can do, but stand with confidence in Your name.

**Great is the Lord, and greatly to be praised;
and his greatness is unsearchable.** Psalm 145:3

OUR WORD *MAJESTY* COMES FROM THE LATIN; it means "greatness." When we ascribe majesty to someone, we are acknowledging greatness in that person and voicing our respect for it: as, for instance, when we speak of "Her Majesty" the Queen.

Now, *majesty* is a word which the Bible uses to express the thought of the greatness of God, our Maker and our Lord. "The Lord reigneth, he is clothed with *majesty*.... Thy throne is established of old" (Psalm 93:1). "I will speak of the glorious honor of thy *majesty*, and of thy wondrous works" (Psalm 145:5). Peter, recalling his vision of Christ's royal glory at the transfiguration, says, "we...were eyewitnesses of his *majesty*" (II Peter 1:16). In Hebrews, the phrase "the majesty" twice does duty for "God"; Christ, we are told, at His ascension sat down "on the right hand of *the majesty* on high," "on the right hand of the throne of *the majesty* in the heavens" (Hebrews 1:3; 8:1). The word *majesty*, when applied to God, is always a declaration of His greatness and an invitation to worship. *J. I. Packer*

When Christian worship is dull and joyless, Jesus Christ has been left out—that is the only possible explanation. *James S. Stewart*

(It is as we turn our eyes upon Jesus we are able to comprehend the glorious and exciting heritage that is ours. As we worship, may we remember the majesty of our King of kings.)

Lord Jesus Christ, to You may all honor and glory be given. We praise You, our blessed Redeemer.

Ye are the salt of the earth.... Matthew 5:13

WE AS CHRISTIANS HAVE A ROYAL RESPONSIBILITY to stand surely and securely upon the Scriptures. We have a mandate from the Most High God to proclaim His desires and decrees to a decadent society.

Without hesitation we should be bold enough to openly advocate high morals, decency and integrity in human affairs. There are some carnal Christians who might prefer to come to some easy accommodation with their contemporaries. But we are not called to compromise, we are instructed to be salt. Salt has a pungency, a potency and a penetrating power that makes it a preservative, repugnant to the forces of evil and decomposition.

This may well mean that we shall not be popular nor acclaimed in the press. But by the same measure it will mark us out as people of positive and purifying influence in the affairs of our world.

Each of us can be a potent, uplifting force for good and for God in any area of the country in which we live, any segment of society in which we serve. *W. Phillip Keller*

A Christian is not one who withdraws but one who infiltrates.
Bill Glass

Almighty God, I pray for Your power to saturate my life as I stand firm in today's society, bringing Your message of decency and love for everyone.

JULY 13

...his servants shall serve him:
and they shall see his face. Revelation 22:3-4

*T*HIS IS THE SUPREME REALITY OF HEAVEN. There will be an intimate relationship between Christ and His Church throughout eternity. He will be "the Lamb which is in the midst of the throne," and He shall feed His own and shall lead them to fountains of living waters.

With this great certainty and assurance, the future holds no terrors we cannot face. Beyond the crisis lies heaven and the utopia of our dreams. Thus the Christian should never be filled with fear, discouragement, or despondency.

If you do not know Christ as Savior, the future is bleak and dark and pessimistic indeed. Surrender your life to the Lord Jesus Christ. Let Him come into your heart and transform you and change you.

Courage, faith and fortitude come from the cross where Christ emptied Himself and humbled Himself, even to the death of the cross. Jesus said, "In the world you will have troubles; but be of good courage, I have overcome the world." *Billy Graham*

To believe in heaven is not to run away from life; it is to run toward it. *Joseph D. Blinco*

Lord Jesus, I cannot even begin to comprehend all the joy that is waiting in heaven, but the fact I shall see You face to face fills me with a joy that will last for all eternity.

...as ye go, preach, saying,
The kingdom of heaven is at hand. Matthew 10:7

◆ ─── ◆

GOD COULD HAVE PUT HIS MESSAGE FOR MANKIND in flaming letters of lightning across the sky. He could have had it sung by angels for the whole world to hear. Instead, He translated Himself into His Son, who walked the hot, dusty roads of Palestine. Today, again, God could translate His message into all the thousands of cultures and languages by running it through some gigantic computer. But He has chosen not to do so. He still chooses to communicate His truth through human personalities. He chooses to walk narrow paths of tropical jungles, hard sidewalks of concrete jungles, and grassy lawns of suburban jungles through translators like you and me, if we will take the risk of letting His treasure be carried to a lost and seeking world in the clay jars of our imperfect lives.

Leighton Ford

He who can tell men what God has done for his soul is the likeliest to bring their souls to God. *Robert Leighton*

Lord Jesus, take this imperfect life and make me a worthy messenger of Your love and redemption.

For the Lamb standing in front of the throne
will feed them and be their Shepherd and lead
them to the springs of the Water of Life. And
God will wipe their tears away. Revelation 7:17 (TLB)

◆ ─── ◆

ONCE I STOOD IN LONDON TO WATCH QUEEN ELIZABETH return from an overseas trip. I saw the parade of dignitaries, the marching bands, the crack troops, the waving flags. I saw all the splendor that accompanies the homecoming of a queen. However, that was nothing compared to the homecoming of a true believer who has said good-bye here to all of the suffering of this life and been immediately surrounded by angels who carry him upward to the glorious welcome awaiting the redeemed in heaven.

The Christian should never consider death a tragedy. Rather he should see it as the angels do: They realize that joy should mark the journey from time to eternity. The way to life is by the valley of death, but the road is marked with victory all the way. Angels revel in the power of the resurrection of Jesus, which assures us of our resurrection and guarantees us a safe passage to heaven.

Billy Graham

There will be no more pain,
no more sorrows, nor tears,
nor crying,
nor parting,
nor death after death.

Age shall not weary them, nor the years erode.
We shall enter into that for which we were created.
It shall be the journey's end for the heart and all its hopes.

Peter Marshall

O Lamb of God, this finite mind cannot begin to grasp the glory of eternity. I imagine Your welcome and the welcome of my loved ones, in You. How magnificent it will be!

JULY 16

**For where your treasure is,
there will your heart be also.** Matthew 6:21

YOU CAN SOON TELL WHERE A MAN'S TREASURE IS by his talk. If it is in heaven, he will not be long with you before he's talking about heaven; his heart is there, and so his speech isn't long in running there, too. If his heart is in money, he will soon have you deep in talk about mines, speculation, stocks, bank rate, and so on. If his heart is in lands, it won't be long before he's talking about real estate, improvements, houses, and so on. Always the same, wherever a man's heart is, there his tongue will be sure to go.

Someone in England said, if you see a man's goods and furniture come down by the luggage train, you're pretty sure he'll be down by the next passenger train; he won't be long after; he'll follow his goods. And so it is with heaven; if your treasure is on before you, you'll be wanting to follow it; you'll be glad to be on the road thither as soon as possible.

D. L. Moody

It is not darkness you are going to, for God is Light.
It is not lonely, for Christ is with you. It is not
an unknown country, for Christ is there.

Charles Kingsley

Lord Jesus, may my conversation convey to another that my heart and soul are blessed with the anticipation of heaven and Your presence.

If a man keep my saying,
he shall never see death. John 8:51

*F*OR ME NOW THE EXPERIENCE OF LIVING IN THIS WORLD is nearly over. My lines, such as they are, have been spoken, my entrances and exits all made. It is a prospect, I am thankful to say, that I can face without panic, fear or undue remorse, confident that, as an infinitesimal part of God's creation, I am a participant in His purposes, which are loving, not malign; creative, not destructive; orderly, not chaotic; and that, however somberly at times the darkness may lour and however men may seem at times to prefer the darkness, the Light that first came to Galilee 2,000 years ago, and through the succeeding centuries has illumined all that was greatest in the work and lives of men, can never be put out.

Malcolm Muggeridge

The truest end of life is to know that life never ends.... Death is no more than a turning of us over from time to eternity. *William Penn*

Father, without fear I can look to my final earthly journey, knowing it will be the beginning of a magnificent heavenly life with You!

Let not your heart be troubled:
ye believe in God, believe also in me. John 14:1

*F*ROM A LIFE OF POVERTY AND HARDSHIP to the glamour of show business, Ethel Waters still found an emptiness—until she gave her life to Jesus Christ. In Him she found completeness of heart and soul and a love that was eternal.

I do understand enough about myself to know that when I get to heaven I'll be overjoyed just to stand in line, knowing at last I'm in His presence. His love does this to us. Love that is always giving. Oh, I just love Him. I love Him. How I *long* for you children to love Him too.

I have loved Jesus Christ all my life, but I think I had to surrender myself to Him before I knew how to love other people. In spite of all my success and all the happiness I tried to give to my audiences, there was no personal happiness in me. I was a high-strung person by nature, but thank heaven I'm under the control of my Savior now. I had no real happiness then. I have it now with Jesus. *Ethel Waters*

Why should I feel discouraged, why should the shadows come,
Why should my heart be lonely and long for heav'n and home,
When Jesus is my portion? My constant Friend is He:
His eye is on the sparrow, and I know He watches me.

Civilla D. Martin

Lord Jesus, thank You for watching over each one of us as we live for You. May Your love spill over from us into the hearts of those who are lonely and sad.

JULY 19

God shall wipe away all tears from their eyes; and there shall be no more death, neither sorrow, nor crying, neither shall there be any more pain: for the former things are passed away. Revelation 21:4

WHEN I THINK OF HEAVEN, I think of a time when I will be welcomed home. I remember when I was on my feet what a cozy, wonderful feeling it was to come home after hockey practice. How pleasant to hear the familiar clanging of bells against our back door as I swung it open. Inside awaited the sights, sounds, and smells of warmth and love. Mom would greet me with a wide smile as she dished out food into big bowls ready to be set on the table. I'd throw down my sweat suit and hockey stick, bound into the den, and greet Daddy. He'd turn from his desk, taking off his glasses, then he'd give me a big "hi" and ask me how practice was.

For Christians, heaven will be like that. We will see old friends and family who have gone on before us. Our kind heavenly Father will greet us with open, loving arms. Jesus, our older Brother, will be there to welcome us, too. We won't feel strange or insecure. We will feel like we're home...for we *will* be home. Jesus said it was a place prepared for us.

Joni Eareckson

There is a land of pure delight,
    Where saints immortal reign;
Infinite day excludes the night,
    And pleasures banish pain.

Isaac Watts

Blessed Savior, when I think of my heavenly home with You and all those I love in Your name, I am overjoyed. The reunions will be wonderful, and we will live together forever and ever!

Lay not up for yourselves treasures upon earth.... Matthew 6:19

◆————————————————————————————————————◆

R EMEMBER, WHEN YOU GIVE TO GOD and spiritual things, you are not giving, you are really "depositing"—"Laying up treasure for yourselves in heaven." What you and I keep, we lose. What we have given away we keep forever.

There is the story of a certain woman who was visiting heaven, a woman who had been of considerable means on earth. She passed a rather modest bungalow, and she said rather lightly to St. Peter, "And whose bungalow is this?" He said, "That is yours, madam." Rather disappointed, they walked on, and she spied a large estate, a costly mansion, and said, "And whose is this?" He said, "That estate belongs to Harry Smith." "Strange," she said, "Harry Smith was the name of my chauffeur." He said, "That's right. It is Harry Smith's. You see, madam, in building the mansions here in heaven, we have only such material to use in their building as is sent up to us. Such material as is given to God. This mansion represents what Harry Smith sent up, and the bungalow what you sent up." She awoke with a start!

Remember, my friends, you cannot take it with you but you can send it ahead. *Louis H. Evans, Sr.*

Death to a good man is but passing through a dark entry out of one little dusky room of his Father's house into another that is fair and large, lightsome and glorious. *Anonymous*

Father, may all my treasures be laid at Your feet, for the greatest sacrifice of Your Son could never begin to be repaid.

The eyes of the Lord are upon the righteous, and his ears are open to their cry. Psalm 34:15

◆————————————————————————————————————◆

G OD DOES NOT ALWAYS DELIVER HIS CHILDREN out of crises and catastrophes. For example, during the trials and tribulations of the '70s, many people in Uganda prayed earnestly to the Lord to deliver them. The evil regime in that country has taken the lives of many believers. The Lord delivered them, but not in the way they had expected. It is up to us as Christians to accept whatever God sends and to be prepared in our hearts and minds for change and revolution—and even torture and death.

Corrie ten Boom tells how, in the midst of the horrors of Ravensbruck prison camp, she learned to pray. Prayer was her constant resort. Through prayer she knew the reality of Christ in her life, even when the burdens were quite overwhelming. She prayed, "Lord, teach me to cast all my burdens upon Thee and go on without them. Only Thy Spirit can teach me that lesson. Give me Thy Spirit, O Lord, and I shall have faith, such faith that I shall no longer carry a load of care."

Billy Graham

The most important part of our task will be to tell everyone who will listen that Jesus is the only answer to the problems that are disturbing the hearts of men and nations. We shall have the right to speak because we can tell from experience that His light is more powerful than the deepest darkness.... How wonderful that the reality of His presence is greater than the reality of the hell about us.

Betsie ten Boom (to her sister, Corrie)

Lord Jesus, such examples of faith strengthen and inspire. The knowledge that You are with us wherever we may find ourselves gives the quiet reassuring peace my heart longs for. I place my life completely into Your strong and loving hands.

JULY 22

***The Lord is my strength and my shield;
my heart trusted in him, and I am helped....*** Psalm 28:7

*W*HERE CAN I FIND JOY? Where peace? Where power? By seeking them, which really means seeking my feelings of joy, peace, power? No. By seeing Him—by faith. He is the joy, peace, power, all. He is that whether or not we feel it. Keep occupied in affirming Him by faith, even though we feel as heavy as lead or as weak as water or as disturbed as a windstorm. Keep believing Him in these conditions. Whether and when they change is His business. If we have Him, we have all. We shall and do experience Him as all these; but I am almost afraid to say that, because we then turn back again and say, "Well, where are they? I don't feel them." And we are back again on the self-level. It is safer to say that I have only Him as my all. How He manifests Himself is entirely His business, and His way is perfect.

So the point is, keep walking with Jesus—by faith—and let everything else fit in as it may.

Norman Grubb

Faith gives a person the true prospect of things past, present and to come, and of things as they are. All our fears and discouragements arise from the fact that men do not see things as they are. If evil be stirring, they think it is greater than it is. If good be stirring, they think it is less than it is. But when faith comes, it opens a person's eyes to see things that are invisible; it is the evidence of things not seen. Faith, true saving faith, sees that in God and in Christ which answers unto all our fears, wants and miseries.   *William Bridge*

Blessed Savior, in faith I come to You believing You are with me, caring and providing for my every need. I praise You, Lord.

JULY 23

...thy word was unto me the joy and rejoicing of mine heart.... Jeremiah 15:16

*W*E CAN'T CHOOSE HAPPINESS either for ourselves or for another; we can't tell where that will lie. We can only choose whether we will indulge ourselves in the present moment, or whether we will renounce that, for the sake of obeying the Divine voice within us, for the sake of being true to all the motives that sanctify our lives. I know this belief is hard; it has slipped away from me again and again; but I have felt that if I let it go forever, I should have no light through the darkness of this life.   *George Eliot*

Know this! Christ never takes our joy away. He gives joy! He says that He came not only to give us life, but to give it to us more abundantly! God tells us that the way of the transgressor is hard, but His ways are ways of pleasantness and all His paths are peace.

The joy that the Lord gives is marvelous. It springs up in sorrow and in trouble like a palm tree springing up in a desert.
          Henrietta C. Mears

(Even when we go through the deepest sorrow, our Lord's joy is in our hearts, comforting and strengthening. We are never alone.)

Lord Jesus, thank You for Your joy which never varies and is not susceptible to my moods. It lightens my days and sustains me in sorrow.

JULY 24

...your life is hid with Christ in God. Colossians 3:3

*T*HE SOUL WHICH HAS BEEN TOUCHED BY GOD will not be drawn up into an other-worldly posture or into bowered ivory towers of private ecstasy but will be deepened in his awareness of the world around him. He will see with his new eyes the beauty of his world; he will hear its music and poetry and know that it is a beautiful world. But he will also find himself in deeper contact with the sadness in the hearts of men. He will notice a new awareness of the reality of his total environment, a new aliveness. As old St. Irenaeus, in the second century, once said: "The glory of God is a man fully alive." The true touch of God results in a new and vital "Yes!" to life.

John Powell, S.J.

There is no life so humble that, if it is true and genuinely human and obedient to God, it may not hope to shed some of His light. There is no light so meager that the greatest and wisest of us can afford to despise it. We cannot know at what moment it may flash forth with the life of God.   *Phillips Brooks*

Almighty God, You have given me a new awareness of Your glorious world as my life has been awakened through the Savior.

──────────────── • **JULY 25** • ────────────────

Study to show thyself approved unto God, a workman that needeth not to be ashamed, rightly dividing the word of truth. II Timothy 2:15

*I*N THE MOVIE *PATTON*, the American general deploys a trap for the enemy. Rommel and his "Afrika Korps" fall into the snare off guard and are defeated, and Hitler's African campaign is destroyed. As Patton looks over the battlefield he says, "Aha, Rommel, I read your book...."

We are always better able to deal with the enemy if we know his philosophy ahead of time. The twentieth-century Christian cannot afford to be ignorant. Let us mature in faith and learn the philosophies of our antagonists. As we become aware of the logic of the Lie, we will hold the Truth with greater security. This knowledge of the anti-Christian position may seldom help us convert our adversaries, but it will prevent us from being debilitated by their logic.

Jesus affirmed that He was the Truth and the Life. We who join the battle must realize the tradition which has preceded us. Our cry is, "Jesus is Christ." To those who yell back across the trenches, "No, He is the Carpenter," we must point to the product of our position: peace, destiny, meaning. If they reply with pity for our superstitions, ask them for the product of their philosophy.   *Calvin Miller*

If you go out to your garden and throw down some sawdust, the birds will not take any notice; but if you throw down some crumbs, you will find they will soon sweep down and pick them up.

The true child of God can tell the difference (so to speak) between sawdust and bread. Many so-called Christians are living on the world's sawdust instead of being nourished by the Bread that cometh down from heaven. Nothing can satisfy the longings of the soul but the Word of the living God.   *D. L. Moody*

Lord Jesus, may I so saturate my mind with Your Word that I will be able to show another, whose beliefs differ, the magnificence of knowing You as Savior.

———→ JULY 26 ←·———

For whatsoever is born of God overcometh the world: and this is the victory that overcometh the world, even our faith. I John 5:4

O NE CANNOT AVOID BEING DEEPLY IMPRESSED by the kind of answer Jesus gave when men came to Him with their questions. When John the Baptist asked Him a question, He said, "Suffer it to be so now." When Peter asked Him a question, He said, "What I do thou knowest not now; but thou shalt know hereafter." And when, on the darkest night of the world's history, the night before His death, they all asked Him questions, He said, "I have yet many things to say unto you, but ye cannot bear them now."

You see, even Jesus did not say, "I have explained the world." What He did say was, "I have overcome the world." And if we can only trust where we cannot see, walking in the light we have—which is often very much like hanging on in the dark—if we do faithfully that which we see to be the will of God in the circumstances which evil thrusts upon us, we can rest our minds in the assurance that circumstances which God allows, reacted to in faith and trust and courage, can never defeat purposes which God ultimately wills. So doing, we shall wrest from life something big and splendid. We shall find peace in our own hearts.   *Leslie D. Weatherhead*

> The calmness bends serene above
>   My restlessness to still;
> Around me flows Thy quickening life,
>   To nerve my faltering will;
> Thy presence fills my solitude;
> Thy providence turns all to good.
> *Henry Wadsworth Longfellow*

Father, for the peace that is in my heart and the victory that is ever in You, I thank You. Bless those whose souls are troubled, I pray.

JULY 27

This people have I formed for myself;
they shall show forth my praise. Isaiah 43:21

◆ ━━━ ◆

YOU HAVE A VERY SPECIAL ASSIGNMENT. You live in a world that needs changing. A world full of people with needs. They need to know who God is, what He is like. They need to know how much He loves them and what He desires to do for them. They need to know how much He wants to make them free from their guilt, their hostility, their fears. They need to know how they can be at peace with God, with themselves, and with others. You are His personal ambassador, representing Him, witnessing to them that He is the answer to these needs. Think of it! *You are a personal representative of the living God on assignment to make God visible to others around you.*

What a calling! What an assignment! What a purpose for living—making God visible to the people of your special world that they might be changed and God glorified! In this way they, too, will be able to fulfill God's purposes for them—to know Him and "to show forth His praise, to glorify His name." *Verna Birkey*

If Christ lives in us, controlling our personalities, we will leave glorious marks on the lives we touch. Not because of our lovely characters, but because of His. *Eugenia Price*

Lord Jesus, control this personality of mine and help me to represent You in my world today.

JULY 28

Take now thy son...whom thou lovest. Genesis 22:2

◆ ━━━ ◆

GOD'S COMMAND IS "TAKE *NOW*," NOT PRESENTLY. To go to the height God shows, can never be done *presently*. It must be done *now*.

"*And offer him there for a burnt offering upon one of the mountains which I will tell thee of.*" The mount of the Lord is the very height of the trial into which God brings His servant. There is no indication of the cost to Abraham; his implicit understanding of God so far outreaches his explicit knowledge that he trusts God utterly and climbs the highest height on which God can ever prove him, and remains unutterably true to Him. There was no conflict; *that was over.* Abraham's confidence was fixed; he did not consult with flesh and blood—his own or anyone else's. He *instantly* obeyed. The point is that, though all other voices should proclaim differently, obedience to the dictates of the Spirit of God at all costs is to be the attitude of the faithful soul.

Always beware when you want to confer with your own flesh and blood—i.e., your own sympathies, your own insight. When our Lord is bringing us into personal relationship with Himself, it is always the individual relationship He breaks down.

If God has given the command, He will look after everything; your business is to *get up and go!*   Oswald Chambers

Faith and obedience are bound up in the same bundle. He that obeys God trusts God, and he that trusts God obeys God.

Charles H. Spurgeon

Almighty God, might I have the attributes that made Abraham a trusting and obedient servant.

———————————————— • JULY 29 • ————————————————

With good will doing service, as to the Lord, and not men. Ephesians 6:7

◆———————————————————————————————————————◆

*A*T THE TIME OF JESUS' LIFE ON EARTH, the world was racked by injustice, hatred, and confusion—just as it is today. But as He went about the countryside, His love and caring changed people, gave them new natures, a new hope. He taught that each person is precious to God. "The very hairs of your head are all numbered" (Matthew 10:30). To those who were ready to listen and accept the Son of God's teachings, His example inspired people everywhere He went.

The call He gave to His disciples is still heard today. It was this call that inspired Mother Teresa of Calcutta to leave the comfort of her home and travel to India to work among the most destitute of all— the emaciated, rotting shells of people dying in the streets. This ministry can only be brought about, as she works amongst the stench and horror of these dear souls, by the love of Jesus Christ in this amazing woman's life.

Florence Nightingale, years before, had heard the same call and had gone to the carnage of the battlefields of the Boer War to give tender and loving aid to the wounded and dying. "We are His glory, when we follow His ways," she said.

Not all of us are called to minister far from home. Around us in our communities are people who need Him. Our compassion, brought about by His Holy Spirit, can reach out to those who have lost hope and who desperately seek an answer to their seemingly unsolvable problems. Ministering through Him we avoid the ego trip that can so easily become our incentive instead of wanting to glorify Him.   *J.W.B.*

My mind is absorbed with the sufferings of man. Since I was 24 there never (has been) any vagueness in my plans or ideas as to what God's work was for me.   *Florence Nightingale*

Lord, may I see this suffering world through Your compassionate eyes and be led by Your Holy Spirit to serve the desperate ones You love.

JULY 30

The grace of the Lord Jesus Christ, and the love of God, and the communion of the Holy Ghost, be with you all.
II Corinthians 13:14

THE PRISONER, THE SICK PERSON, the Christian in exile sees in the companionship of a fellow Christian a physical sign of the gracious presence of the triune God. Visitor and visited in loneliness recognize in each other the Christ who is present in the body; they receive and meet each other as one meets the Lord, in reverence, in humility, and joy. They receive each other's benedictions as the benediction of the Lord Jesus Christ. But if there is so much blessing and joy even in a single encounter of brother with brother, how inexhaustible are the riches that open up for those who by God's will are privileged to live in the daily fellowship of life with other Christians! It is true, of course, that what is an unspeakable gift of God for the lonely individual is easily disregarded and trodden under foot by those who have the gift every day. It is easily forgotten that the fellowship of Christian brethren is a gift of grace, a gift of the Kingdom of God that any day may be taken from us, that the time that still separates us from utter loneliness may be brief indeed. Therefore, let him who until now has had the privilege of living a common Christian life with other Christians praise God's grace from the bottom of his heart. Let him thank God on his knees and declare: It is grace, nothing but grace, that we are allowed to live in community with Christian brethren.   *Dietrich Bonhoeffer*

No matter how great his trials may be, every saved sinner can always find reason for thanksgiving.   *Philip E. Howard, Jr.*

Almighty God, we praise You for Christian fellowship, which we so easily take for granted. Your grace is always more than we deserve.

―――――――――――――― **JULY 31** ―――――――――――――

Faithful is he that calleth you, who also will do it. I Thessalonians 5:24

*I*N A SOCIETY THAT TEACHES YOU to be your own man and do your own thing, it is increasingly difficult not to become deluded with a sense of self-sufficiency. To some extent it is necessary for people to have confidence in their God-given abilities, but deeply ingrained self-trust leads to disaster.

No doubt David became vividly aware of the fact that he was so open to temptation and so prone to wander that self-trust was a luxury he could no longer afford. So he prayed to be "upheld." He evidently did not think it unmasculine to admit weakness. Apparently he did not feel it demeaning to his kingly role to confess inadequacy.

So many people are not free to be honest. They must "save face" at all costs. They must, if they are British, "keep a stiff upper lip." This is no problem to the liberated failure, for he has nothing to hide and is free to be open about his needs and the One who is the answer to his needs.

It is great good news that you don't have to trust your untrustworthy self but the Lord who is faithful, and it is thrilling news to know that you can be free to admit it.   *D. Stuart Briscoe*

God defends me from myself.   *Michel de Montaigne*

Lord, how thankful I am that I do not have to rely on my "prone to failure" self but on You, my faithful, loving Savior!

―――――――――――――― **AUGUST 1** ―――――――――――――

In him was life; and the life was the light of men. John 1:4

*A*UGUSTINE WAS ONE OF THE GREATEST THEOLOGIANS of all time. He was a wild, intemperate, immoral youth. In spite of his mother's pleadings and prayers, he grew worse instead of better. But one day he had a personal encounter with Jesus Christ that transformed his life. His restlessness and the practice of sin disappeared. He became one of the greatest saints of all time.

John Newton was a slave trader on the west coast of Africa. One day in a storm at sea he met Jesus Christ. He went back to England and became an Anglican clergyman. He wrote scores of fine hymns, one of which has become the modern popular song "Amazing Grace."

This is what Christ can do for anyone who puts his trust in Him.

Billy Graham

So the Redeemer came. Somewhere in the mind and heart of God from the very foundation of the earth the Christ had been waiting, hidden in the counsels of eternity until the great bell of the ages should strike; and when at last everything in the world and in the souls of men was ready and prepared, He came, the Word of God made flesh, not a moment early and not a moment late, but exactly on the stroke of the hour. It was the Day of the Lord.

It is still the Day of the Lord whenever another soul enthrones Him. "Even so, come, Lord Jesus."

James S. Stewart

Lord Jesus, whose love changes even the most desperate soul, I praise You, for I know You have transformed the despair of mine.

———————————————— **AUGUST 2** ————————————————

I went down to the potter's house, and I saw him working at the wheel. But the pot he was shaping from the clay was marred in his hands; so the potter formed it into another pot, shaping it as seemed best to him.

Then the word of the Lord came to me: "...can I not do with you as this potter does?... Like clay in the hand of the potter, so are you in my hand....

Jeremiah 18:3-6 (*NIV*)

◆————————————————————————————————————◆

*T*HE LOVING, GRACIOUS HANDS OF GOD are strong enough to rework any life on this earth. Even yours.

Augustine, in his early Church history, was reshaped by God after having a well-deserved reputation of sleeping around with the girls. One day as he was walking down a street, one of his old girl friends spotted him.

"Augustine!" she called.

Augustine didn't answer; he just quickened his pace.

"Augustine," she called again, "it is I!"

Augustine began to run—as he called back to her, "But I am not I!"
Augustine's clay, the original material, was the same, but God had reworked him into a completely different shape, a new pot.

Anne Ortlund

(We all need to be remolded by our Lord. In quiet adoration let us look to Him as we repeat the words of this well-loved hymn.)

> *Have Thine own way, Lord!*
> *Have Thine own way!*
> *Thou art the Potter;*
> *I am the clay.*
> *Mold me and make me*
> *After Thy will,*
> *While I am waiting,*
> *Yielded and still.*

Adelaide A. Pollard

AUGUST 3

For the Son of man is come to seek and to save that which was lost. Luke 19:10

IT WAS A DRAMATIC ENCOUNTER that took place in Jericho between Zacchaeus and Jesus. The Lord said, "Come down quickly, Zacchaeus, for I am coming to visit your house." It was not enough for Zacchaeus to know that Jesus saw into his deepest being. The encounter was not complete until Zacchaeus responded in the center of his soul, saying, "Lord, You can have me."

Zacchaeus came down from that tree, and Jesus went with him to Zacchaeus' house. The Scriptures declare that the tax collector made restitution for his crooked ways, his embezzlement. He arranged to give back to the poor four times as much as he had taken from them. That is repentance. It means an about-face, a willingness to turn from all you know to be wrong. Jesus informed Zacchaeus, "This day salvation has come to your house."

You can find your true self, your identity, by inviting Christ into your heart. For when you receive Him, you are able to accept yourself and become the person you really want to be, and the man or woman God wants you to be.

Ralph Bell

It is hard to find words in the language of man to explain the deep things of God. Indeed, there are none that will adequately express what the Spirit of God works in His children. But...by the testimony of the Spirit, I mean an inward impression on the soul, whereby the

Spirit of God immediately and directly witnesses to my spirit that I am a child of God; that Jesus Christ hath loved me and given Himself for me; that all my sins are blotted out and I, even I, am reconciled to God. *John Wesley*

Almighty God, there are no adequate words to describe the wonder of a changed life through Your Son, Jesus Christ. I praise You for seeking me and changing me.

AUGUST 4

...enter thou into the joy of thy Lord. Matthew 25:21

WHEN GRACE KELLY, A MOVIE ACTRESS from Philadelphia, was married to Prince Ranier III of Monaco, there was a great change in her style of life. A commoner became a princess.

Even more dramatic are the implications for the forgiven sinner who is united to Jesus Christ. This is the fundamental aspect of Christianity. Union with Christ is the unique and essential relationship that provides the potential for Christian growth.

This union with Christ does not mean we lose our identity as persons. Actually, our organic spiritual identification with Jesus Christ enhances our own personality and liberates us from the bondage of our old life of self-centeredness. Despite the many distorted representations by those within and outside the household of faith, the Christian life is a joyous adventure. *Russell T. Hitt*

> My heart is full of Christ, and longs
> Its glorious matter to declare!
> Of Him I make my loftier psalms,
> I cannot from His praise forbear;
> My ready tongue makes haste to sing
> The glories of my heavenly King.
> *Charles Wesley*

Lord Jesus, it is with joy I serve You and walk each day in the freedom of Your forgiveness.

AUGUST 5

I am he that liveth, and was dead; and, behold, I am alive for evermore, Amen.... Revelation 1:18

*I*T WORKS
I've come to one conclusion. A relationship with Jesus Christ changes lives. You can laugh at Christianity; you can mock and ridicule it. But it works. It changes lives. If you trust Christ, start watching your attitudes and actions, because Jesus Christ is in the business of changing lives.

It is your choice

But Christianity is not something that can be forced or shoved down someone's throat. You have your life to live, and I have mine. All I can do is tell you what I've learned. Beyond that, it's your decision. My wife puts it this way: "Because Christ was raised from the dead, He lives. And because He lives, He has that infinite capacity to enter a man or woman's life, forgive him and change him from the inside out." The key element is the resurrection factor. He is risen!

Josh McDowell

Christians all over the world will testify to the truth of Christ's resurrection, for they sense His presence with them—the Living Risen Lord. It is the same Lord who walked in the cool of the garden that first Easter morning and spoke Mary's name. He speaks our names today, for He loves us and longs for our companionship too.

Each time we see the empty cross let it remind us of the suffering of Jesus, but also the *victory*. In the words of Peter Marshall, "Let us never live another day as if *He* were dead!" *J.W.B.*

Jesus, how glorious it is to know I serve a risen Lord...One who understands me and loves my companionship!

AUGUST 6

For if ye forgive men their trespasses, your heavenly Father will also forgive you. Matthew 6:14

---

*T*HE KEY THAT OPENS THE DOOR to the locked rooms of our hearts is forgiveness. It is only when we have experienced forgiveness (and I cannot emphasize strongly enough that I am not talking about the simple nodding of one's head to a preacher's words; I mean being *overwhelmed* by the reality of forgiveness, being able to touch, taste, and smell its results) *that* we find the locks are sprung, the doors flung open, the windows tossed high, the rooms inhabited, and fires lighted on the hearths.

It is then we discover that our hearts are finally free to love. They have become what the Creator intended them to be, places with immense capacity to embrace. We may even hear ourselves saying with surprise, "Do you know, *there isn't anyone I can't love!*" Then we will discover that God has done His work in us. *Karen Burton Mains*

A Christian will find it cheaper to pardon than to resent. Forgiveness saves the expense of anger, the cost of hatred, the waste of spirits. *Hannah More*

Lord Jesus, if ever I needed evidence of Your transforming power in my life, I see it overwhelmingly when You change my unforgiving heart into one of love.

———————————•◦ **AUGUST 7** ◦•———————————

He that believeth on him is not condemned.... John 3:18

•——————————————————————————————•

A STORY THAT HAS BEEN HANDED DOWN from Victorian England tells of a soldier who had been punished many times for major offenses. Now he was in the guardhouse again.

Before he was to enter the colonel's office, a sergeant asked if he could speak for the soldier. "Sir, I know that flogging, solitary confinement, disgrace—everything has been tried to change this man. May I take the liberty of suggesting one other thing?"

"What is that?" asked the officer.

"Sir, he has never been forgiven."

"Forgiven!" exclaimed the officer. But he thought for a few moments and then requested the offending soldier be brought in. Instead of ordering his punishment the colonel looked at the soldier and said, "We forgive you."

The effect was that the soldier, who had shown nothing but contempt and was thought to be completely incorrigible, broke down and wept. The years went on to prove that his life was changed and this act of kindness gave the Queen's regiment a soldier of the finest caliber. The story was told by one who for years had him under close scrutiny. *J.W.B.*

The Gospel comes to the sinner at once with nothing short of complete forgiveness as the starting point of all his efforts to be holy. It does not say, "Go and sin no more, and I will not condemn thee." It says at once, "Neither do I condemn thee: go and sin no more." *Horatius Bonar*

Father, may I ever be aware of the love that forgave me, when I deal with another in need.

Flee also youthful lusts; but follow righteousness,
faith, [love], peace, with them that call on the Lord
out of a pure heart. II Timothy 2:22

*W*HEN THE BIBLE SAYS, "I can do all things through Christ who
strengthens me," where is Christ? He's right here! At that moment of temptation, I don't have to clamor or make a long-distance
phone call, saying, "Lord, can You hear me? Oh, I need Your strength,
Lord. I'm going through this temptation. Can You hear me? Do You
have time to help me?"

No! Christ is as near as my pulse-beat. I can say, "Lord Jesus, here
comes this temptation. Thank You that You are here. Thank You that
You are almighty. And thank You that at this very moment the temptation is over because You live in me." That's it. The power of the
temptation is broken right there—right then—when we turn it
over to the indwelling Jesus Christ.

Romans 6:14 becomes true in your experience when it says, "Sin
shall not have dominion over you: for ye are not under the law, but
under grace" (*KJV*). And grace is really Jesus Christ. "Sin shall not
have dominion over you." It'll try. Sin will come at you. Temptation
will come at you. Satan will come at you. But it shall not have dominion over you because Christ is there within. Luis Palau

Every Christian is endued with a power whereby he is enabled to
resist temptation. Dean Tillotson

My Savior, how I need Your overcoming power when I am faced
with temptation. It is in these moments I see my weakness and Your
strength.

No temptation has overtaken you that is not common
to man. God is faithful, and he will not let you be tempted
beyond your strength, but with the temptation will also
provide the way of escape, that you may be able to
endure it. I Corinthians 10:13 (*RSV*)

I REMEMBER THE FIRST TIME, many years ago, when the full
impact of that verse hit me. God was so aware of what I was to
go through, He had provided "the way of escape" even before the
temptation began.

Jesus, too, was tempted—and angels ministered to Him. *Angel* means "messenger" and those special messengers of His Spirit, along with His earthly children whom He sends to help, will be provided when temptation comes.   *Bill Brown*

Every temptation is an opportunity of our getting nearer to God.
John Quincy Adams

Heavenly Father, I praise You for providing a way to escape so I may conquer temptation. I am so weak, but in Your promised strength I am victorious.

➤ AUGUST 10 ⤛

...conformed to the image of his Son.... Romans 8:29

G OD'S PURPOSE IS THAT WE SHOULD BE "CONFORMED to the image of his Son." That's why He sent Jesus into the world. He died to pour out His life and put it into the believer. We are supposed to do more than admire Jesus—we are to "put Him on!" As Paul wrote to the Ephesians, "Put on the new nature, created after the likeness of God..." that we had at the first; the likeness that we lost by sin is created again in us when our lives are joined to Christ.

Paul the Apostle often spoke of the Christian as being "in Christ." That is true identity—to be in Christ, to know that He has received me into His own life, to know that He has started on a lifelong project of making me like Himself and that someday I "shall also bear the image of the man of heaven" (I Corinthians 15:49, *RSV*).
Leighton Ford

The essence of true holiness consists in conformity to the nature and will of God.   *Samuel Lucas*

Almighty God, may I truly comply with Your desire to see my life bear Jesus' image. There is so much that needs changing.

➤ AUGUST 11 ⤛

You search the scriptures, because you think that in them you have eternal life; and it is they that bear witness to me.... John 5:39 (RSV)

I REMEMBER SOME YEARS AGO attending a performance of Tchaikovsky's *Pathetique* symphony, and at first I was completely unmoved and untouched by the music, even though the auditorium in which I was sitting was filled with glorious harmony.

Later in the program, however, a remarkable change came over me, for I found my heart soaring with the music, my feet tapping to the rhythm, and at the conclusion of the performance my hands were clapping in appreciation. Heart, hands, and feet were affected because the music invaded my soul. The difference in attitude and reaction came about when the music ceased to be *all around me* and managed to get right *into me*.

The teaching of the Scriptures is that we are in Christ—the *realm* of spiritual experience. Scripture also teaches that Christ is in us—the *reality* of Christian experience. The realm of Christian experience is only made reality through the activity of the Lord Jesus Christ Himself living and reigning within the heart of the redeemed sinner. It is when the Lord Jesus gets right *into you* that the heart, hands, and feet move in response to the music of heaven's realm in which you are seated in Christ. *D. Stuart Briscoe*

All the good from the Savior of the world is communicated through this Book. All the things desirable to man are contained in it. *Abraham Lincoln*

Father, my mind was opened when Your Holy Spirit began to reveal to me the wonders of Your Word. No longer foreign to me but abiding deep within my soul.

➤ AUGUST 12 ➤

**Thy word have I hid in mine heart,
that I might not sin against thee.** Psalm 119:11

◆————————————————————————————◆

GOD DOESN'T WANT US TO BE CONFUSED. He chooses to reveal His will because He wants us to know His plan for our lives. For people who want to discover His will, there are several avenues to follow.

Search the Word of God. Daily read the Bible and take notes. God's will never contradicts His own teaching. Much confusion can be eliminated when I know what God is saying in the Scripture. I can know without doubt that I am wrong—God does not contradict His Word.

The same Holy Spirit who inspired the writing of the Bible also inspires the reading of it. Knowing that we want to follow Him, God's Spirit leads us through the Scripture. We don't have to read with a panicky "O God, teach me, show me quick" attitude. We can relax with His Word, enjoy it, and spend time daily pondering and reflecting as we read it. And, as we do, we will begin to be impressed by the ways He supplied needs in other people's lives and realize that He can also do it with us. We discover an aspect of truth about Him that we hadn't known before and sense that he wants to apply that truth in our lives too.   *Roger C. Palms*

The Bible is the one book to which any thoughtful man may go with any honest question of life or destiny and find the answer of God by honest searching.   *John Ruskin*

Almighty God, teach me by Your Holy Word to discover Your will for me each day. Let my heart and life be totally aware of Your leading, I pray.

——————▸ AUGUST 13 ◂——————

For what is a man profited, if he gain the whole world and lose his own soul?... Matthew 16:26

◆—————————————————————————————◆

*T*O MAKE CHRIST LORD is to bring every department of our public and private lives under His control. This includes our career. God has a purpose for every life. Our business is to discover it and do it. God's plan may be different from our parents' or our own. If he is wise, the Christian will do nothing rash or reckless. He may already be engaged in, or preparing for, the work God has for him to do. But he may not. If Christ is our Lord, we must open our minds to the possibility of a change.   *John R. W. Stott*

If you knew there was One greater than yourself, who knows you better than you know yourself, and loves you better than you can love yourself; One who gathered into Himself all great and good things and causes, blending in His beauty all the enduring color of life, who could turn your dreams into visions, and make real the things you hoped were true; and if that One had done one unmistakable thing to prove, even at the price of blood—His own blood—that you could come to Him, would you not fall at His feet with the treasure of your years, your powers, your love? And is there not One such?
                                                              A. E. Whitham

Lord Jesus, the enormity of Your love for me makes it easy to turn all my ambitions, loves, and longings into Your hands—for You want the best for my life. I would give You everything, Lord.

——————▸ AUGUST 14 ◂——————

Righteousness shall go before him: and shall set us in the way of his steps. Psalm 85:13

*H*OW I ASCERTAIN THE WILL OF GOD:
I seek at the beginning to get my heart into such a state that it has no will of its own in regard to a given matter.

Nine-tenths of the trouble with people is right here. Nine-tenths of the difficulties are overcome when our hearts are *ready to do the Lord's will,* whatever it may be. When one is truly in this state it is usually but a little way to the knowledge of what His will is.

Having surrendered my own will, I do not leave the result to feeling or simply impressions. If I do so, I make myself liable to great delusions.

I seek the will of the Spirit of God through, or in connection with, *the Word of God.* The Spirit and the Word must be combined. If the Holy Ghost guides us at all, He will do it according to the Scriptures, and never contrary to them.

Next I take into account *providential circumstances.* These often plainly indicate God's will in connection with His Word and Spirit.

I ask God in prayer to reveal His will to me aright.

Thus, through prayer to God, the study of His Word, and reflection, I come to a deliberate judgment, and if my mind is thus at peace, and continues so after two or three more petitions, I proceed accordingly. In *trivial matters,* and in transactions involving *most important issues,* I have found this method *always effective.*

George Mueller

Our wills are ours, we know not how;
Our wills are ours, to make them Thine.

Alfred, Lord Tennyson

Almighty God, take this will of mine and lead me, I pray.

—◆— AUGUST 15 —◆—

...continuing instant in prayer. Romans 12:12

*T*HE FIRST THING WE HAVE TO DO in building a prayer life is to become humble enough to be willing to pray about little things. When this problem is overcome, it is possible to set up patterns of prayer that can be relied on for larger matters as well.

This is not an easy thing to do, but on it rests the potential for an abundant prayer life. The foundation of prayer is a succession of little prayers answered and thus forged into steel sturdy enough to withstand the shocks of life and all of its emotional storms.

Ruth C. Ikerman

Tell God all that is in your heart, as one unloads one's heart to a dear friend. People who have no secrets from each other never want subjects of conversation; they do not weigh their words, because there is nothing to be kept back. Neither do they seek for something to say; they talk out of the abundance of their hearts, just what they think. Blessed are they who attain to such familiar, unreserved intercourse with God.   *Fénelon*

Dear Father, as I pray to You may I reveal all that is on my heart this day.

———————————————•▸ **AUGUST 16** ◂•———————————————

The Lord hath heard my supplication;
the Lord will receive my prayer. Psalm 6:9

◆———◆

MEN OF GOD WHOSE PRAYERS ARE RECORDED FOR US in the Bible never read a book on prayer, never went to a seminar on prayer, never heard a sermon on prayer. They just prayed.

Satan fears prayer because God hears prayer. Satan will stop at nothing to distract a person from praying or to get him to postpone praying or, failing that, to discourage him in his praying.

Start where you are, as you are, about whatever concerns you, whatever is lying most heavily on your heart, whatever is irritating or frustrating you at present.

Suggestion: Keep a prayer list (small dime-store notebook or an inexpensive diary would do just fine). Make your requests specific and date them. Then date the answer. Like the ungrateful lepers, we tend to forget.

It may be impossible to date the answers to certain requests. For instance, if I pray for patience, I will not find that on such and such a date I suddenly become patient. But if I pray for guidance in a particular problem, or the conversion of a friend, or the resolving of some apparently hopeless difficulty, recording the answer as well as the request will be a cause for worship and a means of strengthening my faith.

Be pointed. Be persistent. Be patient. But pray.   *Ruth Bell Graham*

Prayer is a powerful thing, for God has bound and tied Himself thereto. None can believe how powerful prayer is, and what it is able to effect, but those who have learned by experience.   *Martin Luther*

Father, the words I utter to You, though often said on the run, are heard—and I see the evidence of Your power in such amazing ways.

That it might be fulfilled which was spoken by Esaias the prophet, saying, Himself took our infirmities, and bore our sicknesses. Matthew 8:17

◆————————————————————————————◆

I ALWAYS BELIEVED that Jesus was touched by my infirmities, but I never realized before that He was actually touched by the very *feelings* of my infirmities. Sometimes I really believe no one, not even those closest to me, can understand how I feel. I can try to explain, but the words don't come out right; and sometimes I don't even understand myself, so that I can explain me! I only know I suffer agonies no one seems to understand.

Now then, Jesus my great High Priest has been there because He was taken from among men. He can truly have compassion because He has "felt" my feelings. He knows; He cares; He understands. He is touched with the very feeling of my infirmities, therefore I can come boldly to the throne of grace. And when I come to Him, what will He give me?

Well, we find we have a High Priest who supplies. Supplies what? Mercy and grace to help us in our time of need. What is the difference between mercy and grace? Mercy doesn't give us everything we deserve; grace gives us what we don't deserve. *Jill Briscoe*

> I have a great need for Christ;
> I have a great Christ for my need.
>
> *Charles H. Spurgeon*

Lord Jesus, even when no one else can understand how I feel, You do and the knowledge of Your mercy and grace fills me with thanksgiving.

...when you pray, go away by yourself, all alone, and shut the door behind you and pray to your Father secretly.... Matthew 6:6 (*TLB*)

◆————————————————————————————◆

O UR LORD FREQUENTLY PRAYED ALONE, separating Himself from every earthly distraction. I would strongly urge you to select a place—a room or corner in your home, place of work, or in your yard or garden—where alone you can regularly meet God.

As we observe the prayer life of Jesus, we notice the earnestness with which He prayed. The New Testament records that in Gethsemane, in the intensity of His supplication, He fell to the ground and agonized with God until His sweat became "like drops of blood" (Luke 22:44). What an example of "prayer in suffering" He is—and how He proves the promise that those who are suffering need to look to God even more earnestly. *Billy Graham*

(In the hectic business of living we are often found longing for a time of quiet, alone with God. Awaking, may we seize this moment— remembering His presence goes with us into our often disturbing world.)

> *We kneel how weak, we rise how full of power.*
> *Why therefore should we do ourselves this wrong*
> *Or others—that we are not always strong,*
> *That we are ever overborne with care,*
> *That we should ever weak or heartless be,*
> *Anxious or troubled, when with us is prayer,*
> *And joy and strength and courage are with Thee?*
> *Richard Chenevix Trench*

AUGUST 19

I know whom I have trusted. II Timothy 1:12

GOD TOLD GIDEON TO REDUCE THE NUMBER OF PEOPLE in his band to 300 because He said if there are more than that Israel will "vaunt themselves against me, saying, 'My own hand has delivered me.'" We must trust God and His wisdom that what He does for us will be the best.

Sometimes we ask amiss in prayer and God answers us, and with the answer sends leanness of soul. But if we trust that what He does for us will be right, He will not let us down. The expression, "He gives the very best to those who leave the choice with Him" is true.

We must trust the love of God. The supreme test of faith for the non-Christian is often the question of whether or not God exists. For the Christian, however, it is whether or not God is good. In the face of tragedy only trust in His character will carry us through. It is a great comfort to know that God does not ask us to understand but only to trust Him. *Paul E. Little*

God loves an *uttermost confidence in Himself*—to be *wholly trusted*. This is the sublimest of all the characteristics of a true Christian— the basis of all character.

Is there anything that pleases you more than to be trusted—to have even a little child look up into your face, and put out its hand to meet yours, and come to you confidingly? By so much as God is better than you are, by so much more does He love to be trusted.

There is a Hand stretched out to you, a Hand with a wound in the palm of it. Reach out the hand of your faith to clasp it, and cling to it, for "without faith it is impossible to please God."   Henry Van Dyke

My Lord Jesus, I reach out to You as a trusting, loving child. May I always please You as I place my life into Your nail-pierced hands.

AUGUST 20

Continue in prayer, and watch in the same with thanksgiving. Colossians 4:2

◆————————————————————◆

I REMEMBER ONE PASTOR SAYING the biggest problem with prayer is prayerlessness. This is so true. I have found it so in my own life because prayer, disciplined and regular prayer, is an effect of the will. In my situation I don't have much trouble with spontaneous prayer, nor with the attitude of praying without ceasing. I pray while driving, I pray while doing the laundry, or cooking, or cleaning. I pray as I tuck the children in bed, as I walk or sit in the garden. But to make the necessary effort of my will to pray in a regular, disciplined way, I fall short. Praying without ceasing is important and we are told to do so in I Thessalonians 5:17, but developing a regular disciplined prayer life is also equally important. There is an old saying that I have always loved:

> Satan trembles when he sees
> The weakest saint
> Upon his knees.

And because of this, Satan will do his best to distract and discourage us.   *Gigi Graham Tchividjian*

If you would never cease to pray, never cease to long for it. The continuance of your longing is the continuance of your prayer.
     Augustine

Lord Jesus, may Your Holy Spirit keep me conscious of my need for a disciplined prayer life. Forgive how easily I become distracted, Lord.

AUGUST 21

I will hear what the Lord will speak.... Psalm 85:8

*I*N PRAYING, WE ARE OFTEN OCCUPIED WITH OURSELVES, with our own needs, and our own efforts in the presentation of them. In waiting upon God, the first thought is of *the God upon whom we wait.* God longs to reveal Himself, to fill us with Himself. Waiting on God gives Him time in His own way and divine power to come to us. Before you pray, bow quietly before God to remember and realize who He is, how near He is, how certainly He can and will help. Be still before Him and allow His Holy Spirit to waken and stir up in your soul the childlike disposition of absolute dependence and confident expectation. Wait on God till you know you have met Him; prayer will then become so different. And when you are praying, let there be intervals of silence, reverent stillness of soul in which you yield yourself to God in case He may have aught He wishes to teach you or to work in you.

Andrew Murray

> The holy time is quiet...
> Breathless with adoration...
> The gentleness of heaven broods o'er the sea;
> Listen!...

William Wordsworth

Almighty God, this quiet time with You brings healing to my soul. Now I will stop and listen to Your gentle leadings.

➤ AUGUST 22 ◆

Call unto me, and I will answer thee, and show thee great and mighty things, which thou knowest not.

Jeremiah 33:3

*I*N HAVANA, CUBA, I WAS ONCE A GUEST in a boarding school for girls. There were children from 2 to 17 years. "May I tell the girls something?" I asked after dinner. "No, they still have to do all their homework for tomorrow. You may speak for five minutes, no longer!" After four minutes the lights suddenly went out. "Please, will you continue until the lights go on again? The children cannot work in the dark!" I told about all sorts of adventures, my journeys, meetings with children, happy and sad stories. So I was able to tell about the Lord Jesus, who He was and what He is to us in our wants and joy. He had said: "Lo, I am with you alway, even unto the end of the world" (Matthew 28:20). After an hour the lights came on again. The children started their homework. A little girl came to me, put her arms around my neck and whispered: "I believe that Jesus broke the lights so that you could tell us about Him." In days to come we shall often have to fix our eyes upon the Lord. Often it will seem a lost cause. Often Jesus will have to break the lights so that we can listen to Him.   *Corrie ten Boom*

> The praying spirit breathe,
>   The watching power impart,
> From all entanglements beneath
>   Call off my anxious heart,
> My feeble mind sustain,
>   By worldly thoughts oppressed;
> Appear, and bid me turn again
>   To my eternal rest.
>
> *Charles Wesley*

Lord, thank You for the circumstances in my life that cause me to be still and listen to You.

—————————— **AUGUST 23** ——————————

I am the vine, ye are the branches.... John 15:5

◆ ——————————————————————————————— ◆

W E ARE SET HERE TO REPRESENT CHRIST by "being fruitful in every good work." If we fail, He fails just to that extent of being commended to men. And it is upon this issue that we shall be judged. "Every branch in me that beareth not fruit he taketh away."

It is not what we intended to be, but what we are, that will determine our destiny at the Master's coming. If the thorns and gnarls of unsanctified temper fill the place which God set apart and pruned for the sweet fruits of love and charity, we shall suffer loss; and the shame which the Lord has threatened will come upon us. And if instead of works, good deeds done to the poor, the Gospel preached to the heathen and the sick and afflicted visited in the name of Christ, there be only the spreading leaves of a vain profession, then the "Inasmuch as ye did it not" will fall with fearful emphasis upon our ears.

Oh, we are so careless and drowsy upon the great question of the works and fruits of faith! How we forget that just as there is an abundant faithfulness to which we are exhorted, so there is an abundant entrance to which we are invited.   *A. J. Gordon*

Above all the grace and the gifts that Christ gives to His beloved is that of overcoming self.   *Francis of Assisi*

Lord, give me the gift of Your abiding grace so that I may overcome the deficiencies in this personality of mine.

...Mary hath chosen [the best] part,
which shall not be taken away from her. Luke 10:42

◆————————————————————————————————◆

*C*HRIST DEMANDS THE BEST IN OUR LIVES. I knew a woman who was active in church, taught Sunday school classes, was married to a fine businessman and was a benefactor in the community. One evening she and her husband visited a little country church where a young man just out of seminary was conducting a spiritual emphasis mission. Many things he said impressed her, but especially his question, "Have you ever really committed yourself to Christ unreservedly?"

She leaned over and touched her husband's hand and said, "You know, I've never done that in my life." At the close of the service both of them found their way down the aisle and walked up to the young man. They said to him, "We want to do what you asked us to do."

He said to them, "Make a bundle of all that you are or ever hope to be, and all that you have or ever hope to have, and give it to Him. In the years to come He will take out of that bundle and give back to you what you need to fill your life." Because of that woman, there are today behind the Iron Curtain over 10 million homes that have the Gospel of John. One of her books has been translated into more languages than any other devotional book. Its title is *Streams in the Desert.*

Mary sat at Jesus' feet and learned of Him, and she gave her best to Him. Have you come to Him? Have you sat at His feet and learned of Him? Have you given your best to Him? Do you identify with that woman?
Millie Dienert

I am glad to think
I am not bound to make the world go right;
But only to discover and to do,
With cheerful heart, the work that God appoints.
I will trust in Him,
That He can hold His own; and I will take
His will, above the work He sendeth me,
To be my chiefest good.
Jean Ingelow

Lord Jesus, like Mary I would sit at Your feet and learn more of Your great love so that I may then minister wherever You send me.

Then was Jesus led up of the Spirit into the wilderness to be tempted of the devil. Matthew 4:1

◆━━━◆

*C*AN THE GUIDANCE OF GOD TAKE A PERSON into a wilderness? It took Israel into one. It took them to Marah, where the water was too bitter to drink. It took Jesus into 40 days and nights of harrowing temptation by his archenemy.

How such leading could possibly be the will of God for anyone, even for Jesus, would be a total mystery if we were trying to understand the case in isolation from others. But it was, according to Jesus' own words later, "for their sakes" that He sanctified Himself.

We are not Jesus. We are not even a part of that huge mob of Israelites that moved through the desert toward the Promised Land. But what we learn from them is meant for us because we are going in the same direction—home. I have found it to be true that obedience may lead me not to the fulfillment of my own ideals of spirituality but to very unexpected situations, very "unspiritual" situations in my view, which are meant to teach me to be meek and lowly in heart. If I want to learn of Him, this is what I am going to have to learn. And there, to my surprise, I find rest. I find the chance to recall once more (how many, many times I have to review my lessons) that if I am serious about my primary aim, I may be led elsewhere than my lesser aims would take me, for I do not know what I really need. God sees the "one thing needful," and He alone knows the path that will take me there. *Elisabeth Elliot*

Let us listen to Christ saying, *"Render unto Caesar the things that are Caesar's"*—let duty and work have their place—"and unto God the things that are God's." Let the worship in the Spirit, the entire dependence and continued waiting upon God for the full experience of His presence and power every day, and the strength of Christ working in us, ever have the first place. The whole question is simply this, Is God to have the place, the love, the trust, the time for personal fellowship He claims, so that all our working shall be God working in us? *Andrew Murray*

Almighty God, may You be pre-eminent in my life—in everything I do or say—for each day brings me closer to my eternal home.

My grace is sufficient for thee.... II Corinthians 12:9

*A*N OYSTER IS QUIETLY SLEEPING in the warmth of the sea. A tiny grain of sand is borne along on the current and is caught in the oyster's open shell. An annoyance has entered into the oyster's life; but instead of fighting the intruder, the oyster proceeds to manufacture an exudation of gummy substance which it spins out around the "thorn in its flesh." Thus the thorn becomes a pearl. "A pearl is a garment of patience which encloses an annoyance."

During World War I, Cardinal Desire Joseph Mercier's beautiful cathedral was bombed, his priceless books destroyed, and some of his students slain in cold blood. Out of the experience that great man of God wrote: "Suffering accepted and used will give you a serenity which may well prove the most exquisite fruit of your life."

Milton's blindness resulted in *Paradise Lost.* God's grace wrought "In Memoriam" out of Tennyson's loneliness and *The Angelus* from Millet's poverty. "We shroud the cages of birds," said Jean Paul Richter, "when we would teach them to sing." Or as Lloyd C. Douglas put it, "Sometimes God doesn't save us from the storm but in the storm." Grace is the substance God puts around your thorn and of it makes the pearl of life. *Charles L. Allen*

"He will be very gracious unto thee at the voice of thy cry." That has comforted me often, more than any promise of answer; it includes answers, and a great deal more besides; it tells us what He *is* toward us, and that is more than what He will *do.* And the "cry" is not long, connected, thoughtful prayers, a cry is just an *unworded dart upward* of the heart, and at *that* "voice" He will be very gracious. What a *smile* there is in these words! *Frances Ridley Havergal*

Almighty God, I praise You for Your graciousness to me. In the thorns of my life Your comfort brings healing and peace.

For the eyes of the Lord run to and fro throughout the whole earth, to show himself strong in the behalf of them whose heart is perfect toward him.... II Chronicles 16:9

*W*E OFTEN COMPLAIN THAT WE HAVE NO HELP—and all the while the eyes of the Lord are looking compassionately and longingly at us. He knows the sorrow, trial, or temptation. Nothing would give Him greater pleasure than to show Himself strong on our behalf.

When overcome with failure and sin, when thoroughly discouraged, when overtaken suddenly by temptation, you need to know that even this "care" can be cast upon Him. Believe that He forgives and cleanses and continues to care. Nothing will surprise Him or wear out His patience or nullify His love. He is committed to us—He is our God; we are His people. *Verna Birkey*

The little cares that fretted me,
    I lost them yesterday,
Among the fields above the sea,
    Among the winds at play,
Among the lowing of the herds,
    The rustling of the trees,
Among the singing of the birds,
    The humming of the bees.

The foolish fears of what might pass
    I cast them all away
Among the clover-scented grass
    Among the new-mown hay,
Among the rustling of the corn
    Where drowsy poppies nod.
Where ill thoughts die and good are
    born—
Out in the fields with God!

Elizabeth Barrett Browning

Lord, shed Your compassionate care on all who hurt today, and for myself I ask for Your strength and power to face the temptations of this day.

AUGUST 28

There is no fear in love, but perfect love casts out fear. For fear has to do with punishment, and he who fears is not perfected in love. I John 4:18 (*RSV*)

*W*HAT MAKES YOU AFRAID? We begin life with fear of loud noises. As we grow, we fear darkness or falling. By the time we are adolescents, our emotional circuits are loaded with conditioned fears ingrained by parents and friends. The contagion of fear is epidemic in our society. We fear failure, certain kinds of people, the unexpected and the untried.

Fear, not just hate, is the opposite of love. The same emotional channels which carry the heavy freight of fear were meant to receive and express the liberating power of love. Surrender to our Lord what makes you afraid. Then, picture Him with you in the situation or relationship you fear. Listen to what He said to the disciples on the storming sea: "I am, do not be afraid." Disown the fear; displace it with His love!

Lloyd John Ogilvie

We sleep in peace in the arms of God when we yield ourselves up to His providence in a delightful consciousness of His tender mercies; no more restless uncertainties, no more anxious desires, no more impatience at the place we are in; for it is God who has put us there and who holds us in His arms. Can we be unsafe where He has placed us?

Fénelon

Lord, I surrender all my fears into Your loving hands. With Your courage within me, my days and nights will be lived in quiet assurance.

—— AUGUST 29 ——

Nor height, nor depth, nor any other creature, shall be able to separate us from the love of God, which is in Christ Jesus our Lord. Romans 8:39

*R*OMANS 8 REVEALS AS CLEARLY AS DOES ROMANS 7 that a conflict continues within every believer which never ends as long as one dwells on earth, but it reveals the way of victory. It removes the delusion that the believer can fight the enemy in his own strength and gives spiritual discernment of God's gracious provision of the means of victory. Romans 8 lifts the believer above the clouds of discouragement into the clear sunlight of abiding peace and rest. It assures him at the beginning of the chapter that in Christ there is no condemnation by God as regards his past and at the end that in Christ there is no separation from God as regards the future. All the verses in between proclaim the perfect provision made in Christ for victory over every enemy within and without as regards the present.

Ruth Paxson

When men and women are reduced to dire extremity, when the cares and troubles of the world overwhelm them and life appears to be just too much to endure and they tend to give way under the sheer weight of things, they can overcome if they recall the Scriptures: "In all these things we have complete victory through him who loved us! For I am certain that nothing can separate us from his love: neither death nor life; neither angels nor other heavenly rulers or powers; neither the present nor the future; neither the world above nor the world below—there is nothing in all creation that will ever be able to separate us from the love of God which is ours through Christ Jesus our Lord."   *Norman Vincent Peale*

Almighty God, there is nothing on this earth that can separate me from You. This knowledge fills me with a joy that can never be taken away. I praise Your name.

——•— AUGUST 30 —•——

...I have learned, in whatever state I am, to be content. Philippians 4:11 *(RSV)*

◆————————————————————————————◆

THE CHANGEPOINTS IN THE LIVES of Adam, Noah, Abraham, Sarah, Isaac, Rebekah, Jacob, Rachel, Joseph, Moses, and David (the list is endless) gave each of them times of great tension and the inevitable feeling of being abandoned by God.

The thrilling thing to see, however, was that no matter how change gripped their lives and threatened to paralyze, the sovereignty of God and His great plan was always accomplished. There must have been countless times when those great men and women of God resented the changepoints in their lives, didn't understand them; yet, somehow and by some special God-given grace, they *learned* to accept change. Consequently, God's beautiful purpose was carried out by mere frightened mortals, in spite of their fearsome apprehensions.   *Joyce Landorf*

> You fearful saints, fresh courage take:
> The clouds you so much dread
> Are big with mercy, and shall break
> In blessings on your head.
>
> *William Cowper*

Father, I do not always understand the changes that take place in my life, but I do know You never make mistakes. In faith I trust and am content in Your leading.

*Let your heart therefore be perfect with the Lord
our God, to walk in his statutes, and to keep
his commandments....* I Kings 8:61

*T*HE REAL PROBLEM OF THE CHRISTIAN LIFE comes where
people do not usually look for it. It comes the very moment you
wake up each morning. All your wishes and hopes for the day rush at
you like wild animals. And the first job each morning consists
simply in shoving them all back; in listening to that other voice, taking that other point of view, letting that other larger, stronger,
quieter life come flowing in. And so on, all day. Standing back from
all your natural fussings and frettings; coming in out of the wind.

We can only do it for moments at first. But from those moments
the new sort of life will be spreading through our system: because
now we are letting Him work at the right part of us. It is the difference between paint, which is merely laid on the surface, and a dye or
stain which soaks right through. He never talked vague, idealistic
gas. When He said, "Be perfect," He meant it. He meant that we
must go in for the full treatment. It is hard; but the sort of compromise we are all hankering after is harder—in fact, it is impossible. It
may be hard for an egg to turn into a bird: it would be a jolly sight
harder for it to learn to fly while remaining an egg. We are like eggs
at present. And you cannot go on indefinitely being just an ordinary,
decent egg. We must be hatched or go bad.   *C. S. Lewis*

What is Christian perfection? Loving God with all our heart,
mind, soul and strength.   *John Wesley*

*Almighty God, may I love You in all the ways of this life—totally
surrendered to Your sovereign will.*

*Salvation belongeth unto the Lord:
thy blessing is upon thy people....* Psalm 3:8

*O*NE STORMY SUNDAY, SPURGEON ENTERED a primitive little
Methodist chapel in Colchester, England. A local pastor was
preaching to a dozen or 15 persons. The preacher repeated the text
with hesitant pronunciation, "Look unto me and be ye saved, all the
ends of the earth." The pastor preached on the simple text in a homely

fashion for a few minutes. Then with the freedom of a less conventional age than ours, he looked straight at the young stranger in the congregation and said, "Young man, you look very miserable, miserable in life and miserable in death, if you don't obey my text; but if you obey now, this moment you will be saved. Young man, look to Jesus Christ, look. You have nothing to do but to look and live."

Today a visitor to the little chapel may read on a tablet these words, "Near to this spot C. H. Spurgeon looked and lived." At that place began one of the greatest ministries of the centuries. That was the fountainhead of the mighty man of God from whom people in all parts of the world drank and were refreshed.   *John M. Drescher*

Jesus is what He is said to be. Jesus will do what He says He will do. Therefore we must each trust Him, saying, "He will be to me what He says He is, and He will do to me what He has promised to do. I leave myself in the hands of Him who is appointed to save, that he may save me. I rest upon His promise that He will do even as He has said." This is saving faith, and he that has it has everlasting life.
                                                                      C. H. Spurgeon

Lord Jesus, for the gift of salvation I praise You.

———————————— SEPTEMBER 2 ————————————

***...what wisdom is this which is given unto him,
that even such mighty works are wrought by his hands?***
                                                                      Mark 6:2

◆————————————————————————————————◆

*J*ESUS WAS CARPENTER OF NAZARETH. It is impossible to exhaust the significance of the fact that for a great part of His life on earth the Son of God toiled with His hands, doing a joiner's work. "A workshop," said Henry Drummond, "is not a place for making engines so much as a place for making men." A workshop helped to make the soul of Christ. The devoted skill and labor that went into those Nazareth yokes and ploughs and cottage tables were rendered as an offering to God. Even then Jesus was "about His Father's business." Hence toil has been hallowed forever. The distinction between secular and sacred avocations vanishes. Hard work—whether manual labor or the duty of the businessman—*is* sacred when it is done as under the eyes of God.

> Very dear the cross of shame,
> Where He took the sinner's blame...
> But He walked the same high road,
> And He bore the self-same load

When the Carpenter of Nazareth
Made common things for God.

James S. Stewart

Have thy tools ready. God will find thee work.   *Charles Kingsley*

*Lord Jesus, thank You for making the labor of our hands sacred as
we work each day in Your name.*

Lo, I come to do thy will, O God. Hebrews 10:9

JESUS SAYS, "WHOEVER LOSES HIS LIFE FOR MY SAKE shall
find it"—the absolute antithesis of what most people in our ac-
quisitive society are conditioned to think.

All my life I labored for success, wealth, acceptance and power.
The more I obtained, the less I discovered I had. Surrendering everything in absolute brokenness, however, was the beginning of finding
the identity and purpose for which I had battled so hard. In giving
up my life to Christ, I had found it.

The same thing happened with the prison work. For nine months I
struggled to control it, though in our fellowship we never wanted
our real desires to appear that obvious. Yet the harder I reached for
the reins, the more elusive they were to grasp. When I stepped aside,
gave it all up in honest relinquishment, the Lord gave it back.

Charles W. Colson

God is a kind Father. He sets us all in the places where He wishes
us to be employed, and that employment is truly "our Father's business." He chooses work for every creature which will be delightful to
them if they do it simply and humbly. He gives us always strength
enough, and sense enough, for what He wants us to do; if we either
tire ourselves or puzzle ourselves, it is our own fault. And we may always be sure, whatever we are doing, that we cannot be pleasing
Him if we are not happy ourselves.   *John Ruskin*

*Heavenly Father, in Your will is peace and contentment. Let me not
try to grasp the reins of my life but be totally led by You.*

**...let the beauty of the Lord our God be upon us:
and establish thou the work of our hands upon us....**

Psalm 90:17

*P*EOPLE SOMETIMES SAY that because the world is in such bad shape, it's a sure sign that Jesus is going to come again soon, so they'll just sit down and wait for Him. How foolish! Jesus will come according to *His* timetable, and I for one prefer to be busy working. Remember what the shepherds were doing when the great light shone out to announce Jesus' birth? They were tending their flocks by night, doing their jobs. And what was Moses doing when God came to him and told him He was going to make him a great leader? He was guarding the sheep. None of those to whom God appeared was sitting around idle and useless. They were all working.

God intends for us to work. Our labors should be rewarding, whether we are compensated for them or not. We must find joy in the work we do, whether we work at home or in a career. Then our work will not be a burden to us and we will be free to enjoy whatever other compensation it affords. *Mary C. Crowley*

You have your own special work; make it a work of intercession. Paul labored, striving according to the work of God in him. Remember, God is not only the Creator but the Great Workman who worketh all in all. You can only do your work in His strength, by Him working in you through the Spirit. Intercede much for those among whom you work till God gives you life for them.

Let us all intercede too for each other, for every worker throughout God's Church, however solitary or unknown. *Andrew Murray*

Almighty God, let me find joy in my work wherever I may be. May my prayers be heard for all fellow Christians as together we labor, looking for the return of Your blessed Son.

——• SEPTEMBER 5 •——

Go ye therefore, and teach all nations, baptizing them in the name of the Father, and of the Son, and of the Holy Ghost: teaching them to observe all things whatsoever I have commanded you.... Matthew 28:19-20

*W*E DARE NOT CLOSE OUR EYES TO WORLD EVENTS by relegating them into neatly packaged eschatological schemes that relieve us of any responsibility. We dare not stop our ears to the sobbing moan of the world's hungry by the insulated assertion that these things must occur before the return of Christ. May God give us eyes to see and ears to hear the world in which we live.

What is our world like? Three billion people have yet to hear the redemption that is in Jesus Christ. Nearly two-and-one-half billion are culturally outside the present scope of Christian witness. They die without hearing, without knowing. Business as usual will never accomplish the great irrevocable mandate to world evangelization.

Richard J. Foster

(With so many still needing to hear the message of love and redemption through our Savior, let us ask Him to direct and guide us to these souls.)

> *Use me, God, in Thy great harvest field,*
> *Which stretcheth far and wide like a wide sea;*
> *The gatherers are so few; I fear the precious yield*
> *Will suffer loss. Oh, find a place for me!*
> *A place where best the strength I have will tell:*
> *It may be one the older toilers shun;*
> *Be it a wide or narrow place, 'tis well*
> *So that the work it holds be only done.*

Christina G. Rossetti

⟶• SEPTEMBER 6 •⟵

It is finished.... John 19:30

◆————————————————————————◆

CONSIDER THE MINISTRY OF OUR LORD here on earth. In the eyes of the world the cross was the ultimate in failure, and Jesus' whole life was a wasted effort. But in the eyes of heaven what appeared to be failure was the greatest success this world has ever known. Why was this so? Because Christ was in control of the whole situation...

John 19:30, speaking of the death of Christ, reads: "When Jesus therefore had received the vinegar, he said, 'It is finished: and he bowed his head, and gave up the ghost.'" The phrase *He bowed His head* actually means a deliberate putting of the head into a position of rest. True, He suffered and bled and died, and in His humanity every agony was intensified. But He was not only the Son of God, He was God the Son, and as such He was in control. *John Hunter*

Success is neither fame, wealth nor power; rather it is seeking, knowing, loving and obeying God. If you seek, you will know; if you know, you will love; if you love, you will obey. *Charles Malik*

Savior, You know what I feel when I fail. In failure or success let me seek to find the blessing of trusting in Your sovereign will for my life.

For whom the Lord loveth he chasteneth.... Hebrews 12:6

*B*EFORE ALMOST ANY GOOD THING CAN BE ACHIEVED in our lives, we need to be broken. This involves losing our pride, bowing our wills, and seeing our sinful selves for who we really are. Usually when we first enter God's family, we are full of brokenness. But like a poor man who stumbles upon sudden wealth, we soon forget the pit from which we were lifted. Bit by bit pride and self-sufficiency seep back into our lives and, unlike our first few weeks with Christ, "little" sins slip by unchecked and ignored.

To keep us from totally sliding back down the spiritual hill which we've started to climb, God chastens us. When He does, we may think it's because He's given up on us and wants to "trade us in on a newer model" which will give Him less trouble. But the fact that He disciplines us proves we are His very own children, for a parent doesn't spank a child who isn't his (Hebrews 12:7-8). It also proves He loves us, for wise parents spank their children if they truly love them (Hebrews 12:5-6). Someday when we stand before God's throne to receive our rewards for the lives we lived as Christians, imagine how glad we'll be that God didn't just let us get away with all our sinfulness while still on earth!   *Joni Eareckson*

Power comes by discipline, and by discipline alone.
                                                      E. Stanley Jones

Thank You, Father, for Your gentle disciplining that draws me closer to You.

Every branch in me that beareth not fruit he taketh away:
and every branch that beareth fruit, he purgeth it,
that it may bring forth more fruit. John 15:2

*I*T IS FOR FRUIT IN OUR LIVES that the Husbandman cleanses the branches. Of all the fruit-bearing plants, there is none so ready to produce wild wood, and for which cleansing and pruning are so necessary, as the grape. What is it that the vinedresser cuts away with his pruning-knife? Wood—wild wood. Why cut away this wood? Because it draws away the strength and life from the vine and hinders the flow of sap to the grape. The wood of the branch must decrease that the fruit of the vine may increase. Even so the child of God is a heavenly branch, and there is in us that which seems perfectly good and even legitimate and yet draws out our interest and strength. It must be pruned, cleansed and cut away. How easy it is to let objects and cares of this world possess and over-power us.   Morrow C. Graham

I must always remember that God, who allows every circum-stance in my life, has promised the grace entailed; and He, who never makes mistakes, knows the exact amount of pruning this way-ward heart of mine requires.   J.W.B.

Almighty God, for the pruning in my life that strips the wild wood so that Your strength may flow through me, I praise You.

SEPTEMBER 9

For the redemption of their soul is precious.... Psalm 49:8

S CHUBERT DIED AT 31 YEARS OF AGE and left us a parable of his life and all human life in his *Unfinished Symphony.*

People today still marvel at the genius of Michelangelo. His skills in architecture, painting, and sculpture are known the world around. His finished work such as his statues of Moses and David are well-known. What many do not know is that, because of his tem-peramental nature, he left most of his sculptures unfinished. In the new Sacristy of Michelangelo in Florence, Italy, you may visit an entire hall filled with the unfinished works of Michelangelo.

So many scholars and persons down through the centuries left im-portant parts of their work unfinished. Books and works of art lay incomplete in study and studio. Most had planned to complete their works, but life ended.

Not so with Jesus! He finished the work He came to do. He is called the Author and Finisher of our faith. Nothing more is needed for our salvation.

Christ's earthly work is finished. Ours is not. As long as there is one soul without the Savior our work must go on. Christ did all that divine love could do to redeem the world. He left us the task of shar-ing that love in all of life.   John M. Drescher

How is it possible that you have not been called? You are already a married man or wife or child or daughter or servant or maid.... No-body is without command and calling.... God's eyes look not upon the works, but on the obedience in the work.   Martin Luther

Lord Jesus, stir within me Your love that redeemed my soul so that I will share it with another—this day!

...prepare your hearts unto the Lord, and serve him only....

I Samuel 7:3

S OME TIME AGO IN ENGLAND, there was a group of friends that met in a pub after a hunt. They were talking and sharing the day's activities. One hunter, quite excited, began to relate his story using quite a few gestures. All of a sudden, with one such gesture, he hit a cup of tea and knocked it all over the beautifully whitewashed walls. He was terribly embarrassed, but before he could even apologize, one of the other men jumped to his feet and, pulling a pen from his pocket, began to sketch on the wall. As he sketched, there emerged the most magnificent, majestic stag. That man was Landseer, England's foremost painter of animals. I believe that if Landseer can do that with an ugly brown tea stain, how much more can God make something beautiful out of all our faults and all our failures if we will just give them to Him and allow Him to sketch and work as He sees fit; and we being available, but not getting in His way. *Gigi Graham Tchividjian*

Let us ask Him to prepare us for all that He is preparing for us.

Frances Ridley Havergal

Father, take my heart, with all the faults that mar the beauty You desire, and turn it into a worthy vessel for Your service.

...serving the Lord; rejoicing in hope.... Romans 12:11-12

I MET A WOMAN IN RUSSIA who had multiple sclerosis. Her feet and hands were paralyzed except for one finger. With that one finger she typed out Bible texts and inspirational books.

This woman's husband bound her typewritten message together into books which then went from one person to another. She did this work until the day she died. She is now with the Lord. How happy she is! And I am sure that she has heard from many there who have read her literature, "It was you who invited me here." Do not say you are not healthy or strong enough—you have more than one finger to use for God's work! *Corrie ten Boom*

> I am only one,
> But still I am one.
> I cannot do everything,

But still I can do something;
And because I cannot do everything
I will not refuse to do the something that I can do.

Edward Everett Hale

(There is not one of us who cannot minister in His name. One of the greatest services we can perform for another is to pray for him.)

Almighty God, thank You for the hope we have in You as we work each day. We ask Your blessing on those we know who need Your comfort and strength.

SEPTEMBER 12

With good will doing service, as to the Lord, and not to men. Ephesians 6:7

YEARS AGO IN KOWLOON, HONG KONG, I had the privilege of meeting two of God's choicest servants, Archdeacon and Mrs. Donnithorne. They had been missionaries to mainland China, but when the Communists took over they had had to flee. Both were very elderly when I first met them, but the radiance and joy of serving their Lord was apparent in everything they did.

The tall, venerable Archdeacon could be seen striding through the hot, odorous streets of the notorious old Walled City, where the couple had begun a home for elderly women. When he went to be with the Lord, Mrs. Donnithorne carried on the humanly taxing and exhausting ministry. Although severely crippled with arthritis and having had major surgery, she also climbed to the rooftops of government-provided housing for the refugees from China. There she taught the children about Jesus Christ and the basics of reading, writing and arithmetic.

At a conference in Kowloon a few years later, I sat behind this dedicated, frail-of-body but dominant-in-spirit servant of God and marveled at the way in which He used her. The painfully gnarled arthritic hands clasped her walking stick as she listened to the speaker, whose text was "She has done what she could." I thought, "Lord, if there is anyone I could think of that represents these words today, it is this beautiful child of Yours, Mrs. Donnithorne."

The Donnithornes were Christians whose wholly dedicated lives shone with a radiance that the awesome problems of the world could never dim.

J.W.B.

O Master, let me walk with Thee
In lowly paths of service free;

Tell me Thy secret; help me bear
The strain of toil, the fret of care.

Washington Gladden

Lord, may I serve You in quiet and obedient trust, reaching out to
those who have never known love and understanding.

SEPTEMBER 13

Hereby perceive we the love of God,
because he laid down his life for us.... I John 3:16

I WAS HUNGRY and you formed a humanities club and discussed
my hunger. Thank you.
I was imprisoned and you crept off quietly to your chapel
    and prayed for my release.
I was naked and in your mind you debated the morality
    of my appearance.
I was sick and you knelt and thanked God for your health.
I was homeless and you preached to me of the
    spiritual shelter of the love of God.
I was lonely and you left me alone to pray for me.
You seem so holy, so close to God. But I'm still
    very hungry and lonely and cold.

Author unknown

where people are, needs are hurts,
    searching, hunger.
if Jesus is in me, He can reach out to them.
on a plane, at a bus stop, in a restaurant at the
    shop or school.
He reaches out in things we do.
sir, my seat?
ma'am, take my hand.
did you need a dime?
can i help you with that?
tell me how you feel. i'll listen.
love makes the difference.

Ann Kiemel

Lord Jesus, may I not hesitate to help another in Your name, whether
it be in a small unassuming deed or in some assignment that will
demand my total involvement.

Jesus knowing that the Father had given all things into his hands, and that he was come from God, and went to God; he riseth from supper, and laid aside his garments; and took a towel, and girded himself. After that he poureth water into a basin, and began to wash the disciples' feet, and to wipe them with the towel wherewith he was girded.... Ye call me Master and Lord: and ye say well; for so I am. If I then, your Lord and Master, have washed your feet; ye also ought to wash one another's feet. For I have given you an example, that ye should do as I have done to you. Verily, verily, I say unto you, The servant is not greater than his lord; neither he that is sent greater than he that sent him. If ye know these things, happy are ye if ye do them. John 13:3-5,13-17

◆————————————————————————————◆

*N*OTE THAT JESUS SAYS that if we do these things there will be happiness. It is not just knowing these things that brings happiness, it is doing them. Throughout Jesus' teaching these two words *know* and *do* occur constantly and always in that order. We cannot do until we know, but we can know without doing. The house built on the rock is the house of the man who knows and does. The house built on the sand is the house of the man who knows but does not do.

Christ washed the disciples' feet and dried them with the towel with which He was girded, that is, with His own clothing. He intended this to be a practical example of the mentality and action that should be seen in the midst of the people of God.

Francis A. Schaeffer

All service ranks the same with God.
...There is no last nor first.

Robert Browning

Almighty God, there are so many people who need to know of the sacrificial love of Your Son, Jesus Christ. May my actions toward others bring this love into their longing hearts.

...knowing that of the Lord ye shall receive the reward of the inheritance: for ye serve the Lord [Jesus] Christ.
Colossians 3:24

*W*HEN I THINK OF SERVICE TO THE LORD I remember these simple words of a poor Methodist woman of the eighteenth century.

"I do not know when I have had happier times in my soul than when I have been sitting at work with nothing before me but a candle and a white cloth, and hearing no sound but that of my own breath, with God in my soul and heaven in my eye.... I rejoice in being exactly what I am, a creature capable of loving God and who, as long as God lives, must be happy. I get up and look for awhile out of the window and gaze at the moon and stars, the work of an Almighty hand. I think of the grandeur of the universe and then sit down and think of myself as one of the happiest beings in it."   *J.W.B.*

Do small things as if they were great because of the majesty of Jesus Christ, who works them in us and who lives our life; and great things as small and easy because of His omnipotence.   *Blaise Pascal*

Lord, in everything I do I will remember the most menial task can be glorified if it is performed for You, my Savior.

SEPTEMBER 16

O that thou hadst hearkened to my commandments! Then had thy peace been as a river, and thy righteousness as the waves of the sea. Isaiah 48:18

---

*T*HERE IS PEACE IN GOD'S WILL because it brings to us the approval of a good conscience. I cannot explain exactly what the conscience is or how it works, but I can say that within every one of us there is a voice saying what is right and what is wrong. When we do what God wants us to do, it makes us feel good inside. Really, there is no greater happiness to be found in life than to do what Jesus did when He lifted His eyes to heaven and said, "I have finished the work which thou gavest me to do."   *Charles Allen*

> With eager heart and will on fire,
> I fought to win my great desire.
> "Peace shall be mine," I said; but life
> Grew bitter in the weary strife.
>
> My soul was tired, and my pride
> Was wounded deep: to heaven I cried,
> "God grant me peace or I must die."
> The dumb stars glittered no reply.

Broken at last, I bowed my head,
Forgetting all myself, and said,
"Whatever comes, His will be done":
And in that moment peace was won.

Henry Van Dyke

Almighty God, my willful heart so often desires that which is not in Your plan for my life. Forgive me, Lord God, and restore Your peace, I

...when He, the Spirit of truth, is come, He will guide you into all truth.... John 16:13

---

*W*E CAN'T POSSIBLY OUTGIVE GOD. As we make ourselves available to Him, He allows us to be far more fulfilled and to see greater results than we possibly could outside His will. God owes no man anything, yet His rewards are far more fulfilling and satisfying than any we could possibly imagine. To be available is not always easy, but there is no other way to achieve a more satisfying and glorious life.

God's plan leaves no room for freak accidents. He has created us as we are, with a free will to choose, a mind to create, and time to determine how we will invest our lives even in such a time as this.

Vonette Z. Bright

My life is but a weaving
    Between my God and me;
I do not choose the colors
    He weaveth steadily.
Sometimes He weaveth sorrow,
    And I in foolish pride
Forget He sees the upper
    And I the underside.

Not till the loom is silent
    And the shuttles cease to fly
Will God unroll the canvas
    And explain the reason why
The dark threads are as needed
    In the skillful Weaver's hand
As the threads of gold and silver
    In the pattern He has planned.

Author unknown

Lord, into Your hands I give everything that is dear to me. Guide me in all that I do so that Your will may be done.

...without me you can do nothing. John 15:5

————————————————————————————◆

B ELIEVE IT OR NOT, God does not ask you to live the Christian life. He knows you cannot do it. He will not even help you to live it. There is only one Person who can live the Christian life, and that is the risen Son of God Himself.

Almighty God knows you are not wise enough, clever enough, or strong enough to live an effective Christian life. In risen power the Lord Jesus Christ wants to come into your life, to think with your brain, to look out through your eyes, to listen with your ears, to speak with your lips, to walk with your legs, to work with your hands, to love with your heart. That is what the Christian life is all about. It is nothing more, nothing less, and nothing else.

If you know that you are weak and absolutely unable to meet New Testament standards of righteousness and Christian character, you are a prime candidate for the Christian life and venture. It is as we allow the Lord Jesus to clothe Himself with us that He, through our weakness, demonstrates the greatness of His power that all the honor, glory and praise may be His who alone is worthy to receive it.

Roy W. Gustafson

It is impossible for that man to despair who remembers that his Helper is omnipotent. *Jeremy Taylor*

Lord Jesus, I will not doubt or lose hope for You are with me. Your strength will help me overcome the weaknesses that so often have overtaken me.

For the Lord God is a sun and shield: the Lord will give grace and glory: no good thing will he withhold from them that walk uprightly. Psalm 84:11

————————————————————————————◆

" I WILL ARISE AND GO TO MY FATHER," said the prodigal. "I will," said Paul as he stood on Mars' hill and cried down paganism. "I will," said Martin Luther King, Jr., and he started a second reformation whose influence is felt around the world. "I will," said

James Kwegyir Aggrey as he awakened Western society to the great potential of the African people. Say today, "I will. I ought to serve my God. I will serve my fellowman. I will continue my education. I will be the type of Christian that God wants me to be."

Nearly every person in the world knows enough of duty and of right to be far nobler than he is. It is not for want of clear convictions of duty, it is not for want of recognized models and pattern of life, that people go wrong. It is because these two things are lacking: motives for nobler service and power to do and be what we know we ought to be.

It is precisely here that the grace of God supplies all that we need. For there is nothing that will bend a person's will like the recognition of divine love. Then the will to be noble and good, and the power to carry it out, is from God who works in us through both the willing and the doing. That power comes from the grace of God.

John W. Williams

Grace is not sought nor bought nor wrought. It is a free gift of Almighty God to needy mankind. *Billy Graham*

Father, for Your grace that has come into my unworthy life, I praise and magnify Your glorious name.

—————————————•→ **SEPTEMBER 20** →•—————————————

For with God nothing shall be impossible. Luke 1:37

◆——◆

YOU CANNOT PLAN A BUDGET and expect God to direct your steps until you are willing to honor Him with the firstfruits of your income. In other words, obey God and plan your tithe the very first thing. "Bring the whole tithe into the storehouse, so that there may be food in my house, and test me now in this,' says the Lord of hosts, 'if I will not open for you the windows of heaven, and pour out for you a blessing until there is no more need'" (Malachi 3:10, *NAS*). Now *there* is a promise that you cannot afford to pass up. The Lord says to test Him by giving the whole tithe to Him—and He will bless you until there is no more need. It sounds impossible, but remember that our God deals in the impossible things of life and He challenges you to test Him. *Tim & Bev LaHaye*

A little boy announced very triumphantly that he was going to give his daddy a pair of bedroom slippers for his birthday. His eyes fairly danced with enthusiasm as he told about it.

"Who's going to give you the money to buy them?" someone asked.

"Why, Daddy, of course," was his quick reply.

He had never had anything in his life that his daddy had not given to him, and he could not give back to his father anything that his father had not first given him. Are we not like that in our relationship to God? *Henrietta C. Mears*

Father, all that I have You gave me in love. In gratitude I give You, from a heart that is blessed, the contents of my "storehouse."

———————— ••• **SEPTEMBER 21** ••• ————————

For he knoweth our frame.... Psalm 103:14

◆————————————————————————————◆

*T*HE GREATEST BURDEN WE HAVE TO CARRY IN LIFE is self. The most difficult thing we have to manage is self. Our own daily living, our frames and feelings, our especial weaknesses and temptations, and our peculiar temperaments, our inward affairs of every kind, these are the things that perplex and worry us more than anything else, and that bring us oftenest into bondage and darkness. In laying off your burdens, therefore, the first one you must get rid of is yourself. You must hand yourself and all your inward experiences, your temptations, your temperament, your frames and feelings, all over into the care and keeping of your God, and leave them there. He made you and therefore He understands you, and knows how to manage you, and you must trust Him to do it. *Hannah Whitall Smith*

(May we remember that our heavenly Father, who has created us and cares deeply for His children, desires to guide and protect us in all our ways.)

We know, Lord, we simply know that our life has meaning. And what we are meant to do with Your precious gift of life if we are to fulfill that meaning.

However humble our circumstances or undramatic our talents, our true purpose has been revealed. We were meant to be this person at this time and place. Not only for ourselves, but for You and other people—we were meant to make this particular contribution to the world.

And so we must do it well. Do it with faith and patience, with all our strength and passion. And in so doing discover who we really are.

Thank You, God, that to anyone who really seeks, You will reveal Your purpose. *Marjorie Holmes*

———————— ••• **SEPTEMBER 22** ••• ————————

O come, let us worship and bow down: let us kneel before the Lord our maker. Psalm 95:6

*A*LL OF HIS TIME IS OURS. How much of our time is His? Folks used to have considerable time for God and sermons in the colonial days. Sermons were often two-and-a-half or three hours long and "irksome only to the ungodly." After a minister had preached for three hours, a young man came up to him and said, "You tired me out—you preached too long." The preacher gave the young man a withering look and said, "Young man, you're a little jug and you are very easily filled." We are! We become jumpy when prayers are more than three minutes long. We want "sermonettes by preacherettes." We want everything boiled down. We are in a desperate hurry. We waste time *that belongs to God*, and because of this our souls go hungry, remain immature, and suffer from spiritual malnutrition.

Louis H. Evans, Sr.

> To worship is to quicken the conscience
>   by the holiness of God,
> to feed the mind with the truth of God,
> to purge the imagination by the beauty of God,
> to open the heart to the love of God,
> to devote the will to the purpose of God.

William Temple

Heavenly Father, teach me to be still long enough to feed this hungry soul of mine with Your infinite wisdom and love. I worship You and wait upon Your divine will.

SEPTEMBER 23

...redeeming the time, because the days are evil. Ephesians 5:16

*W*HEN PAUL URGED THE EPHESIAN CHRISTIANS to "redeem the time," he was indicating that in a sense time becomes ours by purchase. There is a price to be paid for its highest employment. We exchange time in the market of life for certain occupations and activities that may be either worthy or unworthy, productive or unproductive. Weymouth renders the sentence thus: "Buy up the opportunities," for time is opportunity, and herein lies the importance of a carefully planned life. "If we progress in the economy of time, we are learning to live. If we fail here, we fail everywhere."

Time can be lost, but it can never be retrieved. It cannot be hoarded; it must be spent. Nor can it be postponed. If it is not used productively, it is irretrievably lost, as these lines that were engraved on a sundial assert:

The shadow of my finger cast
Divides the future from the past;
  Before it stands the unborn hour
  In darkness and beyond thy power;
Behind its unreturning line
The vanished hour, no longer thine;
  One hour alone is in thy hands,
The *now* on which the shadow stands.

J. Oswald Sanders

There is nothing of which we are apt to be so lavish as of time, and about which we ought to be more solicitous, since without it we can do nothing in this world. Time is what we want most, but what, alas! we use worst.   *William Penn*

Father, each second of every day is precious time—a gift from You. May I never show ingratitude by wasting a moment.

SEPTEMBER 24

Nor do men light a lamp and put it under a bushel, but on a stand, and it gives light to all in the house. Matthew 5:15 (*RSV*)

*P*ERHAPS FAR MORE THAN WE REALIZE we Christians have been oblivious to our duty to shine as lights in an otherwise dark place. This is not an obscure theological problem but one of intense daily significance. People do not see Jesus in person; they see Him reflected in the lives of those who have been redeemed by Him. They should see in us love where others hate, a love for the unlovely as well as the lovely. They should see in our lives a joy that has its well-springs in the living Christ. They should see evidence of a peaceful heart, one in which there dwells the peace of God because there is peace *with* God.

Those around us should find in us patience under provocation, kindness and compassion for those in need, faithfulness and gentleness and self-control. The light of Christ, which shines through His own, is in sharp contrast to spiritual darkness.

Jesus laid down the rule of life for Christians in the command, "Let your light so shine before men, that they may see your good works and give glory to your Father who is in heaven" (Matthew 5:16).   *L. Nelson Bell*

Begin at once; before you venture away from this quiet moment, ask your King to take you wholly into His service, and place all the hours of this day quite simply at His disposal, and ask Him to make and keep you *ready* to do just exactly what He appoints. Never mind about tomorrow; one day at a time is enough.   Frances Ridley Havergal

Savior, may my light so shine in this dark world that others will see Your redeeming grace and be drawn to You.

━━━━━━━━━━◆ SEPTEMBER 25 ◆━━━━━━━━━

Then you will call upon me and come and pray to me, and I will hear you. Jeremiah 29:12 (*RSV*)

◆━━━━━━━━━━━━━━━━━━━━━━━━━━━━━━━━◆

WHY IS PRAYER SO STARTLINGLY EFFECTIVE when we admit our helplessness? First, as we have seen, because God insists upon our facing up to the true facts of our human situation. Thus we lay under our prayer-structure the firm foundation of truth rather than self-delusion or wishful thinking.

This recognition and acknowledgment of our helplessness is also the quickest way to that right attitude which God recognizes as essential to prayer. It deals a mortal blow to the most serious sin of all—man's independence that ignores God.

Another reason is that we cannot learn firsthand about God—what He is like, His love for us as individuals, and His real power—so long as we are relying on ourselves and other people. And fellowship with Jesus is the true purpose of life and the only foundation for eternity. It is real, this daily fellowship He offers us.

So if your every human plan and calculation has miscarried, if, one by one, human props have been knocked out, and doors have shut in your face, take heart. God is trying to get a message through to you, and the message is: "Stop depending on inadequate human resources. Let Me handle the matter."   *Catherine Marshall*

All who call on God in true faith, earnestly from the heart, will certainly be heard, and will receive what they have asked and desired, although not in the hour or in the measure, or the very thing which they ask; yet they will obtain something greater and more glorious than they had dared to ask.   *Martin Luther*

Father, I know that I am often completely helpless in the circumstances that invade my life. May I stop relying on anyone, or anything, other than You.

We ought to obey God.... Acts 5:29

THERE ARE TIMES, I HAVE FOUND, when praying is not enough. God says, as it were, "What are you praying for? Do something!"

Moses, hotly pursued by Pharaoh, cried out to God, who replied, "Wherefore criest thou unto me? Speak unto the children of Israel, that they go forward" (Exodus 14:15).

After Israel's ignominious defeat at Ai, the desperate Joshua prostrated himself in prayer before the Lord only to hear Him say, "Wherefore liest thou thus upon thy face? Israel hath sinned" (Joshua 7:10-11).

If our hearts are listening as we pray, we will from time to time hear, "What are you praying for? Do something!" And we will know what it is that we must do. A wrong to put right, a sin to confess, a letter to write, a friend to visit, or perhaps a child to be rocked and read to.

C. S. Lewis suggested that as we pray, Christ stands beside us changing us. "This may send a man," he wrote, "from his prayers to help his wife in the kitchen or to his desk to write a needed letter." And again, "I am often, I believe, praying for others when I should be doing things for them. It is so much easier to pray for a poor man than to go and see him."

And so it is with us. We must be quick to pray, and just as quick to obey. *Ruth Bell Graham*

Grant us grace, Almighty Father, so to pray as to deserve to be heard. *Jane Austen*

Father, teach me obedience to Your will and sensitivity to know when to act upon it.

...lest any root of bitterness springing up trouble you, and thereby many be defiled.... Hebrews 12:15

SOMETIMES WHEN WE FACE HARD SITUATIONS, we find our faith in God faltering. We feel lost and abandoned, wondering why God does not answer our prayers.

It is in these times we become, as someone once said, "bitter or better." A trite remark? Perhaps it is, on the surface, but *very* true.

How we handle our heartaches and trials is watched by those around us. As we keep our faith in these dark moments and release any bitter thoughts to Him, a change takes place in our hearts, and we learn more of His unfaltering grace. Others are drawn closer to Him.

George Mueller, a man whom God used in Victorian England to establish many orphanages through simply trusting in the Lord to supply his financial needs, once said, "The only way to learn strong faith is to endure great trials. I have learned my faith by standing firm amid severe testings."
J.W.B.

The life of faith is not a life of mounting up with wings, but a life of walking and not fainting.... Faith never knows where it is being led, but it loves and knows the One who is leading. *Oswald Chambers*

Heavenly Father, take away any bitterness in my life and grant me faith to look to You in complete trust as I encounter trials in my life.

SEPTEMBER 28

...being made perfect, he became the author
of eternal salvation unto all them that obey him.... Hebrews 5:9

WE KNOW THAT JESUS CHRIST IS RELEVANT to this burdened, bleeding, broken world. The point is that Christ wants to use us to show the world that He is relevant, that He does matter to them, and that they do matter to Him. He has given to us this ministry of reconciliation. In the year 1909, the Hon. Earl Balfour was lecturing at the University of Edinburgh on "The Moral Values Which Unite Nations." He had mentioned diplomatic contacts, commerce, common knowledge, common friendships. At the end there was applause and a question period. Then a Japanese student rose and asked, "But, Mr. Balfour, what about Jesus Christ?" There was dead silence. Everybody felt the irony of the question as a foreign student from a far-off non-Christian land inquired of one of the great diplomatic leaders of the greatest Christian nation of that day, "What about Jesus Christ?"

This is how we make evangelism relevant. We ask of a world wistfully searching for security, forgiveness, purpose, peace, and love, "What about Jesus Christ?" *Leighton Ford*

Lord Jesus Christ, Your glorious message of redemption shines in this dark world. Use me, Savior, to bring hope to someone in despair.

Take my yoke upon you, and learn of me;
for I am meek and lowly in heart: and ye
shall find rest unto your souls. Matthew 11:29

◆————————————————————————————————◆

G ENTLENESS IS THE WORK OF THE SPIRIT. Courtesy of manner, sweetness of disposition, the willingness to give way, come hard to the flesh. Naturally we are hard, rough, rude, bitter, coarse. But such is the work of the gentle Spirit that He is able to transform our whole deportment and give us a charm and sweetness of manner commending Christ and His Gospel.

> Every virtue we possess
> And every victory won,
> And every thought of holiness—
> Are His alone.

This word found its way into what we understand by noble manhood and womanhood; thus the terms *gentlemen* or *gentlewomen*. Are we among God's nobility? Whether we have social superiority or no, do we possess that chivalry and well-bred manners the Holy Spirit can make possible for all God's children?   *Herbert Lockyer*

Jesus Christ alone stands at the absolute center of humanity, the one completed harmonious Man. He is the absolute and perfect truth, the highest that humanity can reach; at once its perfect image and supreme Lord.   *Charles W. French*

Lord Jesus, Your noble life is an example that I need to emulate as each day I live in You. By Your Holy Spirit, fill me with gentleness and humility, I pray.

...the God of love and peace shall be with you. II Corinthians 13:11

◆————————————————————————————————◆

O NE DAY IN THE MOUNTAIN REGION of Scotland, a gigantic eagle snatched a little baby out of his crib and flew away with him. The people of the village ran out after the big bird, but the eagle perched itself upon a nearby mountain crag. Could the child possibly be rescued? A sailor tried to climb the ascent, but he was at last obliged to give up the attempt. A robust Highlander, accustomed to climbing those mountains, tried next and even his strength failed. At last a poor peasant woman came forward. She put her feet upon one shelf of the rock, then on the second, then on the third and in this manner she rose to the very top of the cliff. While all below held their breath for sheer fright, she came down step by step until she stood at the bottom of the rock with the child safely in her arms. Immediately shouts of praise rose from the crowd that had gathered.

Why did that woman succeed when the strong sailor and the experienced mountain climber had failed? Because that woman was the mother of the baby. Her love for her baby had given her the courage to do what the others had failed to do.

If the love of Christ is in your heart, you, too, will find that you will have the courage to do whatever He directs you to do.

Henrietta C. Mears

God Incarnate is the end of fear; and the heart that realizes that He is in the midst, that takes heed to the assurance of His loving presence, will be quiet in the midst of alarm.   *F. B. Meyer*

Beloved Lord, when fears attack me I know that Your love can conquer them and bring peace and quiet courage.

►— OCTOBER 1 —◄

...with everlasting kindness will I have mercy on thee, saith the Lord thy Redeemer. Isaiah 54:8

◆————————————————————————◆

*W*HEN WE ARE DEFEATED, let us remember that it is part of the business of living at its highest. If you never take a chance you will never be defeated—but you will never accomplish anything either. Also, if you never know defeat it means that you were never willing to take a chance, and that should make us more devastated than the fact that we were defeated. Jesus said, "He that findeth his life shall lose it." If you are defeated in life, most of the time it means that you took a chance. If you are afraid to take a chance and only concerned with saving your life and never tasting defeat, it is a certainty that eventually your defeat will be total and permanent. It is just as much a sin to be too careful as it is to take too many chances.

Charles L. Allen

Failure is not a sin. Faithlessness is.   *Henrietta C. Mears*

Lord Jesus, teach me in failure to look to You for the grace to overcome the disappointment. Help me to see the blessing, and may I always be faithful to You.

Casting down imaginations, and every high thing that exalteth itself against the knowledge of God, and bringing into captivity every thought to the obedience of Christ.... II Corinthians 10:5

*D*O YOU WANT TO BE FREE? Do you want to be in control of your emotions and not have them control you and be so afraid of them that they don't have to be avoided? Do you, as a Christian, want your emotions to enhance your spiritual life rather than work against it? You can only do this if you rise up and begin influencing your thoughts. The stream of your thoughts will be the most important factor which influences how you feel. If you can keep your hand firmly on the wheel of your thoughts, you will not be subjected to extremes of emotional buffeting. If you watch, control, and alter your thoughts by patient practice and trace their effects upon you and others, you can move yourself to the place of emotional freedom. ...Solomon was right when he said, "For as a man thinketh in his heart, so is he..." (Proverbs 23:7). *Archibald D. Hart*

When the mind thinks nothing, when the soul covets nothing, and the body acteth nothing that is contrary to the will of God, this is perfect sanctification. *Written in an old Bible, 1599*

(How many times, especially in the night, our thoughts become like "wild horses"! Let us ask God to bring them under His complete control.)

Almighty God, tame these runaway thoughts of mine that keep me from a closer, trusting walk with You, I pray.

...casting all your care upon him; for he careth for you. I Peter 5:7

*I*WAS SADDENED TO READ A STATEMENT in a women's magazine by a well-known actress. She said she despised people who crack under strain. Shakespeare put it very succinctly when he said, "He jests at scars that never felt a wound." Those who have never been wounded by the agonies of the mind can never fully understand the tortures that many go through. But I know this—God understands, for in His life here on earth, Jesus never mocked or belittled those who were weak either in mind or body. He left His scorn for those who felt themselves better than others.

We are all made differently. We are all born with a distinct personality. No two fingerprints are alike, and that is what comforts me. It makes me realize that a God who has taken the time to attend to these minute details cares deeply for the individuals He has created. He cares about all the happenings in our lives, however small or insignificant.

J.W.B.

Lord Jesus, bearer of men's burdens, Comforter of the sorrowful, we would bring to thee all whose hearts are sad. Help us to mediate Thy strengthening sympathy to others, but grant that we may be so continually refreshed by our companionship with Thee that we may not be crushed by the world's burdens. Thou art the burden bearer—not we. Thou art the Redeemer—not we. Thou alone, O Christ, canst in Thy strong heart carry the woes of the world. In this faith, teach us to do our duty day by day as we see it to be Thy will, and save us from the depression of those who try to carry more than man was made to bear, and ever to look to Thee, O Lamb of God who bearest the sins of the world.

Leslie D. Weatherhead

OCTOBER 4

The Lord preserveth all them that love him.... Psalm 145:20

*W*ORRY SEEMS TO BE AN INTEGRAL PART OF LIVING, and if we live we worry. One cannot pick up the newspaper from day to day without realizing that we have a great deal about which we ought to be worrying. We all have been told we shouldn't worry, but there is every reason why we should worry—if God is dead, and if the Bible is not to be trusted, and if we do not have a heavenly Father who watches over us personally and has assumed responsibility for us. If those things are not true, we had better worry. But because we do have a heavenly Father who has a pre-determined plan and purpose for each one of His children, who has assumed responsibility for our food, provision, protection, and care, and who can distinguish each bird in the heavens and each blade of grass in the fields, then we ought to ask ourselves the question: Why worry?

J. Dwight Pentecost

Be Thou, O Rock of Ages, nigh!
So shall each murmuring thought be gone;
And grief and fear and care shall fly,
As cloud before the midday sun.

Charles Wesley

Lord God, may I completely trust You in every phase of my life. Forgive the needless worrying and help me conquer all fears, in Jesus' name.

OCTOBER 5

...godliness with contentment is great gain. I Timothy 6:6

◆——————————————————————————————◆

*T*HERE IS NO PEACE like the peace of those whose minds are possessed with full assurance that they have known God, and God has known them, and that this relationship guarantees God's favor to them in life, through death, and on forever. This is the peace of which Paul speaks in Romans 5:1—"being justified by faith, we have peace with God through our Lord Jesus Christ"—and whose substance he analyses in full in Romans 8. "There is therefore now no condemnation to them which are in Christ Jesus...the Spirit itself beareth witness with our spirit, that we are the children of God, and if children, then heirs...we know that all things work together for good to them that love God...whom he justified, them he also glorified...if God be for us, who can be against us?...Who shall lay anything to the charge of God's elect?...   *J. I. Packer*

> Calm soul of all things, make it mine
> To feel amid the city's jar
> That there exists a peace of thine
> Man did not make and cannot mar.
> *Matthew Arnold*

Almighty God, for the peace that possesses my mind when I think of all Your mercy and goodness, I praise You. May I remember and claim this peace whenever I encounter stress.

OCTOBER 6

**Cast thy burden upon the Lord,
and he shall sustain thee....** Psalm 55:22

◆——————————————————————————————◆

*W*E HAVE THE DESIRE TO BE TOGETHER, and yet we keep falling apart. We know the pains, the pangs, the burdens which shatter human life—parents see their children running away, children see their parents running away.

The loving God has a word for us, and He does everything possible that that word may reach its target. Listen! And look to the One who can put your life's jigsaw puzzle together so that it makes sense to you.

Jesus is saying, "When I am lifted high, I shall draw everyone to me" (John 12:32). Eternal, bleeding Love was lifted high on a cross nearly 2,000 years ago. As you see Him there and are drawn to Him, you know you are completely forgiven. Love draws. Each scattered fragment of your life is finding its place.

Do you feel the drawing of the Holy Spirit in your heart? Are you moving toward this center? Do you see His direction for living in the midst of your "hopeless" circumstances? Have you begun to see the people around you—all of them—as precious? Having been forgiven, do you find you are now forgiving them?

This is the beginning of true community and the end to loneliness.

Festo Kivengere

Before man can live rightly with others, he must first get right with God.

Charles L. Allen

Almighty God, forgive me for not always forgiving others as I should. Teach me Your love so that I may live victoriously and happily with my fellowman.

———————— **OCTOBER 7** ————————

I have loved thee with an everlasting love:
therefore with loving-kindness have I drawn thee. Jeremiah 31:3

◆————————————————————————————————◆

KNOWING THE LOVE THAT GOD HAS FOR US should help us to have a proper and real love for ourselves, a "genuine and joyful" acceptance of ourselves. You should be able to say, "I'm glad to be me." This isn't pride or selfishness, it's just agreeing with God that this part of His creation, too, is very good. "And God saw everything that he had made, and, behold, it was very good..." (Genesis 1:31).

To have a proper love for self is the ability to feel good about yourself. You can recognize and accept your weaknesses and inabilities and deal with your sin. It is to feel comfortable about yourself, to be at peace with yourself, to feel *okay*, acceptable. It is not envying another person's gifts, abilities, temperament. It is to be content to be you, the person you are now for now, but always having the aspiration to become more and more the person God created you to be—more and more like Jesus Christ. It is to have a godly desire to be continually growing as a person, but in the process knowing that you are now a person of worth, of value, acceptable, lovable.

Verna Birkey

Be quiet, soul:
Why shouldst thou care and sadness borrow,
Why sit in nameless fear and sorrow,
    The livelong day?
God will mark out thy path tomorrow
    In His best way.

Author unknown

Lord God, Your loving-kindness gives me the courage to see myself as I really am and to value my life. Much needs changing, but I will not give up hope. I will seek Your help to grow into the kind of person who will glorify You.

OCTOBER 8

...my heart shall not fear.... Psalm 27:3

---

*F*ROM EARLIEST CHILDHOOD NO FEAR IS SO PERVADING as that of being left alone. This fear continues into adulthood in many areas of our life.

This fear struck at the heart of the early disciples as Jesus began to talk about going away. The possibility or even the wisdom of His leaving them was more than they could grasp. They needed Him. Every day new insights and understandings were breaking in upon them. They were discovering that they were really just on the edge of it. There was so much more to learn.

It was at this point in His relationship with them that Jesus began to talk about the Holy Spirit. He was trying to reassure them that His physical absence would be more than compensated for by a gift He was going to send. The reassurance which He tried to communicate to them again and again was that they were not going to be left alone. This is why even after the resurrection when He was sending the believers out to disciple the whole world, He closed the commissioning service with the promise, "And, lo, I am with you alway, even unto the end of the world" (Matthew 28:20).   *Kenneth L. Chafin*

Years ago, when my whole life seemed to be overwhelmed by forces beyond my control, one morning quite casually I opened my New Testament and my eyes fell upon this sentence: "He that sent me is with me: the Father hath not left me alone." My life has never been the same since that hour.   *Joseph R. Sizoo*

Lord, wherever I go You are with me, helping to conquer all my fears. Thank You for Your presence.

Fear not: for I am with thee.... Isaiah 43:5

◆――――――――――――――――――――――――――――――――――◆

*T*HE FIRST HELP IN LEARNING HOW TO HANDLE FEAR is to stop fighting it. My own experience during the Second World War was a tremendous school in learning how to live with fear. Sometimes I had to live for days and weeks in the fear of being killed any minute, almost any second. Every time the roar of the Russian artillery was heard, I knew that within the next few seconds it would be decided whether I would live or die. It was an uninterrupted exercise of living with fear.

I remember that the first help for me was that I stopped fighting fear and learned to admit to myself, "Walter, you are afraid." In that moment the tight grip of fear loosened, and fear became bearable. Yes, it even became a positive force challenging my faith.

Faith did not free me from fear, but fear forced me to believe. Every time I heard the roar of the enemy fire, I threw myself down into the ditch or foxhole where I was. In an act of surrender to the One who has overcome the world, I said, "You have me completely." I can only express it in a paradoxical way: I learned not to be afraid of fear.   *Walter Trobish*

> Peace does not mean the end of all our
>   striving.
> Joy does not mean the drying of our
>   tears;
> Peace is the power that comes to souls
>   arriving
> Up to the light where God Himself
>   appears.
>   G. A. Studdert-Kennedy

Almighty God, surrendered to You I will not be afraid, knowing I am not alone. Your strength surrounds me.

I will never leave thee, nor forsake thee. Hebrews 13:5

◆――――――――――――――――――――――――――――――――――◆

"*I* WILL NEVER LEAVE YOU..."
   Never?
Can we really believe that?
Jesus said it, but it isn't very easy to cling to a blanket promise like

that, not when life gets rough. And sometimes life can get very rough!

There is rarely any visible or tangible sign in our daily living that the Lord is right there with us. Yet, when we move along through life, trusting His promise, and then look back, we find that He kept His Word. He did have every situation in hand.

That's enough to go on one more time, and equips us to say, "God, You handled things before, I'll trust You to handle things again." And, once more, He does.

Roger C. Palms

(Amid all the confusion, the heartaches, the lonely times of our lives, we need to really meditate on the great promise of our Lord that *wherever* we are, *whatever* we face, *He* is with us.)

> *God of our life, through all the circling*
> *years, we trust in Thee;*
> *In all the past, through all our hopes*
> *and fears, Thy hand we see.*
> *With each new day, when morning lifts*
> *the veil,*
> *We own Thy mercies, Lord, which never*
> *fail.*

Hugh T. Kerr

◆ OCTOBER 11 ◆

Greater love hath no man.... John 15:13

◆ ——————————————————————————————————— ◆

*T*HE SMALL BOOTBLACK POLISHED AWAY with enthusiasm. He liked his work—turning a pair of scruffy leather shoes into a shining work of art. He liked the men who called him by name, sat in his chair, and buried their noses in the morning newspaper. He especially liked the little foreign man with the funny accent.

His friendly "Today, how you are?" let him know this man really cared how he was. What the bootblack did not know was that the man with the funny accent was from Soviet Georgia and held three earned doctoral degrees. He just kept polishing away happily.

The day came when the unhappy Ph.D. could stand it no longer. Looking down at the bootblack working so cheerfully and enthusiastically on his shoes, and thinking on his own inner misery, he put down his paper.

"Why always you so happy?" he asked.

Surprised, the bootblack paused in his polishing, sat back on his heels, scratched his head thoughtfully for a moment, then said simply, "Jesus. He loves me. He died so God could forgive my badness. He makes me happy."

The newspaper snapped up around the face of the professor and the bootblack went back to polishing his shoes.

But the brilliant professor could not escape those simple words. They were what brought him eventually to the Savior.

Years later, my husband's college major was anthropology. His beloved and admired professor was the renowned Dr. Alexander Grigolia, who found God through the simple testimony of a bootblack those many years before. *Ruth Bell Graham*

It is said that Tennyson once asked an old Christian woman if there was any news.

"Why, Mr. Tennyson," she replied, "there's only one piece of news that I know, and that is—Christ died for all men."

"That is old news, and good news, and new news," Tennyson responded. *D. L. Moody*

Lord Jesus, for the love for me that took You to the cross, I praise and thank You. May I spread this glorious news each day.

OCTOBER 12

...alive unto God through Jesus Christ our Lord. Romans 6:11

I AM CONVINCED THAT MAN WAS MEANT to live at peace within himself, filled with a deep joy. I am convinced that there should be going on in the heart of every man not a funeral but a celebration of life and love. Prophets of gloom, with their "valley of tears" mentality and vocabulary, have always sounded unreal to me. With good old Irenaeus of the second century I have always believed that "The glory of God is a man fully alive!" Of course, there is no problemless Camelot or painless Utopia. The tension resulting from problems and pain is part of the whole piece, and usually directs our attention to a growing-edge of life, a territory for expansion. For myself, I do not regret the problems or pain in my past life, but only the apathy, the moments when I was not "fully alive." *John Powell, S.J.*

To miss the joy is to miss all. *Robert Louis Stevenson*

Lord Jesus, take away any apathy and make me conscious that to live is joy, for You are with me.

...the God in whose hand thy breath is.... Daniel 5:23

◆━━━◆

"*I*S LIFE WORTH LIVING?" To scores of people, life has ceased to be worth living. To all of you, I have good news. God did not create you to be a defeated, discouraged, frustrated, wandering soul, seeking in vain for peace of heart and peace of mind. He has bigger plans for you. He has a larger orb and a greater life for you. The answer to your problem, however great, is as near as your Bible, as simple as first-grade arithmetic, and as real as your heartbeat. Upon the authority of God's Word, I tell you that Christ is the answer to every baffling perplexity which plagues mankind. In Him is found the cure for care, a balm for bereavement, a healing for our hurts, and a sufficiency for our insufficiency. *Billy Graham*

(God's Word brings each one of us His personal message of love.)

In the beginning was the Word;
　　Athwart the Chaos, night;
It gleamed with quick creative power
　　And there was life and light.

Thy Word, O God, is living yet
　　Amid earth's restless strife,
New harmony creating still
　　And ever higher life.

O Word that broke the stillness first,
　　Sound on, and never cease
Till all earth's darkness be made light,
　　And all her discord peace.

Till selfish passion, strife and wrong,
　　Thy summons shall have heard,
And Thy creation be complete,
　　O Thou Eternal Word.

Henry Wadsworth Longfellow

—••► **OCTOBER 14** ◄••—

...we may boldly say, The Lord is my helper,
and I will not fear what man shall do unto me. Hebrews 13:6

*B*ECAUSE THE HOLY SPIRIT IS TODAY PRESENT in His office on earth, all spiritual presence and divine communication of the Trinity with men are via the Spirit. In other words, while God, the Father, and God, the Son, are present and reigning in heaven, they are invisibly here in the body of the believer by the indwelling God, the Holy Spirit—the Helper.

Yet so long as we are ignorant of the Helper and His work, He cannot be fully operative in our lives. No wonder there is such vagueness and confusion in our minds when we speak or think of the Holy Spirit!

We have no greater need today than to be informed about the Helper. We need to know who He is, why we need Him, what He longs to do for us and our families, for our churches, and how we go about receiving Him. Otherwise we remain orphaned Christians— bereft of His love and of the magnificent fellowship, guidance and help He can give us.   *Catherine Marshall*

The Holy Spirit who is the love whereby the Father loves the Son, is also the love whereby God loves creatures and imparts to them His goodness.   *Thomas Aquinas*

Father, thank You for Your Holy Spirit which helps me in all my ways, giving me strength, wisdom and inner joy.

OCTOBER 15

Thine, O Lord, is the greatness, and the power, and the glory, and the victory.... I Chronicles 29:11

---

*T*HE CHRISTIAN HAS A UNIQUE ADVANTAGE in the contemporary scene. He is secure in the strong certainty that Jesus Christ is Lord, encouraged by close companionship with Him to whom "all power is given in heaven and on earth." The Christian knows that God has spoken in His Son, that God has acted redemptively for men in the life, death and resurrection of Jesus Christ, that God is now working out His redeeming purpose in history, and that one day He will consummate His plan in the return of the Savior when "every knee shall bow...and every tongue confess that Jesus Christ is Lord."

Thus as Christians we act from a position of unshakable security, knowing that even death itself is defeated for us. We do not fight *for* victory but *from* victory. Delivered from concern about ourselves, we are free to give ourselves to the needs of others, and without fear or favor to do the will of God. We live no longer for ourselves, but unto Him who died for us and rose again that we may be cut free from the weight of pride, possessions and personal ambition, to lay out our lives for God and man.   *Robert Boyd Munger*

There is a loftier ambition than merely to stand high in the world. It is to stoop down and lift mankind a little higher.   *Henry van Dyke*

Father, secure in Your love may my eyes turn to the needs of others. Thank You for the freedom from earthly ambitions—my life and desires are Yours.

OCTOBER 16

Nevertheless I have somewhat against thee, because thou hast left thy first love. Revelation 2:4

---

*H*OW LONG HAS IT BEEN since you took time out of your busy schedule to get alone with your Lord, to get down on your knees and look into the face of your loving Lord and say, "Lord, I love Thee"?

I am not asking how long it has been since you asked Him for something. Rather, just when was it that you actually told the Lord how much you love Him, and then, alone in prayer and with the Word of God, you felt His presence and His power?

How long has it been since you remained in His presence and felt the burning heart that can come only from Him?

When I travel, every now and then I receive letters from my wife and children. When those letters arrive I don't throw them aside and say, "I'll look at them later." No, immediately I get alone and open them up and read them. They mean everything to me because they are letters from my loved ones.

You and I have God's Word, which is His love letter to all His children. He wants us to get alone with Him and read this letter of love, and learn about His care and His will for us.   *Howard O. Jones*

It is in the Word that we receive and embrace Him, and so where the Word of Christ dwells richly, there Christ dwells. If the Word be in us at home, then we abide in Christ, and He in us. The ground of our hope is Christ in the world, but the evidence of our hope is Christ in the heart.   *Matthew Henry*

Father, forgive the times I neglect to read Your Word, which brings such comfort and joy. Restore to me the desire to learn more of Your message of love and wisdom. Thank You for this gift.

OCTOBER 17

Beloved, think it not strange concerning the fiery trial which is to try you, as though some strange thing happened unto you.... I Peter 4:12

---

*W*HOEVER GOT THE IDEA that the Christian is an alien to hardship and suffering? These things are God's tools to shape us according to His plan. It is for us as it was for Jesus: first death, then resurrection; first the cross, then the crown; first the suffering and then the glory!

"God had one Son without sin," said the wise Augustine. "He has no sons without suffering."

This hope of God's plan gives me the courage to confront life with a complete faith that nothing occurs outside of God's purpose. The trivial things, the tragic things—everything that happens—provide an opportunity to prepare to meet God!

Listen to this triumphant assertion from Peter: "Now for a season, if need be, you are in heaviness through manifold temptations: that the trial of your faith, being much more precious than of gold that perishes, though it be tried with fire, might be found unto praise and honor and glory at the appearing of Jesus Christ...."   *Leighton Ford*

> When peace, like a river, attendeth my way,
> When sorrows like sea billows roll—
> Whatever my lot, Thou hast taught me to say,
> It is well, it is well with my soul.
>
> *H. G. Spafford*

Lord Jesus, suffering comes roaring into our lives and we are left bewildered, but Your comfort helps us to triumph and trust in Your loving care as we experience the fiery trials of life.

OCTOBER 18

And we know that all things work together for good to them that love God, to them who are the called according to his purpose. Romans 8:28

*D*ON'T EVER LET ANYBODY TEACH YOU that Christianity says that tragedy is good. It is not good! When my mother died, that was a tragedy in my own life. When my father died, that was a tragedy in my own life. I am not excited about the fact that my parents died. That bothers me. I do not like that which was not good, but together with something else it brought about good *for me*. We know that *all* things—every piece of garbage that comes into your life, every little irritation throughout the day you face, every circumstance that gets you down—God will cause to work *together* with something else for the purpose of good.

God will use that trial (no matter the cause) to make you a better person—a more valuable person. The trial that you experience—divorce, bankruptcy, abortion, rape, death of a loved one, disease—could move you toward intense loneliness with all its pain. But there is an alternative. You can find the handle on that same potentially destructive trial and respond properly to it. This builds a quality into your own life and enables you to empathize and counsel with others who experience the same kinds of trials.

We know that God causes all things to work together for good to those who love God, to those who are called according to His purpose, to those who are plugged into an active relationship with God.

Tim Timmons

No sorrow touches man until it has been filtered through the heart of God.

Joseph D. Blinco

Almighty God, help me to respond positively to all the tragedies I may encounter. Let me not shut out the blessing of Your mercy and love at such times, but may I be able to tell another You care.

--------- **OCTOBER 19** ---------

Thou wilt keep him in perfect peace, whose mind is stayed on thee: because he trusteth in thee. Isaiah 26:3

*O*NE OF THE BRIGHTEST YOUNG MEN ever to graduate from my collegiate alma mater was deeply devoted to the Lord. He felt called to become a medical missionary, and he directed every energy toward that objective. After graduating cum laude from college, he enrolled in medical school and finished his first year at the very top of his class, academically. Then during the spring of that year he began to experience a curious and persistent fatigue. He was examined by a physician who made the diagnosis of leukemia. The promising student was dead a few months later.

How can a tragedy like that be explained? The Lord seemed to call him to the mission field where his healing talents were desperately needed. He was accepted into medical school despite fierce competition. Every step seemed to be ordered by God. Then, suddenly, he was taken. What did the Lord have in mind from the beginning? Why did He seem to give him a definite call and then frustrate its culmination? I have no idea. I simply offer this illustration as one of thousands where God's actions are difficult for us to explain in simplistic terms. And in these moments we have to say with Job, "Though he slay me, yet will I trust in him." *James Dobson*

(We cannot understand the heartbreaks that tear into our souls, but one day when we see our Lord we will know the answer and see He made no mistakes. Until then, we trust Him.)

> *Precious Lord, take my hand,*
> *Lead me on, help me stand;*
> *I am tired, I am weak, I am worn;*
> *Thru the storm, thru the night,*
> *Lead me on to the light,*
> *Take my hand, precious Lord, lead me home.*
> *Thomas A. Dorsey*

OCTOBER 20

Blessed are they that mourn: for they shall be comforted. Matthew 5:4

A FATHER WHO SUFFERS THE BEREAVEMENT of a beloved child may go through his personal catastrophe dry-eyed. He may consider any betrayal of emotion to be a sign of weakness or even of lack of faith. He may sternly "carry on" his daily life without interruption. In such an experience even though we may not mourn outwardly, our bodies do. In odd, strange ways, not always healthy, the heart serves notice that it is dressed in black; for man is mortal, and he cannot help mourning his mortality. How much better that grief should express itself in normal fashion; how much more comfort in true mourning!

The Scriptures suggest a link between human nature (the problem of sin) and human destiny (the certainty of death). "By one man sin entered into the world, and death by sin; and so death passed upon all men, for that all have sinned" (Romans 5:12). Without going into all the implications of the passage, we can see that Paul is suggesting that the shortness of life is bound up with the evil in the world. When Mary Magdalene stood weeping at the tomb of Jesus, her heart was broken not only because of the Life that had been extinguished, but because of the deed that caused it. To mourn for sin and to mourn for death are but two sides of the same cloth. The poets have always known it. It is important for us to learn it too.   *Sherwood Eliot Wirt*

> Anger and just rebuke, and judgment given,
> That brought into this world a world of woe,
> Sin and her shadow Death, and Misery,
> Death's harbinger.
>
> *John Milton*

Lord Jesus, for the sin of our world that sent You to the cross, we grieve. For loved ones who are no longer with us, we mourn. But for the victory of Your resurrection we rejoice and are comforted!

OCTOBER 21

...I have replenished every sorrowful soul. Jeremiah 31:25

---

*D*URING THE U.S. CIVIL WAR, a man who had lost his wife and had several children to care for was drafted. He did not want to go, so a young man in the community volunteered to go in his place. He was killed in the war. But as a result, the man with a family did not have to go to war. There was no way the government could force him to go to battle, because he had already gone in the person of the young man. Someone had taken his place. In the same way, Jesus Christ was hanged on the cross in our place. He bore our sins and transgressions, accepting the punishment due us for our sin.

Yet Jesus also bore something else, our negative emotions. Isaiah 53:4 clearly states, "Surely our griefs he himself bore, and our sorrows he carried." Christ not only died that you could be forgiven and free from sin, but He also bore your sorrow, your rejection, and your hurt. Consequently, all of those ugly emotions that rise up within you to make you miserable may be carried away. As a result you can say, "Thank God, I am free."   *Erwin Lutzer*

There is no circumstance, no trouble, no testing, that can ever touch me until, first of all, it has gone past God and past Christ, right through to me. If it has come that far, it has come with a great purpose, which I may not understand at the moment. But I refuse to become panicky, as I lift up my eyes to Him and accept it as coming from the throne of God for some great purpose of blessing to my own heart. *Alan Redpath*

Lord Jesus, I put my complete trust in You, my Savior, and look for the blessing in every sorrow I experience.

―――――――――――――― ● OCTOBER 22 ●――――――――――――

**This is my comfort in my affliction:
for thy word hath quickened me.** Psalm 119:50

◆―――――――――――――――――――――――――――――――――◆

THE MOTTO OF THE NEWSPAPERMAN, Joseph Pulitzer, owed much to Jesus: "Comfort the afflicted and afflict the comfortable." Jesus does just that! He comforts those who mourn over their own, others', and the world's suffering. The Greek word for comfort means "to call to the side of." Christ stands by our side when we become sensitive to the needs of our world and our part in it. When we become comfortable in any other security than Him, He unsettles us with His disturbing exposure of what life was meant to be.

Only Christ knows when we need to be comforted and when we need to be afflicted. He knows when to assure and when to alarm. Our own judgment of our needs is often wrong. When we think we need comforting, He often comes with a disturbing challenge which gets us on our feet. Then, too, when we do not know our need for fortification, He builds us up in love to face some imminent difficulty we must go through. *Lloyd John Ogilvie*

Afflictions are but the shadow of God's wings. *George MacDonald*

Almighty and everlasting God, under the shadow of Your wings I am strengthened with love as I face the afflictions of each day.

―――――――――――――― ● OCTOBER 23 ●――――――――――――

**...seek ye first the kingdom of God, and his righteousness;
and all these things shall be added unto you.** Matthew 6:33

◆―――――――――――――――――――――――――――――――――◆

WILLIAM HUNT, A GREAT ARTIST, was coaching a class in landscape painting. It was in the late afternoon and he had suggested that they paint the sunset. As the sun was sinking below the horizon, he looked over the shoulder of one of his most promising art pupils and noticed, to his dismay, that the young man, instead of painting the glorious sunset, had spent all his time painting an old red barn with decaying shingles. In alarm, the great artist and teacher exclaimed, "Son, son, it won't be light long! You haven't time for both shingles and sunsets. You must choose!" Let us not spend our days, our hours, our energies, our purses on painting old barns and shingles—the mundane earthly things of life—for it will not long be light. Rather, splash the sun, the spiritual things on the canvas of your life while it still is light. Then hope will rise above the destroyed cities and the scarred lands of this world with healing in its wings!

Quietly now, is this the purpose of your life, honestly to seek "first the kingdom of God, and his righteousness"? Then yours is the royal life. You are not merely existing, you are living!   *Louis H. Evans, Sr.*

(How we need to sift through the unimportant activities of our lives and dedicate ourselves to the priorities of our Lord's Kingdom.)

> *Lord, I have given my life to Thee,*
> *And every day and hour is Thine,*
> *What Thou appointest let them be;*
> *Thy will is better, Lord, than mine.*
>
> *A. Warner*

OCTOBER 24

God, who at sundry times and in divers manners spake in time past unto the fathers by the prophets, hath in these last days spoken unto us by his Son....
Hebrews 1:1-2

GET WITH CHRIST. He is the One who can make things happen. When Jesus Christ came, things happened—things that never happened before. That is what the writer of the Epistle to the Hebrews told his people (Hebrews 1:1-3). It is what we have to tell our people today. It is what we have to tell ourselves.

God has spoken in His Son. World, listen! Church, listen! People, listen! This is what we are saying during these days to ourselves and to everyone associated with us in the Christian enterprise! Listen to the Word of the living God! Listen to Christ!

The time has come to listen. The world is in a mess. High-sounding talk is not the answer to our problems. Fancy programs will not change things. Mere organizing and reorganizing lead down a dead-end street. Nothing will do except to "get with" Christ, the living Son of the living God, crucified for the sins of our world and raised again from the dead to be the Son of God with power.

"With great power gave the apostles witness to the resurrection."

His men have always told people about Jesus Christ. In telling they changed the world. His men always followed Christ and in following Him they led the world into a new age. "Awake from your sleep-walking," said the Apostle Paul, and all the other apostles echoed him. "Arise from the dead! Christ will give you light!"

Oswald C. J. Hoffman

In His death He is a Sacrifice, satisfying for our sins; in the resurrection, a Conqueror; in the ascension, a King; in the intercession, a High Priest.

Martin Luther

Lord Jesus Christ, as I live each day in the light of Your Word, my heart is at peace and I am fully alive!

——•— OCTOBER 25 —•——

...it is not the will of your Father which is in heaven, that one of these little ones should perish. Matthew 18:14

*O*FTEN AS I LET MY MIND WANDER BACK to the great storms and blizzards that we went through on my ranches, I recall scenes full of pathos and power. Again and again I would come home to our humble cottage with two or three tiny, forlorn, cold lambs bundled up within the generous folds of my big, rough wool jacket. Outside hail, sleet, snow and chilling rain would be lashing my face and body. But within my arms, the lambs were safe and sure of survival. Part of the great compensation for enduring the blizzards...was to pick up lost lambs. And as I picked them up I realized in truth I was taking up my own life again in them.... It is as I am found in Him that He, too, revels and rejoices in my being found. No wonder there is such rejoicing in heaven over one lost soul who is brought home.

W. Phillip Keller

Not father or mother has loved you as God has, for it was that you might be happy He gave His only Son. When He bowed His head in the death hour, love solemnized its triumph; the sacrifice there was completed.

Henry Wadsworth Longfellow

Lord Jesus, tender Shepherd who has led me out of the storms and given me peace and eternal life, I worship and praise You.

——•— OCTOBER 26 —•——

The Lord is my shepherd.... Psalm 23:1

*W*HILE I WAS WORKING ON MY DAD'S FARM I remember him saying to me, "Well, that bee stung me, son; you don't have to worry about him." And it was true. Once a worker bee stings, his stinger is gone. There is no need to fear it. In the case of death, the last enemy, Jesus Christ has done that for us; He has removed the sting of death, as Paul says, by dying for our sins.

The Christian has no fear of death, for he is following the Great Shepherd. Like many of you, I have stood at the bedside of a child of God as he came to the moment of death. With a smile of joy on his face he quoted this Psalm, and like you, I murmured, "Thank God." There was no fear. Death for him was a mere stepping stone into eternity; he was just a sheep heading for the green pastures.

Perhaps you are facing a dark valley today. Remember this: In the valley there is Christ; in the valley there is fruit; in the valley there is the joy of the Lord. When you know the reality of a relationship with the Shepherd, nobody can take that relationship away from you. He anoints our head with oil so that our cup runs over.   *Cliff Barrows*

Not *was*, not *may be*, nor *will be*. "The Lord is my shepherd" *is* on Sunday, *is* on Monday, and *is* through every day of the week; *is* in January, *is* in December, and every month of the year; *is* at home, and *is* in China; *is* in peace, and *is* in war; in abundance, and in penury.   *J. Hudson Taylor*

Lord Jesus, forever Your presence is with me, leading me to my eternal home. In You I will trust.

OCTOBER 27

...he led them on safely, so that they feared not.... Psalm 78:53

---

*W*HEN THE LORD CREATED SHEEP, He must have had in mind the use He would make of them one day to teach spiritual truths. In their nature He put characteristics that closely resemble those of the Christian life. He seems to say: "If you want to know how to live the Christian life, watch the sheep. If you wish to see Me, watch some faithful shepherd."

A little girl attempting to quote the first verse said, "The Lord is my Shepherd, and that's all I want." She did not make a serious mistake, for if the Lord is our Shepherd, what more do we want?

We shall not want for rest: "He maketh me to lie down in green pastures." We shall not want for guidance: "He leadeth me in the paths of righteousness for his name's sake." We shall not want for courage: "Yea, though I walk through the valley of the shadow of death, I will fear no evil."

We shall not want for companionship: "Thou art with me." We shall not want for comfort: "Thy rod and thy staff, they comfort me." We shall not want for necessities: "Thou preparest a table before me in the presence of mine enemies." We shall not want for joy and gladness: "Thou anointest my head with oil; my cup runneth over." We shall not want for any good thing in this life: "Surely goodness and mercy shall follow me all the days of my life." We shall not want for any good thing in the life to come: "I shall dwell in the house of the Lord forever."

Roy W. Gustafson

The Shepherd knows what pastures are best for His sheep, and they must not question nor doubt, but trustingly follow Him. Perhaps He sees that the best pastures for some of us are to be found in the midst of opposition or of earthly trials. If He leads you there, you may be sure they are green for you, and you will grow and be made strong by feeding there.

Hannah Whitall Smith

Heavenly Father, thank You for Your love that leads me each day. Your goodness surrounds me, and I know this will be for always.

———————————— • OCTOBER 28 • ————————————

...without faith it is impossible to please him.... Hebrews 11:6

•——————————————————————————————————•

*W*E HAVE AN OIL PAINTING of my husband's favorite verse on one of our walls, and every time I walk by it I am reminded of how the Lord accomplishes this changing, this transforming in me: "For it is *God* who worketh in you both to will and to do of his good pleasure" (Philippians 2:13). The Source of wisdom to change me is also the Means. It is God Himself who is working in me, producing the change. When I try to pick myself up by my own bootstraps, I can fall flat on my face. Even when I know how to change, doing it myself is practically impossible.

But there is a Person involved. A divine Means. Back in November 1971 I wrote: "Lord, change me" in the margin of my Bible by Hebrews 11:6. Then I added, "I believe You will do it." "Without faith it is impossible to please (God)," but the faith is not in the seeking or the changing process; faith is in a Person. God will reward me and work in me when I diligently seek Him. God is the divine Means for my changing.

Evelyn Christenson

My most cherished possession I wish I could leave you is my faith in Jesus Christ, for with Him and nothing else you can be happy, but without Him and with all else you'll never be happy.   *Patrick Henry*

Almighty God, I am thankful that I do not have to do the changing in my life, but it is You who gives me the strength and wisdom needed. In faith I live each day in the power of Your Son, Jesus Christ.

─────────────────── **OCTOBER 29** ───────────────────

...by whom also we have access by faith into this grace wherein we stand, and rejoice in [the] hope of the glory of God. Romans 5:2

◆───◆

*L*IVING FAITH IS ALWAYS IN THE PERSON OF JESUS CHRIST. The Chinese word for faith, *hsin*, has several interesting root characters. On the left side stands a man, on the right side is a small squarish opening out of which spring several short lines, denoting a mouth and the words being spoken. So then, faith is the confidence one has in a man and his words.

Do you believe in Jesus Christ? Then you have faith. Faith to ask Him for anything because you believe in Him. You will know what to ask and how and where, because you believe in Him and love Him. Your greatest need can be your greatest asset, for need is the golden door through which He comes close to His loved ones. Christ promised, "Lo, I am with you all the days — perpetually, uniformly and on every occasion — to the (very) close and consummation of the age" (Matthew 28:20, *Amplified*).

Jesus Christ is our "point of contact," and as we touch Him, alone or with others, power is released and our prayers are answered.
Rosalind Rinker

Keep Thou my feet; I do not ask to see
The distant scene — one step enough for me.
John Newman

Lord Jesus, I love You and believe in Your love and redeeming power. Your words bring me hope and an underlying joy as I live each day in You.

─────────────────── **OCTOBER 30** ───────────────────

Get thee behind me, Satan: for it is written, Thou shalt worship the Lord thy God, and him only shalt thou serve. Luke 4:8

S ATAN DELIGHTS TO ENGAGE OUR THOUGHT with ourselves, our sins, our worthlessness, our failures; for when we are so engaged, we are looking back, and our furrow goes crooked at once. The backward pull greatly hinders straight ploughing, and Paul was thinking of it when he wrote about "forgetting those things which are behind, and reaching forth unto those things which are before" (Philippians 3:13).

Or perhaps we cannot have everything we want, and do not quite understand why we cannot have it. This word meets us there. It says, Do not let your thoughts linger about the thing which you want to have. This is a matter of the will. Fix your desires on the track ahead. Look on. Go on.

Amy Carmichael

Lead on, O King Eternal,
    The day of march has come;
Henceforth in fields of conquest
    Thy tents shall be our home.
Through days of preparation
    Thy grace has made us strong,
And now, O King Eternal,
    We lift our battle song.

Ernest W. Shurtleff

Almighty God, forgive the time I spend in defeated thoughts. May I always keep my mind on You, my strength and my King.

OCTOBER 31

Thine, O Lord, is the greatness, and the power, and the glory, and the victory.... I Chronicles 29:11

I F WHAT JESUS HAD TO SAY ABOUT THE DEVIL IS TRUE, then he is something more than an idea for a Halloween costume. But if what Jesus taught about the Evil One is merely superstitious nonsense, then how could we take authoritatively anything else Christ said?

In Christ's eyes the stakes here are desperately high:
        your immortal soul and mine,
where we shall spend eternity—either in the Father's house or lost from ourselves, our Maker, and our fellows.

Jesus warns us that the devil's techniques are insidious.

In our time we have heard a great deal about infiltration.
But the Communists did not invent it.
It started back in the Garden of Eden when a snake slithered
his way into Paradise...

and this technique has been used ever since.

Peter Marshall

"Checkmate!" is an old painting depicting the so-called triumph of the devil in a chess game. He is shown delighting in the apparent failure of his opponent. The young man, seated at the chessboard, seemingly has lost. His expression is one of utter dejection and hopelessness.

A renowned chess player was fascinated by this painting and decided to see if there were any way the young man could win. Setting the chess pieces in exactly the same way on his own chess board, the expert pondered over them. Suddenly he jumped up and shouted, "The painting is wrong! There is a way out!"

For Christians, Jesus Christ is the way out and it is the devil who eventually will lose. In the power of Jesus' name we can triumph over any satanic power he tries to unleash. *J.W.B.*

Lord Jesus, we praise You that we have victory over any wiles of the devil. It is in Your name we win the battle.

NOVEMBER 1

**Blessed is that man that maketh
the Lord his trust.** Psalm 40:4

*W*E CAN NEVER BE TOO OLD to give our lives to Jesus Christ. I remember my grandmother would say, "It's too late for me to change" whenever I talked to her about making a commitment to Him. She had cared for people all her life, given of herself unstintingly—the traits of a Martha—without complaint. How I longed for her to know the joy that Mary knew as she sat at the feet of Jesus!

It was my privilege to see my grandmother come to know our Lord just a few hours before she died. In her hospital room I prayed with her as she accepted Him. The joy that came into her eyes was absolutely beautiful to see and illuminates my memory of her. The last words she spoke were, "I'm not afraid to die anymore." She knew she was going to be with Jesus Christ and the delight of a heavenly home He had been preparing for her. *J.W.B.*

I came to love You late, O Beauty so ancient and so new; I came to love You late. You were within me and I was outside, where I rushed about wildly searching for You like some monster loose in Your beautiful world. Your were with me, but I was not with You. You called me, You shouted to me, You broke past my deafness. You bathed me in Your light, You wrapped me in Your splendor, You sent my blindness reeling. You gave out such a delightful fragrance, and I drew it in and came breathing hard after You. I tasted, and it made me hunger and thirst; You touched me, and I burned to know Your peace.

Augustine

Lord Jesus, thank You for Your love and forgiveness that welcome us as we give ourselves into Your saving power.

NOVEMBER 2

For God sent not his Son into the world to condemn the world; but that the world through him might be saved.
John 3:17

I HAD AN UNCLE WHO PASSED AWAY a couple of years ago. He had been a church member all his life, but it was only toward the end that he really had assurance of salvation.

One of our grandsons was 5 at the time. When he heard of Uncle Herm's passing he said, "Uncle Herm is up there with the good guys. There was only one bad guy up there, and God drove him out."

How did God love the world? "For God so..." That little word *so* expresses both the quantity and the quality of God's love and the affection He has for the sinner in order that he may be saved.

How did He love? God loved as only God can love—the miracle and marvel of it all. "God so loved the world." All His divine attributes are in this fact. He created the world, He maintains and manages it. Because He created us, He can maintain and manage us—if we but let Him.

How did God love? "God so loved the world." The highest of all His attributes expended upon a needy world.

He gave His all, His only. He loves the world and wraps it around with the latitude and longitude of His divine compassion and inexhaustible love. "He so loved the world." *George M. Wilson*

(It is in God's love we find absolute assurance of eternal life through Jesus Christ. All our strivings, all our longings can find peace in Him.)

> *O Love that wilt not let me go,*
> *I rest my weary soul in Thee;*

I give Thee back the life I owe,
That in Thine ocean depths its flow
May richer, fuller be.

George Matheson

NOVEMBER 3

...*he knoweth our frame; he remembereth that we are dust.*

Psalm 103:14

---

*H*AVE YOU COME TO THE END OF A VERY IMPERFECT DAY, when everything has gone wrong, unable at night to put together a sensible prayer? Finally, you gave up trying and lumped the whole tangled mess and committed it to an understanding God, while you sighed very lamely, "Lord, You know how it is."

He does. And what a blessed relief to know that when we do the best we can, not faultlessly but blamelessly, He takes all the loose ends and ragged edges and binds them into a perfect whole. For we are complete in Him.

> And I smiled to think God's greatness
> Flows around our incompleteness;
> 'Round our restlessness His rest.

He makes up all the deficiencies, and rounds out all the broken corners. He knows the heart's intent and credits the soul's sincere desire, though it be poorly expressed in the deed. As Whittier put it, He judges our frailty by the life we meant.

This affords no ground for slovenliness. Do your very best. But remember that your very best is very poor. He will perfect it in Himself.

He knows how it is. *Vance Havner*

> At night, my weary body aches,
> My mind is torn by questions deep,
> But while I rest my Father takes
> And mends my raveled soul with sleep.

Fred Bauer

Father, how wonderful to know You are aware of all my frailties and yet You still love me. This knowledge gives me hope when my day has been filled with failure and frustration.

NOVEMBER 4

Simon, Simon, Satan has asked to have you, to sift you like wheat, but I have pleaded in prayer for you.... Luke 22:31-32 (TLB)

*J*ESUS PRAYED FOR PETER! And in praying for Peter, Jesus still saw possibilities in Peter, though he was weak and undependable...

Gutzon Borglum, the sculptor who carved the famous bust of Lincoln, had a cleaning woman who dusted the block of marble from which the great carving was sculpted. To the cleaning woman, the chunk of marble was simply one of the many shapeless blocks amidst the clutter. One day, after Borglum had started sculpturing the block, chipping until the unmistakable profile of Lincoln began to emerge, the cleaning woman studied the block, then rushed to Borglum's secretary, asking, "Ain't that Abraham Lincoln?" When told it was, she exclaimed, "Well, how in the world did Mr. Borglum know that Lincoln was in that piece of marble?"

How did Jesus know that an apostle was in that fickle fisherman, Peter? He knew through praying. How may you know that a disciple is in that block of flesh which is your friend, who is slipping? Again, you know through praying. *William P. Barker*

> More things are wrought by prayer
> Than this world dreams of. Wherefore, let thy voice
> Rise like a fountain for me night and day.
> For what are men better than sheep or goats
> That nourish a blind life within the brain,
> If, knowing God, they lift not hands of prayer
> Both for themselves and those who call them friend?
> For so the whole round earth is every way
> Bound by gold chains about the feet of God....
>
> *Alfred, Lord Tennyson*

Heavenly Father, thank You for breaking through the facade and melting the hardness of my heart. I praise and worship You. Bless those who need Your love and give me grace to pray and care for them.

NOVEMBER 5

...we know not what we should pray for as we ought: but the Spirit itself maketh intercession for us with groanings which cannot be uttered. Romans 8:26

*O*H, HOW GOD HAS SPOKEN TO ME in prayer times and taught me to be honest with myself, with Him, and then with those against whom I have sinned. Prayer has revealed my poverty of spirit, my bigoted attitudes toward those I am sent to serve. In prayer God has shattered the ice of my soul and set me free to love! He has answered my prayers—not as I told Him to, praise God—but with a whale of a storm, a group of difficult people, or a seemingly impossible assignment. He has listened deeper than my superficial request and answered the hidden needs of my character. He has ignored my petitions for physical ease, and yet strangely answered them by giving me rest in distress, comfort in adversity, and joy in the midst of a Nineveh situation. *Jill Briscoe*

Prayer is something deeper than words. It is present in the soul before it has been formulated in words, and it abides in the soul after the last words of prayer have passed over our lips. Prayer is an attitude of our hearts, an attitude of mind. Prayer is a definite attitude of our hearts toward God, an attitude which He in heaven immediately recognizes as prayer, as an appeal to His heart. Whether it takes the form of words or not does not mean anything to God, only to ourselves. *O. Hallesby*

Lord, there are times when I canot find words to tell You all that is in my heart, but You hear my longings and I praise You.

NOVEMBER 6

For every one that asketh receiveth; and he that seeketh findeth.... Luke 11:10

*O*NE DAY AS I WAS DRIVING home from town with our youngest son, he kept urging me to hurry. "Go faster, Mother!" he insisted. But he was too young to read the road sign that said 45 m.p.h.

And again, "Pass him, Mother." But he was too small to see that there was a double yellow line.

Then I began applying the brake. "Why are you stopping?" he demanded.

"There's a school bus ahead that has stopped," I replied.

I thought to myself, "When God is at the wheel we may request, but never insist. We are too young to read certain road signs, too small to see what lies ahead."

George Macdonald writes, "There is a communion with God that asks for nothing, yet asks for everything. He who seeks the Father more than anything He can give, is likely to have what he asks, for he is not likely to ask amiss."

There may be a long interval between the two clauses, "Ask, and ye shall receive...that your joy may be full." But the end of true prayer is always joy. *Ruth Bell Graham*

Even such as ask amiss may sometimes have their prayers answered. The Father will never give the child a stone that asks for bread; but I am not sure that He will never give the child a stone that asks for a stone. If the Father says, "My child, that is a stone; it is not bread," and the child answers, "I am sure it is bread; I want it," may it not be well that he should try his "bread." *George Macdonald*

Father, forgive the times I try to run ahead of You. By Your grace, I will wait patiently trusting in Your sovereign plan for my life.

NOVEMBER 7

**Watch ye and pray, lest ye enter into temptation.
The spirit truly is ready, but the flesh is weak.** Mark 14:38

"WATCH" AND "PRAY" GO TOGETHER—"praying always...and watching with perseverance." It demands spiritual energy. I must not allow myself to be careless or neglectful.

It is well to accustom oneself to stated seasons of prayer, and to refuse to allow even pressing business to turn one aside. Who has not heard of the white handkerchief in front of General "Chinese Gordon's" tent? The sentry pacing to and fro allowed no courier to enter, no matter how urgent, till that kerchief was removed. It indicated that Gordon was having an audience with God, and all other matters must wait. *H. A. Ironside*

(The most important time of our day—one in which the rest of our activities revolve—is when, like General Gordon, we give our complete attention to our Lord.)

> *Spirit of God, descend upon my heart;*
> *Wean it from earth, through all its pulses move;*
> *Stoop to my weakness, mighty as Thou art,*
> *And make me love Thee as I ought to love.*
>
> *I ask no dream, no prophet ecstasies,*
> *No sudden rending of the veil of clay,*
> *No angel visitant, no opening skies;*
> *But take the dimness of my soul away.*
>
> *George Croly*

...knowing what was done in her, came and fell down before him, and told him all the truth. Mark 5:33

◆──◆

T HE STORY OF THE WOMAN who had been so desperately ill
for 12 long years and believed that if she could just touch Jesus
she would be healed is one of the great accounts of faith found in the
Bible.

Even though she must have been weak, she was determined to
push through the great crowd that thronged around the Savior.
When He asked the disciples who had touched Him, she became
afraid. She knew something incredible had happened to her, and she
told Jesus *all* the truth. His loving words, "Daughter, thy faith hath
made thee whole; go in peace and be whole of thy plague," apply to
us today. It is when we come to Him in absolute faith and trust,
pouring out all our needs, our hurts, our longings, that He heals our
troubled minds of whatever is plaguing us.

The communion that comes when we are totally honest as we
pray is a glorious experience. He knows us—our thoughts, our
motives—yet so often we try to hide all that is in our hearts from
Him. In doing so we miss much. Our Lord is always waiting to commune with us. We are never alone in sorrow, conflict, or joy. *J.W.B.*

The prayer preceding all prayer is, "May it be the real I who speaks.
May it be the real Thou that I speak to." *C. S. Lewis*

*Lord Jesus, from the very depths of my heart I would give You all my
feelings—the hurts, the anger, the lack of faith that keep me from
close communion with You. May I be completely honest with You, my
beloved Savior.*

Let us walk honestly.... Romans 13:13

◆──◆

H ONESTY OF HEART IS ONE THING GOD RESPECTS. The char-
latan, the pretender, the hypocrite is an abomination unto
Him. To the most pretentious religious people of His time He said:
"Woe unto you, scribes and Pharisees, hypocrites! for ye are like unto
whited sepulchres, which indeed appear beautiful outward, but are
within full of dead men's bones, and of all uncleanness" (Matthew
23:27).

When Jesus performed one of His miracles, Simon Peter fell down at His knees, saying, "Depart from me; for I am a sinful man, O Lord."

For his honesty of heart, Jesus said to Simon: "Fear not; from henceforth thou shalt catch men," and Simon Peter became the Great Fisherman.

Your life is full of potentialities. You may become much more than you are, and honesty is the key. If we face our inner need, if we stop pretending, if we will dare to be honest with God—a miracle can happen in our heart. "If we confess our sins, he is faithful and just to forgive us our sins, and to cleanse us from all unrighteousness."

Lee Fisher

An honest man's the noblest work of God. *Alexander Pope*

Almighty God, You know every thought, every motive of this heart of mine. With Your strength may I walk each day with honesty, seeing myself as You see me.

——•— NOVEMBER 10 —•——

Thou shalt be perfect with the Lord thy God. Deuteronomy 18:13

◆————————————————————————◆

*I*N THE OLD TESTAMENT, sincerity and integrity were enjoined on Israel. Sincerity is transparency of character, an unconscious quality that is self-revealing.

In the early years of his ministry, Billy Graham was invited to an interview with Sir Winston Churchill. When he went to his appointment, to his dismay he found himself in the presence of the British cabinet. As he left the room after the interview, Churchill turned to his colleagues and said, "There goes a sincere man."

In reply to a question, a prominent businessman said, "If I had to name the one most important quality of a top manager, I would say, *personal integrity*"—sincere in promise, faithful in discharge of duty, upright in finances, loyal in service, honest in speech.

J. Oswald Sanders

He that does as well in private between God and his own soul as in public, hath given himself a testimony that his purposes are full of honesty, nobleness and integrity. *Jeremy Taylor*

Almighty God, may I examine my heart and see whether every intention of mine is in Your perfect will. I ask that Your Holy Spirit invade me and show the flaws.

Cease from anger, and forsake wrath:
fret not thyself in any wise to do evil. Psalm 37:8

I SEE UNACCEPTABLE ANGER as that which motivates us to hurt our fellowman—when we want to slash and cut and inflict pain on another person. Remember the experience of the Apostle Peter when Jesus was being crucified. His emotions were obviously in a state of turmoil, seeing his beloved Master being subjected to an unthinkable horror. However, Jesus rebuked him when he severed the Roman soldier's ear with a sword. If there ever was a person with an excuse to lash out in anger, Peter seemed to be justified; nevertheless Jesus did not accept his behavior, and He compassionately healed the wounded soldier.

There is a vitally important message for all of us in this recorded event. Nothing justifies an attitude of hatred or a desire to harm another person, and we are treading on dangerous ground when our thoughts and actions begin leading us in that direction. Not even the defense of Jesus Christ would justify that kind of aggression.

James Dobson

I shall never permit myself to stoop so low as to hate any man.

Booker T. Washington

Lord Jesus, take from my heart any anger or hatred toward anyone and fill it with Your love.

Doest thou well to be angry? Jonah 4:4

L ET OUR TEMPER BE UNDER THE RULE of the love of Jesus; He can not alone curb it, *He can* make us gentle and patient. Let the vow that not an unkind word of others shall ever be heard from our lips be laid trustingly at His feet. Let the gentleness that refuses to take offense, that is always ready to excuse, to think and hope the best, mark our intercourse with all. Let our life be one of self-sacrifice, always studying the welfare of others, finding our highest joy in blessing others. And let us, in studying the divine art of doing good, yield ourselves as obedient learners to the guidance of the Holy Spirit. By His grace, the most commonplace life can be transfigured with the brightness of a heavenly beauty, as the infinite love of the Divine nature shines out through our frail humanity. *Andrew Murray*

(Each of us feels anger within us at times. We feel misunderstood, unloved, unjustly accused, frustrated. In giving this emotion over to our Lord, He can take it and in exchange give us His peace and joy once more.)

> O Holy Spirit, enter in
> And in our hearts Thy work begin,
> Thy temple deign to make us;
> Sun of the soul, Thou Light Divine,
> Around and in us brightly shine,
> To joy and gladness wake us.
> That we, in Thee truly living,
> To Thee giving prayer unceasing,
> May in love be still increasing.

Michael Schirmer

NOVEMBER 13

...the meekness and gentleness of Christ.... II Corinthians 10:1

JESUS WAS A GENTLE PERSON. When He came into the world, there were few institutions of mercy. There were few hospitals or mental institutions, few places of refuge for the poor, few homes for orphans, few havens for the forsaken. In comparison to today, it was a cruel world. Christ changed that. Wherever true Christianity has gone, His followers have performed acts of gentleness and kindness.

The word *gentleness* occurs only a few times in our English Bible. It is spoken of in connection with the three Persons of the Trinity. In Psalm 18:35, it is the gentleness of God; in II Corinthians 10:1, the gentleness of Christ; and in Galatians 5:23, the gentleness of the Holy Spirit.

Charles Allen points out: "In one's disdain of sin, one can be harsh and unkind toward a sinner.... Some people seem to have such a passion for righteousness that they have no room left for compassion for those who have failed."

Billy Graham

The heart of the gentle is the throne where the Lord reposes.

John Climacus

Lord Jesus, Your gentle life compels me to be gentle with those I encounter. Teach me Your love and consideration, I pray.

Put on therefore...kindness, humbleness of mind,
meekness, long-suffering.... Colossians 3:12

*I*T IS A MATTER OF HISTORIC RECORD that the two great English evangelists John Wesley and George Whitefield disagreed on doctrinal matters. Both of them were very successful, preaching to thousands of people and seeing multitudes come to Christ. It is reported that somebody asked Wesley if he expected to see Whitefield in heaven, and the evangelist replied, "No, I do not."

"Then you do not think Whitefield is a converted man?"

"Of course he is a converted man!" Wesley said. "But I do not expect to see him in heaven—because he will be so close to the throne of God and I so far away that I will not be able to see him!" Though he differed with his brother in some matters, Wesley did not have any envy in his heart, nor did he seek to oppose Whitefield's ministry.

Warren W. Wiersbe

(Jesus' true humility can keep our hearts from envying another and make us realize we will only be content as we fix our eyes on Him.)

> *Plant in us an humble mind,*
> *Patient, pitiful, and kind;*
> *Meek and lowly let us be,*
> *Full of goodness, full of Thee.*

Charles Wesley

And he said unto me, My grace is sufficient
for thee: for my strength is made perfect in weakness....
II Corinthians 12:9

*H*ISTORY IS FULL OF EXAMPLES OF GOD using for His greatest work those who seem most insignificant in man's eyes. There was the obscure Christian in Damascus—Ananias—who baptized Paul, the great propagator of the faith. Ananias was unknown before and never heard of again.

Charles Haddon Spurgeon, the great scholar and preacher, whose writings are treasured today, was converted by the testimony of a simple working man whom Spurgeon heard when he stepped into a small church to escape a raging storm.

Dr. Abraham Kuyper, Dutch scholar and theologian, had just finished an erudite sermon when a peasant woman, her head wrapped in a shawl, approached him. "Dr. Kuyper, that was an excellent sermon, but you need to be born again," she said softly. He soon was and thereafter kept a picture of a peasant woman on his desk as a constant reminder.

A butcher in England, Henry Varley, who also was a lay preacher, told evangelist Dwight Moody, "The world has yet to see what God will do with a man fully consecrated to Him." Moody, who had been led to Christ by Edward Kimball, an obscure salesman in a shoe store, prayed that he might be that man. His ministry then exploded on two continents. Monuments are built to Moody's honor while the names of Kimball and Varley are found only in footnotes.

I like Richard Halverson's statement that "the strong need the weak so they can be close to God's strength." He so often uses people whose names may never appear in the *New York Times* but I'm convinced are printed in bold letters in the "Book of Life."

Charles W. Colson

Christ can triumph in a weaker man than I am, if there be any such. Samuel Rutherford

Almighty God, take my weak life and make it strong for Your service.

---———— **NOVEMBER 16** ————---

Let all bitterness, and wrath, and anger, and clamor, and evil speaking, be put away from you.... Ephesians 4:31

◆————————————————————————————◆

*I*F, WHEN WE FEEL WE MUST DISAGREE as true Christians, we could guard our tongues and speak in love, in five or ten years the bitterness could be gone. Instead of that, we leave scars—a curse for generations. Not just a curse in the church, but a curse in the world. Newspaper headlines bear it in our Christian press, and it boils over into the secular press at times—Christians saying such bitter things about other Christians.

The world looks, shrugs its shoulders and turns away. It has not seen even the beginning of a living church in the midst of a dying culture. It has not seen the beginning of what Jesus indicates is the final apologetic—observable oneness among true Christians who are truly brothers in Christ. Our sharp tongues, the lack of love between us—not the necessary statements of differences that may exist between true Christians—these are what properly trouble the world.

How different this is from the straightforward and direct command of Jesus Christ—to show an observable oneness which may be seen by a watching world!   *Francis A. Schaeffer*

They (the Christians) know one another by secret marks and signs, and they love one another almost before they know one another.
                                                               Statius Caecilius

(Do we show by our actions to fellow Christians this love that Rome saw and was amazed by?)

Lord Jesus, often I get discouraged and do not show my brothers and sisters in You the love that should transcend our petty differences. Forgive me.

———————————— ►► **NOVEMBER 17** ◄◄ ————————————

Let no corrupt communication proceed out of your mouth, but that which is good to the use of edifying, that it may minister grace unto the hearers. Ephesians 4:29

◆———————————————————————————————◆

"*I* WOULD RATHER PLAY WITH FORKED LIGHTNING," says A. B. Simpson, "or take in my hands high-voltage wires with their fiery currents, than to speak a reckless word against any servant of Christ, or to repeat idly the darts which other Christians, to the hurt of their own souls and bodies, are hurling on their fellows."

Too often we accuse others of doing things that we ourselves are guilty of committing, although we may not know it. "You may wonder, perhaps, why your sickness is not healed," Dr. Simpson adds, "or why your spirit is not filled with the joy of the Holy Ghost, or your life not blessed and prosperous. It may be that some dart which you have flung with angry voice, or tossed during an idle hour of thoughtless gossip, is pursuing you on its way, as it describes the circle which always brings every shaft of bitterness and every idle and evil word back to its source.

"The evil influence of talebearing has permeated every stratum of society, from the palace to the slum, and it rears its ugly head in the Church, as many Christians have known by painful experience. The tongue of the gossiper has destroyed empires and has cast down mighty men. Ruined lives, blighted homes, broken hearts, sundered friendships have been caused by idle chatter. Too late, people learn what harm has been wrought by giving too ready an ear to rumor."

May God help us to live, think, act and speak in the light of eternity. Then, instead of getting our eyes on man and judging him, watching for virtues and faults, we will keep our eyes fixed on the Christ who indwells him, and we will see no man save Jesus only.   *Oswald J. Smith*

Never believe anything bad about anybody unless you positively know it to be true; never tell even that unless you feel that it is absolutely necessary—and that God is listening while you tell it.

Henry van Dyke

Lord God, may my tongue be kept under control by the power of Your Holy Spirit.

——→ NOVEMBER 18 →——

....*the tongue is a fire, a world of iniquity....* James 3:6

*I*T IS IMPOSSIBLE FOR A LEADER—or any person for that matter—with a sensitive spirit not to be hurt by a rumor. I don't care how strong a leader you are, you will experience times when the cutting remarks really hurt. Afterward, when you've picked up the pieces and put things back together, you'll be able to move on.

Let me say something to those who gossip. If your tongue is a loose tongue, God is going to have to deal with it. You see, gossip is a major reason for disunity in the family of God. The body has no stronger muscle than the one in our mouths!

What should we do then when we have disagreements that need to be expressed? We need to take them to the leaders who can do something about them, to those who will really listen, evaluate, and respond to what we have to say.

If you work in a corporation and are bad-mouthing your boss, you're wrong. You need to express that gripe to someone in authority in a tone that is loving and not harsh.

I believe every telephone ought to have written beside it the words of Ephesians 4:29:

> Let no foul speech whatever come out of your mouth,
> but only what serves well to improve the occasion,
> so as to add blessing to the listeners (*MLB*).

Charles R. Swindoll

> If aught good thou canst not say
> Of thy brother, foe, or friend,
> Take thou, then, the silent way,
> Lest in word thou shouldst offend.

Author unknown

Father, when I am hurt by an unkind remark may I learn to bridle my tongue in all situations. Forgive the times I have been guilty of destructive gossip.

***...the Lord bindeth up the breach of his people,
and healeth the stroke of their wound.*** Isaiah 30:26

*N*O DOUBT YOU HAVE EXPERIENCED the nasty sensation of discovering that friends are sometimes absent in time of trouble. When all was well, they were with you. But when things started to come apart at the seams, they suddenly became conspicuous by their absence. Such people may have a tough time coping with their own difficulties and have no intention of getting involved in the troubles of others. Not so the Lord. He is a very present help in trouble.

Down through the history of the Church, there have been men and women who have proved this conclusively. When the Covenanters were being hauled across the glens by the English dragoons, they took great comfort from the Psalms, not least the one that assured them that the Lord was "very present."

When Martin Luther was up to his ears in trouble with the Pope, he rejoiced in God's presence and wrote his most famous hymn, "Ein Feste Burg Ist Unser Gott" ("A Mighty Fortress Is Our God") because of the inspiration of this psalm.

Luther and the Covenanters in their moments of stress and distress came to know the Lord in a deeper dimension and so does everyone who takes the occasion to be still and know that He is God.

D. Stuart Briscoe

When some friend has proved untrue—betrayed your simple trust; used you for his selfish end, and trampled in the dust the past, with all its memories, and all its sacred ties, the light is blotted from the sky—for something in you dies.

Bless your false and faithless friend, just smile and pass along— God must be the judge of it; He knows the right and wrong.... Life is short—don't waste the hours by brooding on the past; His great laws are good and just; Truth conquers at the last. *Patience Strong*

Lord Jesus, let me trust in You completely. When a friend fails me, help me not to harbor grudges; for he is like me, human, and in need of Your forgiveness and love.

***And the Lord God called unto Adam, and said unto him,
Where art thou?*** Genesis 3:9

*T*HAT GOD MADE MAN TO BE HIS FRIEND appears from the third chapter of Genesis, where we find God walking in the garden in the cool of the day, looking for Adam to join Him and share His company (Genesis 3:8). That, despite sin, God still wants human friends appears from Christ's statement that God seeks true worshipers (John 4:23); for *worship*, the acknowledging of *worth*, is an activity of friendship at its highest (hence "with my body I thee *worship*" in the marriage service). God wants men to know the joy of the love-relationship from which worship springs, and of the worship itself in which that relationship finds its happiest expression. The supreme example of such a relationship with God is that of Abraham, who worshiped God and trusted and obeyed His word even to the point of being willing to surrender his son for sacrifice— and Abraham, we are told, "was called *the friend of God*" (James 2:23, alluding to Isaiah 41:8, cf. II Chronicles 20:7). It is to make us His friends, as Abraham was, that God has spoken to us.   *J. I. Packer*

> May His Counsels Sweet uphold you,
> And His Loving Arms enfold you,
> As you journey on your way.
>
> May His Sheltering Wings protect you,
> And His Light Divine direct you,
> Turning darkness into day.
>
> May His Potent Peace surround you,
> And His Presence linger with you,
> As your inner, golden ray.
>
> *Author unknown*

Lord God, thank You for Your almighty presence that shelters and guides me each day. I worship You, Father, and praise Your holy name.

---———— **NOVEMBER 21** ————

Grace be unto you, and peace, from God our Father, and the Lord Jesus Christ. I Thessalonians 1:1

*J*OHN HENRY JOWETT SAID, "The will of God will never lead you where the grace of God cannot keep you." This means that the Lord won't demand something of you which He doesn't intend to help you implement.

I hope that this will be of encouragement to those who are facing struggles in this and related matters of self-control. The Christian experience is not an easy way of life—in no instance does the Bible teach that it is. Considerable discipline is required to love our enemies and maintain a consistent prayer life and exercise sexual control and give of our income to the work of the Lord—to name but a few of the many important areas of Christian responsibility. God doesn't expect instant maturity in each of these matters, but He does require consistent growth and improvement. The beautiful part is that we are not abandoned to struggle in solitude; the Holy Spirit "pities us as a father pities his child" (Psalm 103:13), tenderly leading and guiding us in the paths of righteousness. *James Dobson*

Have you ever thought that in every action of grace in your heart you have the whole omnipotence of God engaged to bless you?
Andrew Murray

Heavenly Father, thank You for Your grace that leads me each moment. Grant me Your peace, I pray.

―――――――――・― **NOVEMBER 22** ―・・――――――――

...he satisfieth the longing soul,
and filleth the hungry soul with goodness. Psalm 107:9

◆――――――――――――――――――――――――――――――――◆

*H*OW CLEVERLY PAUL TURNED THE TABLES on all those who taught that "godliness is a means of gain" by replying that "there is great gain in godliness with contentment" (I Timothy 6:5-6). He saw that the problem with material gain is its inability to bring contentment. John D. Rockefeller was once asked how much money it would take to be really satisfied. He answered, "Just a little bit more!" And that is precisely our problem—it always takes a little more; contentment always remains elusive.

But the wonderful thing about simplicity is its ability to give us contentment. Do you understand what a freedom this is? To live in contentment means we can opt out of the status race and the maddening pace that is its necessary partner. We can shout "No!" to the insanity which chants, "More, more, more!" We can rest contented in the gracious provision of God. *Richard J. Foster*

Get up early, go to the mountains and watch God make a morning. The dull gray will give way as God pushes the sun toward the horizon, and there will be tints and hues of every shade as the full-orbed sun bursts into view. And as the king of the day moves forward majestically flooding the earth and every lowly vale, listen to the music of heaven's choir as it sings of the majesty of God and the glory of the morning. In the hush of the earthly dawn, I hear a voice saying, "I am with you all the day. Rejoice! Rejoice!" *Mrs. Charles E. Cowman*

Almighty God, the glories of Your creation fill me with delight. May I always see that true contentment is in You and not material possessions.

NOVEMBER 23

For all things are for your sakes, that the abundant grace might through the thanksgiving of many redound to the glory of God. II Corinthians 4:15

◆──◆

*W*E RECOGNIZE THAT EVERYTHING NOBLE and praiseworthy comes from God.

Has He not given beauty to gold, to silver, to ivory, to marble? Has He not given us many things which we esteem even though they are not essential to us? Can we think that our Lord would have given to flowers such beauty as presents itself to our eyes if it were not intended that we should feel pleasure as we look on them? Can we think He would have given them such an attractive aroma if it had not been His wish that we should delight in smelling them?

Let us then not forget those outstanding blessings of the divine Spirit which He has dispensed to whomever He wills for the common good of mankind. *John Calvin*

This way of seeing our Father in everything makes life one long thanksgiving and gives a rest of heart, and, more than that, a gaiety of spirit, that is unspeakable. Someone says, "God's will on earth is always joy, always tranquility." And since He must have His own way concerning His children, into what wonderful green pastures of inward rest, and beside what blessedly still waters of inward refreshment is the soul led that learns this secret. If the will of God is our will, and if He always has His way, then we always have our way also, and we reign in a perpetual kingdom. He who sides with God cannot fail to win in every encounter; and, whether the result shall be joy or sorrow, failure or success, death or life, we may, under all circumstances, join in the Apostle's shout of victory, "Thanks be unto God which always causeth us to triumph in Christ!"

Hannah Whitall Smith

Lord God, I give my thanksgiving to You for all that You have provided. My eyes see Your blessings everywhere. You have given the most glorious gift of all in Your Son, Jesus Christ, my Savior.

Let us come before His presence with thanksgiving....

Psalm 95:2

WHEN I THINK OF MY OWN UPBRINGING, the love and care that were lavished on me in my youth, the kind of home into which I was born, the community in which I was reared, the gracious influences that were brought to bear on me, the examples that were held up before me, the kind of teaching I was given, the signposts that awaited me at every turn of the road, the fences that were set to keep me from wandering from the way, the warnings that were given me against every pitfall, the words in season so often spoken to me—when I think of all these things, and in spite of my shame for having so little profited from them, I must indeed prostrate myself in gratitude before the memory of my parents, my teachers, my wonderful friends, and those who wrote the books I was given to read, who rendered me this inestimable service.

Yet I know that they themselves had it all from Christ. Nothing of it would have been there if Christ had not come to seek and to save that which was lost. I cannot say that I "wot not who it was."

John Baillie

Now thank we all our God
  With heart and hands and voices,
Who wondrous things hath done,
  In whom His world rejoices;
Who from our mother's arms,
  Hath blessed us on our way
With countless gifts of love,
And still is ours today.

Martin Rinkart

Father, all that I have is from You, and I thank You for Your faithfulness that has followed me all my life.

Come home with me, and refresh thyself.... I Kings 13:7

WHEN I FIRST VISITED THE HOME of Dr. and Mrs. Nelson Bell, the parents of Mrs. Billy Graham, I sensed a warmth—a feeling that love was pre-eminent. As I watched the tender way this couple responded to each other, I saw the reason their home was so welcoming. Through their love for Jesus Christ and each other, the joy of their caring spilled over to everyone who came through their front door. Visitors left encouraged and refreshed, ready to face their own particular problems.

Victor Hugo wrote in his poem "House and Home":

> A house is built of logs and stone,
> Of tiles and post and piers;
> A home is built of loving deeds
> That stand a thousand years.

Both Dr. and Mrs. Bell are now with the Lord, but the memory of their home nestled in the mountains of North Carolina lives on as a reminder of what a house, an apartment, or even a room, can become if the occupants reflect the beauty of Jesus Christ.   *J.W.B.*

The Bible does not say very much about homes; it says a great deal about the things that make them. It speaks about life and love and joy and peace and rest. If we get a house and put these into it, we shall have secured a home.   *John Henry Jowett*

Lord Jesus, for the beauty of homes that give us a glimpse of what our heavenly home will be like, we thank You.

———————————— **NOVEMBER 26** ————————————

Bless the Lord, O my soul; and all that is within me, bless his holy name! Bless the Lord, O my soul, and forget not all his benefits.... Psalm 103:1-2 (*RSV*)

◆——————————————————————————————————◆

*W*E ARE DEPENDENT UPON GOD FOR EVERYTHING. We could not breathe a breath, think a thought, move a muscle, work a day, or develop our lives without His moment-by-moment provision. Put your finger on your pulse; thank God for your life. Breathe in, saying, "Bless the Lord, O my soul"; breathe out, saying, "And all that is within me, bless His holy name."

List what is yours from God's loving provision. Praise Him for food, your body, the people of your life, the opportunities and the challenges of today. Daily bread is more than food to eat. Through the Bread of Life, Jesus Christ, all things we have and are become an evidence of unmerited favor from a Lord who knows our needs. Make this a day of unmerited favor from a Lord who knows our needs. Make this a day for "flash prayers" in which you repeatedly say, "Thank You, Lord," for the abundant mercies in every moment of life.   *Lloyd John Ogilvie*

Cherish thankfulness with prayer. St. Paul gives us in two words this secret of peace. "In everything" (he excepts nothing, so do not you), "by prayer and supplication with *thanksgiving* let your requests be made known unto God. And the peace of God which passeth all understanding *shall* keep your hearts and minds through Christ Jesus." He does not say it as a benediction only; he tells us it "*shall* keep your hearts and minds." Do the one and God will do the other.

E. B. Pusey

Almighty God, I praise You for all Your hand provides. For peace of mind and heart that Your presence brings I thank You.

NOVEMBER 27

Religion that is pure and genuine in the sight of God the Father will show itself by such things as visiting orphans and widows in their distress and keeping oneself uncontaminated by the world. James 1:27 (*Phillips*)

THERE ARE THOUSANDS OF LONELY SHUT-INS: in homes for the aged; in hospitals for incurables; in wards for the mentally deranged; in jails, prisons, and penitentiaries where you can go to them but they can't come to you. Go and sing to them, or just go in and talk to them. Talk to them about Jesus. But talk to them also about anything and everything which is wholesome. Listen to them. Laugh with them, cry with them, empathize with them, share with them. That is your social privilege. It is your spiritual responsibility. Jesus said: "I was in prison and ye visited me!"

And then there are disasters: fires, earthquakes, landslides, traffic accidents, hurricanes, floods, and crime victims. Don't just watch them on the news or read about them in the papers. So many who have been involved have complained that the only people to turn up are reporters, cameramen, firemen, and doctors. They need you.

Billy Graham

There are a great many different ways of doing good. A lady once visited a hospital and noticed with what pleasure the patients would smell and look at the flowers sent to them. Said she: "If I had known that a bunch of flowers would do so much good, I would have sent some from home."

As soon as she got home, she sent some flowers out of her garden. It was a little thing—a bouquet of flowers. It might be a very insignificant work—very small; but if it was done in the right spirit, God accepted it. A cup of water given in His name is accepted as given to Himself. Nothing that is done for God is small. *D. L. Moody*

Lord, instill in my heart Your love and lead me to those with whom I can share it.

...a certain Samaritan, as he journeyed, came where he was: and when he saw him, he had compassion on him, and went to him, and bound up his wounds, pouring in oil and wine, and set him on his own beast, and brought him to an inn, and took care of him. Luke 10:33-34

◆——————————————————————————————————————◆

WITHOUT DEEP CARING, THE WORDS WE SAY about Jesus' peace will ring rather hollow. But with God-given *koinonia*, we can expect people to be drawn to the body of Christ.

Recently a young man picked me up to go to a meeting in Los Angeles. I discovered that he was Jewish and had moved to California from Canada several years before. He had become very successful in business, yet was conscious of an inner void in his life. A girl invited him to go with her to church. "I don't remember a thing the preacher said the first Sunday" he told me. "In fact, I couldn't tell you anything he said for several weeks. But I kept coming back because I was so impressed with the way these people related to each other, with a warmth and love and quality of caring to which I was a stranger. Finally it hit me that what the man in the pulpit was talking about was the reason for this love. And," he finished, "that's what brought me to Jesus Christ."

The world today is starved for community. We live in a nation of strangers, characterized by empty homes, lonely faces, and alienation. Our greatest social problem may be loneliness. A rediscovery of the fellowship of the Holy Spirit will be a powerful tool for sharing our faith. *Leighton Ford*

The way from God to a human heart is through a human heart. *S. D. Gordon*

Lord Jesus, teach me to care and reach out to those in my community who are hurting and lonely.

And my soul shall be joyful in the Lord.... Psalm 35:9

*J*OY IS PRAYER—Joy is strength—Joy is a net of love by which you can catch souls. She gives most who gives with joy.

The best way to show our gratitude to God and the people is to accept everything with joy. A joyful heart is the inevitable result of a heart burning with love.

We all long for heaven where God is, but we have it in our power to be in heaven with Him right now—to be happy with Him at this very moment. But being happy with Him now means:

> loving as He loves,
> helping as He helps,
> giving as He gives,
> serving as He serves,
> rescuing as He rescues,
> being with Him for all the 24 hours,
> touching Him in His distressing disguise.

Mother Teresa

Joy is not happiness so much as gladness; it is the ecstasy of eternity in a soul that has made peace with God and is ready to do His will.

Sherwood E. Wirt

Almighty God, may Your joy fill my heart as I minister in Your name.

NOVEMBER 30

We saw certainly that the Lord was with thee....

Genesis 26:28

*O*NE DAY MALCOLM MUGGERIDGE WATCHED Mother Teresa board a train in Calcutta. As he walked away, he said he felt as though he were leaving behind all the beauty and all the joy of the universe. "She has lived so closely with her Lord that the same enchantment clings about her that sent the crowds chasing after Him in Jerusalem and Galilee."

Lives that are completely yielded to our Savior cannot help but leave a touch of His love wherever they go. Even though Corrie ten Boom could not speak the language of many of the women in Ravensbruck concentration camp, they could sense Christ's love in her, and they were blessed. In her 80s, stricken by several strokes and unable to speak as she once did, Corrie still led people to her Lord. It was the glow of His presence in her life that spoke to the needy, longing heart of a woman who came to clean Corrie's home. Watching Corrie each day, she saw His love in her eyes and knew Corrie was praying for her. It was inevitable that she accept the Lord Jesus Christ.

Are our lives so transparent that when we are with others they sense His presence? In our daily walk with the Lord, can people—those in our home or outside—tell that we have been with the King of kings?   *J.W.B.*

Our Lord does not care so much for the importance of our works as for the love with which they are done.   *Teresa of Avila*

Lord Jesus, may I walk so closely to You that others will know that I am living joyously in Your presence.

DECEMBER 1

For the law was given by Moses, but grace and truth came by Jesus Christ. No man hath seen God at any time; the only begotten Son, which is in the bosom of the Father, he hath declared him. John 1:17-18

◆───◆

*T*HERE *IS* EVIDENCE FOR THE DEITY OF JESUS—good, strong, historical, cumulative evidence; evidence to which an honest person can subscribe without committing intellectual suicide. There are the extravagant claims which Jesus made for Himself, so bold and yet so unassuming. Then there is His incomparable character. His strength and gentleness, His uncompromising righteousness and tender compassion, His care for children and His love for outcasts, His self-mastery and self-sacrifice have won the admiration of the world. What is more, His cruel death, and the circumstantial evidence for His resurrection is most compelling.

Supposing Jesus was the Son of God, is basic Christianity merely an acceptance of the fact? No. Once persuaded of the deity of His Person, we must examine the nature of His work. What did He come to do? The biblical answer is, He "came into the world to save sinners." Jesus of Nazareth is the heaven-sent Savior we sinners need. We need to be forgiven and restored to fellowship with the all-holy God, from whom our sins have separated us. We need to be set free from our selfishness and given strength to live up to our ideals. We need to learn to love one another, friend and foe alike. This is the meaning of "salvation." This is what Christ came to win for us by His death and resurrection.   *John R. W. Stott*

As all the sweetness that is in the flowers of the field and in the garden is brought by the bees into the hive, and is there embodied in one hive; so all the attributes of God and the sweetness of them are hived in Christ, in whom all the fullness of the Godhead dwells bodily. *William Bridge*

Lord Jesus, Son of God, I praise You for the gift of my salvation. In You, and You alone, I am forgiven and have eternal life.

―――――― • **DECEMBER 2** • ――――――

...in him dwelleth all the fullness of the Godhead bodily.
Colossians 2:9

♦―――――――――――――――――――――――――――♦

WHEN CHARLES H. SPURGEON WAS ONLY 20 YEARS OLD he spoke these words of comfort and maturity:

"Nothing will so enlarge the intellect, nothing so magnify the whole soul of man, as a devout, earnest, continued investigation of the great subject of the Deity.

"And, whilst humbling and expanding, this subject is eminently *consolatory*. Oh, there is, in contemplating Christ, a balm for every wound; in musing on the Father, there is a quietus for every grief; and in the influence of the Holy Ghost, there is a balsam for every sore. Would you lose your sorrow? Would you drown your cares? Then go, plunge yourself in the Godhead's deepest sea; be lost in His immensity; and you shall come forth as from a couch of rest, refreshed and invigorated. I know nothing which can so comfort the soul; so calm the swelling billows of sorrow and grief; so speak peace to the winds of trial, as a devout musing upon the subject of the Godhead. It is to that subject that I invite you this morning...."
J.W.B.

> Art thou weary, art thou troubled,
>   Art thou sore distrest?
> "Come to Me," saith One, "and, coming,
>   Be at rest."

John M. Neale

Blessed Savior, Your comfort is deep within my heart and I find, even in the turbulence of life, Your peace.

―――――――― • **DECEMBER 3** • ――――――――

The night is far spent, the day is at hand: let us therefore cast off the works of darkness, and let us put on the armor of light. Romans 13:12

A GAIN WE FACE A DARK TIME in the history of God's people. In spite of some encouraging signs, the forces of evil seem to be gathering for a colossal assault on the work of God in the world. Satan has unleashed his power in a way perhaps unparalleled in the history of the Christian Church. If ever there was a time we needed renewal, it is now. Only God can thwart the plans of Satan and his legions, because only God is all-powerful. Only His Holy Spirit can bring true spiritual awakening which will stem the tide of evil and reverse the trend. In the darkest hour God can still revive His people, and by the Holy Spirit breathe new vigor and power into the body of Christ.

Our world needs to be touched by Christians who are Spirit-filled, Spirit-led, and Spirit-empowered. Are you that kind of Christian? Or is there in your own life the need for a new touch of the Spirit? Do you stand in need of genuine spiritual renewal within your own life? If so, know that God the Holy Spirit wants to bring that renewal to you right now. *Billy Graham*

(In this quiet time might we open our hearts completely to the renewing power of the Holy Spirit.)

> *Breathe on me, breath of God;*
> *Fill me with life anew,*
> *That I may love what Thou dost love,*
> *And do what Thou wouldst do.*
>
> *Edwin Hatch*

DECEMBER 4

If my people, which are called by my name,
shall humble themselves, and pray, and seek my face,
and turn from their wicked ways; then will I hear
from heaven, and will forgive their sin, and will heal
their land. II Chronicles 7:14

O UR VERSE IN II CHRONICLES INDICATES THE PEOPLE through whom revival comes. God specifies, *"My people!"* He does not say, "the Anglican church" or "the Roman Catholic church" or "the Protestant church" or "the Jewish church." But He does say, "If my people which are called by my name..." And God has His people in all the churches, those who have received His Son as Savior and Lord.

All the infidels and agnostics and skeptics and scoffers and repro-bates and unbelievers in the world cannot hold back the blessing and the power of God if God's people are willing to pay the price of spiritual awakening.

The Bible teaches that the burden of responsibility for revival any-where in the world is upon the shoulders of God's people. If you do not have a spiritual revival in your town or community, don't blame the bartender; don't blame the infidel; don't blame those who are protesting, demonstrating or rioting. Blame yourself, if you are a child of God, because God says, "*My people*" must do certain things. He has not left us in the dark. He has given us a blueprint for revival.

Grady Wilson

Revival is nothing else than a new beginning of obedience to God.

Charles G. Finney

Almighty God, cleanse me of my sins and give a sacrificial dedica-tion to pray for my country and the world. May I be completely obedi-ent to Your holy will.

———————————•▸ **DECEMBER 5** ◂•———————————

Him that overcometh will I make a pillar in the temple of my God.... Revelation 3:12

S LOWLY, THROUGH ALL THE UNIVERSE, that temple of God is being built. Wherever, in any world, a soul, by free-willed obedience, catches the fire of God's likeness, it is set into the growing walls, a living stone. When, in your hard fight, in your tiresome drudgery, or in your terrible temptation, you catch the purpose of your being, and give yourself to God, and so give Him the chance to give Himself to you, your life, a living stone, is taken up and set into that growing wall.... Wherever souls are being tried and ripened, in whatever commonplace and homely ways; there God is hewing out the pillars for His temple. Oh, if the stone can only have some vision of the temple of which it is to lie a part forever, what patience must fill it as it feels the blows of the hammer, and knows that success for it is simply to let itself be wrought into what shape the Master wills.

Phillips Brooks

David Brainerd, dedicated missionary to the American Indian, wrote of his experience one Sunday night as he totally dedicated his life into God's service:

"It was raining and the roads were muddy; but this desire grew so strong that I kneeled down by the side of the road and told God all about it. While I was praying, I told Him that my hands should work for Him, my tongue speak for Him, if He would only use me as His instrument—when suddenly the darkness of the night lit up, and I knew that God had heard and answered my prayer; and I felt that I was accepted into the inner circle of God's loved ones."   *J.W.B.*

Almighty God, by Your infinite love and wisdom show me the obstacles that stand like a barrier between my surrender and total dedication, I pray.

DECEMBER 6

Behold, I stand at the door, and knock: if any man hear my voice, and open the door, I will come in to him, and will sup with him, and he with me. Revelation 3:20

*T*O PRAY IS TO LET JESUS INTO OUR LIVES. He knocks and seeks admittance, not only in the solemn hours of secret prayer when you bend the knee or fold your hands in supplication, or when you hold fellowship with other Christians in a prayer meeting; nay, He knocks and seeks admittance into your life in the midst of your daily work, your daily struggles, your daily "grind." That is when you need Him most. He is always trying to come into your life, to sup with you. He sees that you need His refreshing presence most of all in the midst of your daily struggles. Listen, therefore, to Jesus as He knocks in the midst of your daily work or rest. Give heed when the Spirit beckons you to look in silent supplication to Him who follows you day and night.   *O. Hallesby*

How rare to find a soul still enough to hear God speak.

Fénelon

Heavenly Father, in the stillness of these moments I wait to hear You speak. My heart delights in Your presence, O God.

DECEMBER 7

...grow in grace, and in the knowledge of our Lord and Savior Jesus Christ. II Peter 3:18

*T*HE SCRIPTURES GIVE THE KEY to two kinds of knowledge— the knowledge of God, and the knowledge of men and nature. The great Reformation confessions emphasize that God revealed His attributes to man in the Scriptures and that this revelation was meaningful to God as well as to man. There could have been no

Reformation and no Reformation culture in northern Europe without the realization that God had spoken to man in the Scriptures and that, therefore, we know something truly about God, because God has revealed it to man.

It is an important principle to remember, in the contemporary interest in communication and in language study, that the biblical presentation is that though we do not have exhaustive truth, we have from the Bible what I term "true truth." In this way we know true truth about God, true truth about man and something truly about nature. Thus on the basis of the Scriptures, while we do not have exhaustive knowledge, we have true and unified knowledge.

Francis A. Schaeffer

The Bible is the book of all others to be read at all ages and in all conditions of human life.... I speak as a man of the world to men of the world, and I say to you, "Search the Scriptures."

John Quincy Adams

Almighty God, how I praise You for Your holy Word that brings me hope and the strength and knowledge I need each day.

DECEMBER 8

They helped every one his neighbor.... Isaiah 41:6

MANY PEOPLE IN OUR WORLD HAVE GROWN WARY of all religion. Only patient, loving service can earn us the right to speak to them. Those who work in the teeming slum areas of great cities tell us of the suspicion with which people greet any visitor. The door opens just a crack. The cautious face looks out. The obvious question is, "What are they trying to sell me now?" If the caller mentions the church, the immediate reaction is, "I don't have time to go" or "I don't have anything to give." Perhaps the first step to reach such people is not to ask them to do anything, or to start preaching, but just to sit down and find out how things are going and how one can help, for Jesus' sake. *Leighton Ford*

If any man's sorrows need our sympathy, his bodily or spiritual wants our help, let us think no more of asking whether he belongs to our country or family, our party or church, than if we saw him stretching out his hands from the window of a burning house, or found him, like the object of the Samaritan's kindness, wallowing in a pool of blood. Thus Christ loved us; and thus He teaches us to love one another. *Thomas Guthrie*

Lord Jesus Christ, give me a heart that can love without counting any cost and that will reach out to my neighbor.

By this shall all men know that ye are my disciples, if ye have love one to another. John 13:35

◆————————————————————————————————————◆

*P*EOPLE ARE PEOPLE. They have a nature that craves love and belonging and harmony with God. But most never find it. The world hasn't got it to give. But occasionally people do see love—God's love—as God's people care for each other without conditions.

Seeing how Christians care and help one another has always drawn people to Christ. It still does. A young attorney named Frank is a good example.

With two diplomas already hanging on his wall and well into his law-school studies, Frank was not at peace. But he knew young people his age who were at peace. So he went to a church retreat with them hoping that through that experience he would find an answer to two basic questions: "Is there a God?" "Will He care for me?"

At the retreat the lectures were scholarly and the discussion groups relevant. Still his questions persisted. But over in a different part of the camp another group was also having their retreat. Nearly 100 retarded teenagers were learning about Jesus and praising Him.

For two days Frank watched those young people and their counselors, listened to their spirited singing and noted their eager responses to Bible lessons. And he saw something else—something more.

On the last night of the retreat at the campfire, Frank stood up to make an announcement: "I've given my heart to Jesus."

Roger C. Palms

When iron is rubbed against a magnet it becomes magnetic. Just so love is caught, not taught. One heart burning with love sets another on fire. The Church was built on love; it proves what love can do.

Frank C. Laubach

Lord Jesus, may I not be guilty of ever delaying someone from coming to You because I did not love.

Love worketh no ill to his neighbor: therefore love is the fulfilling of the law. Romans 13:10

*W*E MUST NEVER FORGET that to be a follower of Jesus is to be dominated by love. We may not be well versed in Scripture, or have a seminary background; we may be timid and unsure of ourselves. But we have arms and hearts that were meant to be used. We must ask ourselves, Do I treat people as royalty walking the earth? My parents, my spouse, my roommate, the student on the floor that I can't stand? Do I believe that by merely seeing me God would break into a run and embrace me? Does my life reflect only religious activity, or does it bear the mark of profound love? When our lives are characterized by the love of Christ, we can begin to interest people in the Gospel. *Rebecca Manley Pippert*

Love is the inner motivation of all sound Christian living, and the complete surrender of ourselves to love is the secret of the Christian extra.

But where do we find this love?... It is suggested in a phrase in Matthew 5:44: "I say to you." The secret of love...and the strength of love are to be found in the Person of Christ who, through His Spirit, dwells within the Christian.... You must have the living Christ if you are to live by His teachings. He didn't say, "Without My precepts you can do nothing," or, "Without My ideals you can do nothing." [What our Lord] said [was], "Without *Me* ye can do nothing." *Paul Rees*

Beloved Savior, how often I find out that I am nothing without You! Forgive the times I fail You, and restore to me Your true, unselfish love, which will come into a longing heart yielded completely to You.

―――――――――― **DECEMBER 11** ――――――――――

Love...does not hold grudges.... I Corinthians 13:5 (*TLB*)

*R*ESENTMENTS ARE LIKE SNOWDRIFTS and forgiveness is the snowplow. You see, in the eyes of many people, forgiveness is simply a matter of passive acquittal. But in the Christian context, forgiveness is a snowplow—opening the road, removing barriers, permitting communication to be restored.

There are a lot of resentments that can build up in our lives in the course of a day. And the only way to put joy on your face and in your heart is to find an overwhelming love that can remove resentments and fill you with *forgiveness*.

"I forgive you" is the language of love! *Robert H. Schuller*

"I can forgive, but I cannot forget" is only another way of saying, *"I will not forgive."* A forgiveness ought to be like a cancelled note, torn in two and burned up so that it can never be shown against the man. *D. L. Moody*

Lord God, help me to tear up all the resentments that seep into my heart and replace them with the balm of Your love and forgiveness.

DECEMBER 12

I came that they might have life and might have it abundantly. John 10:10 (ASV)

T HE PERFECT TENSE EXPRESSES THE CONTINUANCE of completed action. Our love is the continuance of our Lord's completed love. His life in us is the secret source of our loving. He promised the abundant life to His followers. The abundance is more of Him!

The more we experience Christ, the more we will know of life as He meant it to be. When we find it difficult to love, the answer is not to condemn ourselves or search for some hidden psychological cause. Rather, it's a time for prayer. In the quiet we can open our need to Christ, tell Him our inadequacy and impotence to love profoundly. The amazing delight will be a new power flowing into us beyond our capacity. Inadvertently, a fresh flow of love for people will surprise us—and the people we long to love. *Lloyd John Ogilvie*

> Beloved, let us love: love is of God;
> In God alone hath love its true abode.
>
> Beloved, let us love: for love is rest,
> And he who loveth not dwelleth in night.
>
> Beloved, let us love: for only thus
> Shall we behold that God who loveth us.
> *Horatius Bonar*

Almighty God, as I contemplate and accept the love that sent Your Son to die for me, I am able to love in His name.

DECEMBER 13

...the Lord shall guide thee continually.... Isaiah 58:11

RECKON WITHOUT GOD? To do so would be as nonsensical as ignoring the sun as we watch a shifting pattern of sunlight and shadow on the ground.

Reckon without God? We'd better not, not in any area of life, if we are serious about knowing reality and about achieving our full potential. For our God never considers our work as merely a way to earn a living—so much an hour, so much a year. He has given each of us the gift of life with a specific purpose in view. To Him work is a sacrament, even what we consider unimportant, mundane work. When done "as unto the Lord," it can have eternal significance.

It is therefore important to Him that we discover what our particular aptitudes and talents are; then that we use those talents to His glory and their maximum potential during our all-too-brief time on earth.

For each of us, He does have a plan. What a joy to find it and even out of our helplessness, let Him guide us in its fulfillment.

Catherine Marshall

He leads me where the waters glide,
　　The waters soft and still,
And homeward He will gently guide
　　My wandering heart and will.

J. Keble

Heavenly Father, there is nowhere on this earth that I can ever be separated from Your love and guidance. This knowledge gives such joy!

DECEMBER 14

I am the good shepherd, and know my sheep, and am known of mine. John 10:14

WHEN DR. J. WILBUR CHAPMAN WAS TRAVELING through the Scottish highlands, he met a little shepherd boy tending his sheep. "Do you know the Twenty-third Psalm?" he asked the boy. He did not, and so Dr. Chapman gave him the first five words—"The Lord is my shepherd"—and told him to have a word for each finger of his hand. Months later Dr. Chapman traveled through the same section and decided to visit the boy. Not finding him, he inquired at a nearby hut, where he found the lad's mother. She told him the story of how her boy had perished in a fearful blizzard during the winter. He had always treasured the five words of the psalm, and he was specially impresséd by the fourth word, "*my*." He would frequently say the words and, holding onto his fourth finger, would repeat: "My Shepherd, My Shepherd." "When his body was found in the deep snow," said his mother, "his two hands were seen projecting from the snow. He was clasping his fourth finger—and we knew what that meant." Perhaps there are many who repeat the opening words of this psalm who cannot say from the heart: "Jesus is my Shepherd."

Keith L. Brooks

(In times of sorrow or joy, our Savior, the tender Shepherd, leads us and we are always in His loving care.)

O Lord, who art our Guide even unto death, grant us, I pray Thee, grace to follow Thee whithersoever Thou goest. In little daily duties to which Thou callest us, bow down our wills to simple obedience, patience under pain or provocation, strict truthfulness of word or manner, humility, kindness; in great acts of duty or perfection, if Thou shouldest call us to them, uplift us to self-sacrifice, heroic courage, laying down of life for Thy truth's sake, or for a brother. Amen.

Christina G. Rossetti

➤ DECEMBER 15 ◄

For all have sinned, and come short of the glory of God....

Romans 3:23

THIS EARTH WAS NOT ALWAYS PLEASANT FOR HIM—*nothing* compared to the glories and comforts of heaven, where He was surrounded by praise and honor. Here He was mocked, ridiculed, misunderstood, mistreated, spit upon, beaten, and finally nailed to the cross. Even before He came He knew all this would happen to Him, yet He considered us persons of value, of worth. He loved us and wanted to redeem us so that we might be restored to a place of fellowship with Him to love Him and enjoy Him. He knew that only in this way could we realize our true worth and be happy and fulfilled and bring glory to His name, as we were created to do. "But God commendeth his love toward us, in that, while we were yet sinners, Christ died for us" (Romans 5:8).

As we recognize that to Him we have always been persons of worth, we do not wish in any way to diminish how deeply we are fallen. The Bible clearly describes the depth of human sin—your sin and mine. "But we are all as an unclean thing, and all our righteousnesses are as filthy rags..." (Isaiah 64:6).

Verna Birkey

The love of God is greater far
Than tongue or pen can ever tell;
It goes beyond the highest star,
And reaches to the lowest hell.
The guilty pair, bowed down with care,
God gave His Son to win;
His erring child He reconciled,
And pardoned from his sin.

O love of God, how rich and pure!
How measureless and strong!
It shall for evermore endure
The saints' and angels' song.

F. M. Lehman

Almighty God—because of Jesus—Your love is leading me, unworthy as I am.

DECEMBER 16

And when they were come to the place, which is called Calvary, there they crucified him, and the malefactors, one on the right hand, and the other on the left. Luke 23:33

WHAT A SHATTERING BLOW the crucifixion must have been to Jesus' disciples during those first hours. What cruel irony to hear Him say, "Father, into thy hands I commend my spirit." What Father? Where now was the God who saw the sparrow fall? What was He doing when Jesus was crucified? Jesus (so it could have seemed to them) was either the Great Deceiver or the Great Deceived. God had let Him down. Had He Himself not cried out, "My God, why?"

Do you not believe such thoughts must have assailed the citadel of the disciples' faith? Was it not this that sent Peter in despair back to his fishing boat?

Yes, until...until that morning when God raised His Son from that tomb, when Jesus appeared to Peter and the other disciples. Then faith unfurled its flag, never again to lower its colors!

Leighton Ford

I know not how that Bethlehem's Babe
Could in the Godhead be;
I only know the Manger Child
Has brought God's life to me.

I know not how that Calvary's cross
A world from sin could free;
I only know its matchless love
Has brought God's love to me.

I know not how that Joseph's tomb
Could solve death's mystery;
I only know a living Christ,
Our immortality.

Major Harry W. Farrington

Lord Jesus, living Savior, I praise You for Your sacrifice for me. In conquering death You have given eternal life to all who love You!

————————•► **DECEMBER 17** ◄•————————

For since he himself has now been through suffering and temptation, he knows what it is like when we suffer and are tempted, and he is wonderfully able to help us. Hebrews 2:18 (*TLB*)

*N*O ONE AROUND US SEEMS TO UNDERSTAND the personal anguish of suffering we often experience. But Jesus does!

Jesus understands lack of wealth. His delivery room was a stable. His occupation was that of a lowly, underpaid carpenter. During His ministry, the Bible tells us He had nowhere to lay His head.

Jesus understands separation and loneliness. His disciples forsook Him and fled. In His death, He died alone, with His heavenly Father turning away from Him.

Jesus understands tiredness. We're told in the Scriptures that He became "wearied." On one occasion He was so tired He slept on a boat during a violent storm.

Jesus understands suffering and pain. Even before bearing the pain of the cross, He suffered indescribable physical and mental anguish as He was ridiculed, whipped, and crowned with thorns.

Herbert Lockyer has said, "The Christ who had never known suffering would not be the Christ for broken hearts." Because He's been there, He cares. And in caring, He offers the comfort needed to ease the ache that is trying to defeat you. *Bill Brown*

The Lord Jesus paid a tremendous price for you and me. He left heaven and came here just for one reason—to love you so you may love Him, to accept you so that you may accept Him. He has a right to claim you because if anyone ever loved you, it is the Lord Jesus.

Just as the servant of Abraham showed them his master's beautiful things, so you have been shown the beautiful peace that Jesus can give, the forgiveness He freely offers you, the love poured out on Calvary for you. Have you seen how He can heal broken relationships and bring joy and sweetness to your life? I know because He has filled my very empty life!

Festo Kivengere

Lord Jesus, thank You for bringing such joy into my life. Even in my saddest moments Your loving presence gives hope and peace. For all Your suffering for me, I give You all my love and devotion.

———•◦ DECEMBER 18 ◦•———

...the Lord Jehovah is my strength and my song; he also is become my salvation. Isaiah 12:2

*W*HEN I WAS A LITTLE GIRL I longed for God to change me— into an angel. My sister, brother, and I each had a special Christmas tree ornament that was our very own. We could hang it anyplace we wanted on the tree. Mine was a beautiful pink angel. And I would hang it on a low branch, way inside, near the tree trunk where it could not be seen except from my favorite, private spot— under the tree. Lying on my back, I spent hours gazing at that lovely, fragile, glass angel and dreaming my favorite dream: "If only I could be an angel!" How I wished I had been made an angel instead of a little girl.

But the words in a song, "Holy, holy, is what the angels sing," that became popular when I was a young teenager, brought it all into focus for me:

> But when I sing redemption's story,
> They will fold their wings;
> For angels never knew the joys
> That our salvation brings.

No, created in all their beauty, power and intelligence, no angels will ever have the privilege I have of being changed by God, step-by-step, into conformity to the image of His dear Son, Jesus (Romans 8:29). The angels probably aren't going through the often hard, deep and fiery changing process, but neither are they *becoming conformed to Jesus' image*! Nor have they been promised someday *to be like Him.*

Evelyn Christenson

I never knew true joy until my heart experienced the love of Jesus Christ. His forgiveness has turned my darkest days into ones of glorious light.

J.W.B.

Lord Jesus, as we prepare for the celebration of Your birth, our hearts are filled with joyous expectancy. May this joy be shared with others that they too will know Your gift of salvation.

──────────────────── **DECEMBER 19** ────────────────────

...in all things he might have the pre-eminence. Colossians 1:18

◆──◆

*A*T THIS TIME OF CHRISTMAS, with so much that is counterfeit being passed as part of the sacred festival of the birthday of Christ, let me refresh the minds of believers by asking:

Do we give Him His place in our lives, or are we like Diotrophes, who, according to John, loved to have the pre-eminence and to hold the place for self?

Do we give Him His place as the Son over God's house?

Do we give Him His place as Lord and Head of the Church?

Do we give Him His place in our homes and in our service to humanity?

Do we give Him His place in our customary gatherings?

Too many of us are pointing to our brothers and asking, like Peter, "What shall this man do?" We are like James and John, wondering about the seating order of other people and about our own status, instead of giving the Man Christ Jesus His place.

John the Baptist had it right. He understood the meaning of the parable. Pointing to the Lamb of God, he said, "He must increase, but I must decrease." *Roy W. Gustafson*

Lord Jesus, I give everything to You in adoration and love. May You have first place in all the ways of my life.

──────────────────── **DECEMBER 20** ────────────────────

I will run the way of thy commandments, when thou shalt enlarge my heart. Psalm 119:32

◆──◆

*T*HE CHRISTMAS SPIRIT DOES NOT SHINE OUT in the Christian snob. For the Christmas spirit is the spirit of those who, like their Master, live their whole lives on the principle of making themselves poor—spending and being spent—to enrich their fellowman, giving time, trouble, care and concern, to do good to others—and not just their own friends—in whatever way there seems need. There are not as many who show this spirit as there should be. If God in mercy revives us, one of the things He will do will be to work more of this spirit in our hearts and lives. If we desire spiritual quickening for ourselves individually, one step we should take is to seek to cultivate this spirit. "Ye know the grace of our Lord Jesus Christ, that, though he was rich, yet for your sakes he became poor, that ye through his poverty might be rich." "Let this mind be in you, which was also in Christ Jesus."

J. I. Packer

Christmas is based on an exchange of gifts: the gift of God to man— His unspeakable gift of His Son; and the gift of man to God—when we present our bodies as a living sacrifice and, like the Macedonians (II Corinthians 8:5), first give ourselves to God. No one has kept or can keep Christmas until he has had a part in this two-way transaction.

Vance Havner

Lord Jesus, in all the rush and preparation for Christmas I need to keep in perspective the real meaning of this celebration. May Your love be apparent in me as I rejoice in the wonder of the most blessed gift of all.

DECEMBER 21

...we also joy in God through our Lord Jesus Christ, by whom we have now received the atonement. Romans 5:11

◆ ——————————————————————————————— ◆

*T*HIS CHRISTMAS, ONCE MORE, there will be a soft knock at the door of many hearts and homes—perhaps a soft knock at your door. And as we peep out the window, we see Jesus standing there with nail-scarred hands, seeking entrance into our lives: "Behold, I stand at the door, and knock: if any man hear my voice, and open the door, I will come in to him, and will sup with him, and he with me." Two thousand years ago there was no room for him, and for many today there will be no room either.

Thank God there will be many others, however, who will bid Him enter, and know the true meaning of this wonderful season. Those who let Him in when He lived on earth were never the same again. Jairus let Him in, and his funeral dirge was changed to a resurrection anthem. Mary Magdalene let Him in, and she began to walk in newness of life. Zacchaeus let Him in, and there was great joy in that house. Saul of Tarsus let Him in, and shouted: "There is therefore now no condemnation to them which are in Christ Jesus."

Billy Graham

> Though Christ a thousand times
> In Bethlehem be born,
> If He's not born in thee
> Thy soul is still forlorn.

Angelus Silesius

Lord Jesus, I praise the day I asked You into my life! Help me show others how to accept Your glorious present of eternal life.

---◆— **DECEMBER 22** —◆---

**...the Lord himself shall give you a sign;
Behold, a virgin shall conceive, and bear a son,
and shall call his name Immanuel.** Isaiah 7:14

◆————————————————————————————————◆

*A*MONG THE MOST REASSURING PROMISES of Scripture are the "I-Am-With-You" promises. They begin in Genesis where God says to Isaac, "Fear not, for I am with you." And they occur again and again—in Genesis 28:15; Deuteronomy 31:3,6,8 and 23; Joshua 1:5,9; Judges 2:18, 6:12; Psalm 23:4; Isaiah 43:2. And they reach a glorious climax in Matthew 1:23: "and they shall call his name Emmanuel, which means, 'God with us.'"

Once again at the close of Matthew, as the risen Lord prepares to return to heaven, He leaves His disciples with the promise, "Lo, I am with you alway."

This happy season will be even happier as we bear in mind the words of the writer to the Hebrews, "Let your conversation be without covetousness; and be content with such things as ye have: for he hath said, I will never leave thee, nor forsake thee." Having so great a Gift places all lesser gifts in proper perspective.

And all of time is marching toward that glorious fulfillment when, as He said, "I will come again, and receive you unto myself; that where I am, there ye may be also."

He with us here—we with Him there.

Emmanuel!   *Ruth Bell Graham*

> Rejoice! Rejoice!
> Emmanuel shall come to thee,
> O Israel!

Latin hymn

Lord, You are with me and my heart is glad! How glorious is the Christmas message.

---◆— **DECEMBER 23** —◆---

...to guide our feet into the way of peace. Luke 1:79

◆————————————————————————————————◆

*O*NE OF THE GREATEST MINISTERS America has ever produced was Phillips Brooks. Several times when I have been in Boston, I have stood at the front of Trinity Church and looked at the statue of that great preacher who preached there for so many years. Whenever I visit Bethlehem, I always think of the song he wrote:

> O little town of Bethlehem,
> How still we see thee lie!
> Above thy deep and dreamless sleep
> The silent stars go by.

It is one of the most beautiful of all the Christmas carols. Once Phillips Brooks said that one of the most important lessons he ever learned was when he was a young boy. He was at the family dinner table. Times were hard, and the Brooks household was having difficulties. His mother, in a moment of despair, spoke bitterly about the injustices of it all. When she had finished, he remembered that his father said quietly, "I have trusted the Lord for 40 years, and I do not mean to stop now."

When you take all of your troubles and face up to them in the most practical and reasonable way, you truly can find peace in the valley.

Charles L. Allen

Sons of men, why are you so heavy-hearted? Now that Christ the Life has descended to you, why don't you ascend with Him and start living?

Augustine

Lord Jesus, You have brought abundant life and peace into my soul. May I always be grateful for all You have provided.

———————•→ **DECEMBER 24** →•———————

Thanks be unto God for his unspeakable gift. II Corinthians 9:15

◆————————————————————————————————————◆

*I*N GOD'S PERFECT TIMING His gift of Jesus was born to a despairing world—in God's perfect place. In the Church of the Holy Sepulchre in Jerusalem there is a spot that is pointed out to visitors as being "the center of the world." Nearby in Bethlehem, in a squalid stable, the Son of God was born. When men's hearts and souls most needed it, from out of the heart and mind of God came the Messiah.

A Savior had been prophesied down through the ages. Men had sung songs predicting His coming. Surely their King would appear clothed in robes of great majesty—not wrapped in swaddling clothes, lying in a humble manger. How very different it all was from what had been expected!

Most of us as children loved to hear the story of Jesus' birth. Christmas was such a wonderful time. As we excitedly anticipated all the gifts we were going to receive on Christmas Day, the reality of its meaning seemed to get lost. It will always elude us until, by faith, we receive the Savior and come to know Jesus. God's immeasurable love reaching out to all mankind is His gift to us. *J.W.B.*

The life of Christ that appeared on this earth at the first Christmas is the most invaluable gift to be cherished both here and in the hereafter. It is the secret of a Christian's victory over the predicaments of earthly existence and his participation in "the inheritance of the saints in light" (Colossians 1:12). It is the only source of true joy to man, to nature and to the entire universe, all of which are equally subject to decay and disintegration.

> Joy to the world! the Lord is come:
> Let earth receive her King;
> Let every heart prepare Him room,
> And heaven and nature sing.
>
> *Akbar Abdul-Haqq*

Almighty God, Your gift of Jesus Christ brings true joy into the heart of every believer. It is with adoration and thanksgiving we remember the eve of His birth.

DECEMBER 25

...unto you is born this day in the city of David a Savior, which is Christ the Lord. Luke 2:11

*T*HE PROMISE THAT THE ANGELS SANG is the
most wonderful music
the world has ever heard...
It is a promise—God's promise—of what
one day will come
to pass.
The years that are gone are graveyards in
which all the
persuasions of men have crumbled
into dust.
If history has any voice, it is to say that
all these ways of
men lead nowhere.
There remains one way—The Way—
untried
untested
unexplored fully...

the way of Him who was born a Babe in
Bethlehem. *Peter Marshall*

Let us never forget that standing at either end of the life of Christ is
a greater miracle: the virgin birth at the beginning and the resurrection at the end. *Calvin Miller*

*Lord Jesus, on this Your birthday we praise You and rejoice in the
miracle that brought You to this world. We worship and adore You,
loving Savior.*

-------------------- ► **DECEMBER 26** ◄--------------------

*And the Word was made flesh, and dwelt among us,
(and we beheld his glory, the glory as of the
only begotten of the Father,) full of grace and truth.*

John 1:14

◆———————————————————————————◆

*L*ET US BE CAREFUL NOT TO LIMIT that mysterious joining of
divine with human to an infant wailing piteously on the straw.
Let us struggle to understand that the Word becomes flesh in all of us
who believe. It dwells among us, tabernacled within us. God incar-
nates us with the nativity of Himself. We are born again as His Spirit
births within. This is the reality of incarnation, this mystery of being
en-godded, the human joined with the spiritual. Now it too is full of
grace and truth—incarnation occurs over and over again.

We must force our feeble human perceptions to understand that
the Word still comes. God still speaks. He "comes unto" us, our day,
our times, our places. It is not He who is the aphasiac. It is not His
muteness which causes the breakdown of language between Creator
and creature. It is our deafness that is responsible, our inattentive-
ness, our deliberate rebellion of holding our fingers in our ears.

God is not silent. He never has been. He will never be. It is we who
have "ears to hear but do not hear." It is our disability that prevents
discourse, our very own. *Karen Burton Mains*

The truths of the Bible are like gold in the soil. Whole generations
walk over it and know not what treasures are hidden underneath. So
centuries of men pass over the Scriptures and know not what riches
lie under the feet of their interpretation. Sometimes when they discover them, they call them new truths. One might as well call gold,
newly dug, new gold.

The Bible, without a spiritual life to interpret it, is like a trellis on
which no vine grows—bare, angular and in the way. The Bible with

a spiritual life is like a trellis covered with luxuriant vine—beautiful, odorous, and heavy with purple clusters shining through the leaves.
Henry Ward Beecher

Almighty God, the gift of Your Holy Word, through which we find the forgiveness and love of Jesus, is more precious than gold to us.

DECEMBER 27

Looking for that blessed hope, and the glorious appearing of the great God and our Savior Jesus Christ.... Titus 2:13

---

*H*E WAS GOD IN THE PERSON OF HIS SON, come to take away the sins of the world, to bear our griefs and carry our sorrows, to be wounded for our transgressions and bruised for our iniquities; for the sins of men He was to be stricken, and God in infinite love and compassion was to lay on His sinless body the iniquity of us all.

There is a new note of gladness to "Joy to the World" when we look beyond the Bethlehem fields to Calvary, and then on to the mount across the Kidron in the east. When, knowing that He has saved us from our sins, we hear the words of angels again: "This same Jesus... shall so come in like manner," and know that at that time we will meet Him in the glorious company of the redeemed.
L. Nelson Bell

The entire Book of Revelation is given over to the teaching of the Second Coming of Jesus Christ. When minds are full of pessimism and gloom, when all seems lost, it represents the promise of a wonderful future. Many people wail, "What is to become of us? Where are we drifting?" to which the Bible gives a sure, straight answer, saying that the consummation of all things shall be the coming again of Jesus Christ and all the rewards that await the elect of God!
Billy Graham

Lord Jesus, each day I look for Your return! May my life reflect the joy of this hope to everyone I meet.

DECEMBER 28

...the day of his return will soon be here. Romans 13:12 (TLB)

---

*T*HE LORD IS COMING. But until He comes to catch away the Church, every member of that body should be about the Lord's business. Our hearts and our houses should be clean. Our accounts should be up-to-date. Our prayers should be fully said. Our witnessing should be current. Our beings should be filled with the Holy Spirit. And our lips should be framing the words: "Even so, come, Lord Jesus."

Harold Lindsell

> Beyond the war-clouds and the reddened ways,
> I see the Promise of the Coming Days!
> I see His Sun arise, new charged with grace
> Earth's tears to dry and all her woes efface!
> Christ lives! Christ loves! Christ rules!
> No more shall Might,
> Though leagued with all the Forces of the Night,
> Ride over Right. No more shall Wrong
> the world's gross agonies prolong.
> Who waits His Time shall surely see
> The triumph of His Constancy;
> When without let, or bar, or stay,
> The coming of His Perfect Day
> Shall sweep the Powers of Night away;
> And Faith, replumed for nobler flight,
> And Hope, aglow with radiance bright,
> And Love, in loveliness bedight,
> *Shall greet the morning light!*

John Oxenham

Lord Jesus Christ, how I long for that perfect day when every eye will see You! May every fiber of my being be ready for Your return.

⸺•⸺ DECEMBER 29 ⸺•⸺

...*abide in him; that, when he shall appear, we may have confidence, and not be ashamed before him at his coming.* I John 2:28

◆━━━━━━━━━━━━━━━━━━━━━━━━━━━━━━━━━━━━◆

*W*HAT A JOY TO KNOW THAT "THE BEST IS YET TO BE," and if Jesus tarries yet we know that one day He *will* come and we shall see Him face to face. I long for that day to come. Why? Because I love Him.

My father was a very dear man and, I believe, the best father anyone could have in the whole world. He often had to go away on business and, although we were not sure when he would return, flowers were placed in his room every day. Oh, the joy when he did return home. My place at the oval dinner table was opposite his, which meant that I could look into his eyes. With these lovely eyes and a long beard he had just the sort of face I imagined a patriarch would have. Why was I so happy? Because I loved him.

There is fear in the heart of a disobedient servant when the master returns, but there is joy in the heart of an obedient child when the father comes home. How I should love it if Jesus should come today. Just imagine how wonderful it would be not to have to be sick, to die or to pass through the valley of the shadow of death.

O joy, O delight, should we go without dying;
No sickness, no sorrow, no sadness, no crying;
Caught up in the clouds to meet Him in glory,
When Jesus receives His own.

Corrie ten Boom

The Second Advent is possible any day, impossible no day.

Richard Trench

Lord Jesus, the anticipation of Your return fills me with happiness! May I not be ashamed of my life upon that blessed day.

DECEMBER 30

For whosoever shall do the will of God, the same is my brother, and my sister, and mother. Mark 3:35

---

*L*AID ON THINE ALTAR, O MY LORD, DIVINE,
Accept this day my gift for Jesus' sake.
I have no jewels to adorn Thy shrine,
Nor any world-famed sacrifice to make;
But here I bring within my trembling hand
This will of mine: a thing that seemeth small;
And only Thou, dear Lord, canst understand
That when I yield Thee thus, I yield Thee all.
It hath been wet with tears and dimmed with sighs,
Clenched in my clasp, till beauty it hath none.

Now from Thy footstool, where it vanquished lies,
The prayer ascendeth: "Let Thy will be done."
Take it, O Father, ere my courage fail,
And blend it so with Thine own will, that e'en
If in some desperate hour my cry prevail,
And Thou giv'st back my gift, it may have been
So changed, so purified, so fair have grown,
So one with Thee, so filled with peace divine,

I may not know nor feel it as my own,
But gaining back my will may find it Thine.

Author unknown

I gave up all for Christ, and what have I found?
I have found everything in Christ!

John Calvin

Lord God, the year is almost drawing to a close, and I realize there is still so much of my life that needs changing. In humble adoration I come to You bringing my will and all my ambitions. Take them, Lord, and for Jesus' sake may they be wholly surrendered to You.

══════════════ DECEMBER 31 ══════════════

These things have I spoken unto you, that my joy might remain in you, and that your joy might be full. John 15:11

I LOVE GOD'S MATHEMATICS: Joy adds and multiplies as you divide it with others, and in laughing, loving, and learning, we have helped countless others to find real joy—and to discern the difference between happiness and joy. *Happiness* comes from the same root word as *happenings*: Happiness so often depends on happenings—atmosphere—environment—others' actions—external things— no one can be happy all the time. A mother cannot be happy if her child is seriously ill. A person cannot be happy with a toothache or a painful ailment. A man can't be happy when he's just lost his job— but one can have *joy*—which comes from the knowledge that God loves me—God cares for me. God has His hand on my life—I am going somewhere, and no matter if the year has been rough—if obstacles loom larger, I can have *joy*—as a sunrise colors the new day!

Mary C. Crowley

We have come to the end of another year. As we look back we will remember times of joy and sorrow, days of defeat and success. In all these circumstances we can see that our Lord's presence has been with us, consoling, caring and watching over us.

Some of our experiences may have hurt deeply. We have "whys?" in our hearts. Why did a loved one have to die or be sick? Why did so many things go wrong? Corrie ten Boom was asked why she and her family had had to suffer so during World War II—they were so dedicated to the Lord. Her answer was honest: "I do not know why now, but one day I will when I stand in the presence of my Savior." Her life was bruised, but she did not sink under her persecution, she rose up and became a person wholly and utterly consecrated to Jesus Christ, and He has used her mightily.

As we look forward to the new year, let us resolve that we will enter it filled with devotion to our Lord as we ask Him to use us to bring many into the joy that is eternal.   J.W.B.

Lord Jesus Christ, thank You for caring for me each day of this past year. With this reassuring knowledge I will go into the new year with quiet confidence, knowing that I shall be surrounded by Your love. Use my life, Lord, to touch others and tell them that in Your presence is fullness of joy forevermore!

━━━━ ACKNOWLEDGMENTS ━━━━

The author and publisher wish to acknowledge the following publishers and individuals for quotes used by permission. The publisher has made every effort to credit sources properly. If there are any questions concerning this, please contact the publisher and corrections will be made in future editions.

Abingdon Press, 201 Eighth Avenue South, Nashville, Tennessee 37262; *A Time to Seek* by Lee Fisher, © 1972 Abingdon Press, Used by permission; *River of Life* by James S. Stewart, © 1972 James S. Stewart, Used by permission; *The Will of God* by Leslie D. Weatherhead, © 1972 Leslie D. Weatherhead, Used by permission.

Accent Books, 12100 West Sixth Avenue, Denver, Colorado 80215: *Soul Free* by Ralph Bell, © 1976 B/P Publications, Used by permission.

African Enterprise, P. O. Box 988, Pasadena, California 91102: Excerpts by Festo Kivengere, © Outlook, Used by permission.

Argus Communications, One DLM Park, Allen, Texas 75002: *He Touched Me* by John Powell, S.J., Used by permission; *The Secret of Staying in Love* by John Powell, S.J., © 1974 Argus Communications, Used by permission.

Augsburg Publishing House, 426 South Fifth Street, Minneapolis, Minnesota 55415: *God Holds Your Tomorrows* by Roger C. Palms, © 1976 Augsburg Publishing House, Used by permission.

Broadman Press, 127 Ninth Avenue North, Nashville, Tennesse 37234; *The Reluctant Witness* by Kenneth L. Chafin, © 1974 Broadman Press, Used by permission; *Finding God's Best* by John Hunter, © 1975 Broadman Press, Used by permission.

Chosen Books, Lincoln, Virginia 22078: *Life Sentence* by Charles Colson, © 1979 Charles Colson, Used by permission; *Adventures in Prayer* by Catherine Marshall, © 1975 Catherine Marshall, Used by permission; *Heaven Can't Wait* by Catherine Marshall, © 1963 Catherine Marshall, Used by permission; *The Helper* by Catherine Marshall, © 1978 Catherine Marshall, Used by permission; *Meeting God at Every Turn* by Catherine Marshall LeSourd, © 1981 Catherine Marshall LeSourd, Used by permission; *Let's Keep Christmas* by Peter Marshall, © 1953 Catherine Marshall, Used by permission.

Christian Herald Books, 40 Overlook Drive, Chappaqua, New York 10514: *Let Prayer Help You* by Ruth C. Ikerman, © 1980 Ruth C. Ikerman, Used by permission; *Managing Your Emotions* by Erwin Lutzer, © 1981 Christian Herald Books, Used by permission.

Christian Literature Crusade, P. O. Box C, Fort Washington, Pennsylvania 19034: *Thou Givest, They Gather* by Amy Carmichael, © 1958, Used by permission; *Approved Unto God* by Oswald Chambers, © 1962, Used by permission of CLC and the Oswald Chambers Association of Great Britain; *God Unlimited* by Norman Grubb, © Christian Literature Crusade, Used by permission; *Marching Orders for the End Battle* by Corrie ten Boom, © 1969 Christian Literature Crusade, London, Used by permission; *Plenty for Everyone* by Corrie ten Boom, © Christian Literature Crusade, Used by permission.

Christianity Today, 465 Gundersen Drive, Carol Stream, Illinois 60187: Article by Ruth Bell Graham, © 1981 Christianity Today, Used by permission.

Christians, Inc., P. O. Box 2040, Orange, California 92669: Excerpts by Corrie ten Boom, © The Hiding Place Magazine, Used by permission.

Church of Scotland Committee on Youth, 121 George Street, Edinburgh 2, Scotland: *The Life and Teachings of Jesus Christ* by James S. Stewart, © 1933, Used by permission.

David C. Cook Publishing Company, 850 North Grove, Elgin, Illinois 60120: *Good News Is for Sharing* by Leighton Ford, © 1977 David C. Cook Publishing Company, Used by permission; *The Key to a Loving Heart* by Karen Burton Mains, © 1979 David C. Cook Publishing Company, Used by permission.

Doubleday and Company, 245 Park Avenue, New York, New York 10017: *While Men Slept* by L. Nelson Bell, © 1970 L. Nelson Bell, Used by permission; *Who Am I God?* by Marjorie Holmes, © 1970, 1971 Marjorie Holmes Mighell, Used by permission.

William B. Eerdmans Publishing Company, 255 Jefferson S.E., Grand Rapids, Michigan 49503: *Convictions to Live by* by L. Nelson Bell, © 1966 William B. Eerdmans Publishing Company, Used by permission; *Love Within Limits* by Lewis B. Smedes, © 1978 William B. Eerdmans Publishing Company, Used by permission.

Harcourt Brace Jovanovich, Inc., 757 Third Avenue, New York, New York 10017: *The Four Loves* by C. S. Lewis, © 1960 Harcourt Brace Jovanovich, Used by permission.

Harper & Row Publishers, 10 East 53rd Street, New York, New York 10022: *Life Together* by Dietrich Bonhoeffer, © 1954 Harper & Row Publishers, Used by permission; *These Strange Ashes* by Elisabeth Elliot, © 1975 Elisabeth Elliot, Used by permission; *The Christian Persuader* by Leighton Ford, © 1966 Leighton F. S. Ford, Used by permission; *Celebration of Discipline* by Richard J. Foster, © 1978 Richard J. Foster; *Freedom of Simplicity* by Richard J. Foster, © 1981 Richard J. Foster, Used by permission; *Jesus* by Malcolm Muggeridge, © 1975 Malcolm Muggeridge; *When the Wood Is Green* by Arthur F. Sultz, © Harper & Row Publishers; *A Gift for God* by Mother Teresa, © 1975 Mother Teresa's Missionaries of Caring, Used by permission; *To Me It's Wonderful* by Ethel Waters, © 1972 Ethel Waters, Used by permission.

Harvest House Publishers, 1075 Arrowsmith, Eugene, Oregon 97402: *The Beauty of Love* by Lloyd John Ogilvie, © 1980 Harvest House Publishers, Used by permission; *Loneliness Is Not a Disease* by Tim Timmons, © 1981 Shasta Press, Used by permission.

Here's Life Publishers, Inc., Box 1576, San Bernardino, California 92402, Used by permission; *Answers to Tough Questions* by Josh McDowell and Don Stewart, © 1980 Campus Crusade for Christ, Int., Used by permission; *The Resurrection Factor* by Josh McDowell, © 1981 Campus Crusade for Christ, Int., Used by permission.

Hodder & Stoughton Ltd., London, England: *New Testament Christianity* by J. B. Phillips, © J. B. Phillips, Used by permission; *The Secret of Serenity* by Gordon Powell, © 1957 Hodder & Stoughton, Used by permission; *River of Life* by James S. Stewart, © 1972 Hodder & Stoughton, Used by permission.

Hope Publishing Company, Carol Stream, Illinois 60187: *Great Is Thy Faithfulness* by Thomas O. Chilsholm, © 1923, Renewal 1951 Hope Publishing Company, All rights reserved, Used by permission; *Have Thine Own Way, Lord* by Adelaide A. Pollard, © 1907, Renewal 1935 Hope Publishing Company, All rights reserved, Used by permission.

Ideals Publishing Corporation, 11315 Watertown Plank Road, Milwaukee, Wisconsin 53201: *Sound Sense for Successful Living* by D. Stuart Briscoe, © 1979 D. Stuart Briscoe, Used by permission; *Thank You, Lord, for My Home* by Gigi Graham Tchividjian, © 1979 Gigi Graham Tchividjian, Used by permission.

InterVarsity Press, Box F, Downers Grove, Illinois 60515: *Prayer* by O. Hallesby, © 1948 InterVarsity Press, Used by permission; *God Has Spoken* by J. I. Packer, © 1979 J. I. Packer, Used by permission; *Knowing God* by J. I. Packer, © 1973 J. I. Packer, Used by permission; *Out of the Saltshaker and Into the World* by Rebecca Manley Pippert, © 1979 InterVarsity Christian Fellowship, Used by permission; *Escape From Reason* by Francis A. Schaeffer, © 1968 InterVarsity Fellowship, London, Used by permission; *The Mark of the Christian* by Francis A. Schaeffer, © 1970 L'Abri Fellowship, Used by permission; *No Little People* by Francis A. Schaeffer, © 1974 L'Abri Fellowship, Used by permission; *Basic Christianity* by John R. W. Stott, © 1958 InterVarsity Press, London, Used by permission; *Love Is a Feeling to Be Learned* by Walter Trobisch, © 1971 Editions Trobisch, Used by permission; *Love Yourself: Self Acceptance and Depression* by Walter Trobisch, © 1976 Editions Trobisch, Used by permission.

Littlebrook Publishing, Inc., 6 Littlebrook Road, Princeton, New Jersey 08540: *Poems* by Fred Bauer, © 1981 Littlebrook Publishing Company, Inc., Used by permission.

Loizeaux Brothers, Box 277, Neptune, New Jersey 07753: *Though the Mountains Shake* by Amy Carmichael, © Loizeaux Brothers, Used by permission; *Mission of and Praying in the Holy Spirit* by H. A. Ironside, © Loizeaux Brothers, Used by permission.

MacMillan Publishing Company, Inc., 866 Third Avenue, New York, New York 10022: *Letters and Papers From Prison*, Revised Edition, by Dietrich Bonhoeffer, © 1953, 1967 SCM Press Ltd., Used by permission; *Mere Christianity* by C. S. Lewis, © 1943, 1945, 1952 MacMillan Publishing Co., Copyrights renewed, Used by permission; *Good News* by J. B. Phillips, © 1963 J. B. Phillips, Used by permission; *Plain Christianity* by J. B. Phillips, © 1954 MacMillan Publishing Co., Used by permission.

Moody Press, 2101 West Howard Street, Chicago, Illinois 60645: *Life on the Highest Plane* by

Ruth Paxson, © 1928, Used by permission; *Man's Problems—God's Answers* by J. Oswald Chambers, © 1967, 1980 Moody Bible Institute, Used by permission.

Multnomah Press, 10209 S.E. Division Street, Portland, Oregon 97266: *The Moment to Shout* by Luis Palau, © 1977 Luis Palau, Used by permission.

Thomas Nelson, Inc., 407 Seventh Avenue South, Nashville, Tennessee 37214: *The Holy Spirit of God* by Herbert Lockyer, © 1981 Herbert Lockyer, Used by permission; *Hand Me Another Brick* by Charles Swindoll, © 1978 Charles R. Swindoll, Used by permission; *Three Steps Forward, Two Steps Back* by Charles Swindoll, © 1980 Charles R. Swindoll, Used by permission.

Oxford University Press, 200 University Avenue, New York, New York 10016: *How Christians Grow* by Russell T. Hitt, © 1979 Oxford University Press.

Regal Books, 2300 Knoll Drive, Ventura, California 93003: *Emotions* by James Dobson, © 1980 Regal Books, Used by permission; *431 Quotes* by Henrietta Mears, Compiled by Eleanor L. Doan, © 1970 Gospel Light Publications, Used by permission; *Autobiography of God* by Lloyd John Ogilvie, © 1979 Gospel Light Publications, Used by permission; *Life as It Was Meant to Be* by Lloyd John Ogilvie, © 1980 Regal Books, Used by permission.

Fleming H. Revell Company, 184 Central Avenue, Old Tappan, New Jersey 07675: *The Charles L. Allen Treasury,* © 1970 Fleming H. Revell Company, Used by permission; *Perfect Peace* by Charles L. Allen, © 1979 Charles L. Allen, Used by permission; *Victory in the Valleys of Life* by Charles L. Allen, © 1981 Charles Allen, Used by permission; *To Pray Is to Live* by William P. Barker, © 1977 Fleming H. Revell Company, Used by permission; *You Are Very Special* by Verna Birkey, Used by permission; *For Such a Time as This* by Vonnette Bright, © 1976 Fleming H. Revell Company, Used by permission; *Some Run With Feet of Clay* by Jeannette Clift, © 1978 Jeanette Clift George, Used by permission; *Women Who Win* by Mary C. Crowley, © 1979 Mary C. Crowley, Used by permission; *You Can Too* by Mary Crowley, © 1976, 1980 Fleming H. Revell Company, Used by permission; *Hide or Seek* by Dr. James Dobson, © 1974, 1979 Fleming H. Revell Company, Used by permission; *The Mark of a Man* by Elisabeth Elliot, © 1981 Elisabeth Elliot Gren, Used by permission; *Love Is an Everyday Thing* by Colleen Townsend Evans, © 1974 Fleming H. Revell Company, Used by permission; *They Call Me Mother Graham* by Morrow C. Graham, © 1977 Fleming H. Revell Company, Used by permission; *The Kingdom Is Yours* by Louis H. Evans Sr., © 1962 Fleming H. Revell Company, Used by permission; *Feeling Free* by Archibald D. Hart, © 1979 Archibald D. Hart, Used by permission; *Day By Day* by Vance Havner, © 1963 Fleming H. Revell Company, Used by permission; *Ocean Glory* by W. Phillip Keller, © 1980 W. Phillip Keller, Used by permission; *Spirit Controlled Family Living* by Tim and Beverly LaHaye, © 1978 Tim and Beverly LaHaye, Used by permission; *Changepoints* by Joyce Landorf, © 1981 Joyce Landorf, Used by permission; *Dark Threads the Weaver Needs* by Herbert Lockyer, © 1979 Herbert Lockyer, Used by permission; *Mr. Jones, Meet the Master: Sermons & Prayers of Peter Marshall,* Edited by Catherine Marshall, © 1949, 1959 Fleming H. Revell Company, Renewed 1976, 1977 Catherine Marshall LeSourd, Used by permission; *The Light and the Glory* by Peter Marshall and David Manuel, © 1977 Peter J. Marshall Jr. and David B. Manuel Jr., Used by permission; *Children Are Wet Cement* by Anne Ortlund, © 1981 Anne Ortlund, Used by permission; *Victorious Christian Living* by Alan Redpath, © 1955 Fleming H. Revell Company, Used by permission; *Where He Leads* by Dale Evans Rogers, © 1975 Fleming H. Revell Company, Used by permission; *Affliction* by Edith Schaeffer, © 1978 Edith Schaeffer, Used by permission.

The Rodeheaver Company: *He Lives,* © 1933 Homer A. Rodeheaver, Renewed 1961 Rodeheaver Company, All rights reserved, Used by permission.

Tyndale House Publishers, 366 Gundersen Drive, Wheaton, Illinois 60187: *I Love the Word Impossible* by Ann Kiemel, © 1976 Tyndale House Publishers, Used by permission; *The Gathering Storm* by Harold Lindsell, © 1980 Harold Lindsell, Used by permission; *Karen! Karen!* by Karen Burton Mains, © 1979 Karen Burton Mains, Used by permission; *Givers, Takers, and Other Kinds of Lovers* by Josh McDowell and Paul Lewis, © 1980 Josh McDowell and Paul Lewis, Used by permission; *The Cup of Wonder* by Lloyd John Ogilvie, © 1976 Tyndale House Publishers, Used by permission of author; *The Positive Power of Jesus Christ* by Norman Vincent Peace, © 1980 Norman Vincent Peale, Used by permission; *Leighton Ford: A Life Surprised* by Norman Rohrer and Leighton Ford, © 1981 Norman Rohrer and Leighton Ford, Used by permission; *Hidden Art* by Edith Schaeffer, © 1971 Edith Schaeffer, Used by permission.

Victor Books, 1825 College Avenue, Wheaton, Illinois 60187: *What Works When Life Doesn't* by Stuart Briscoe, © 1976 Scripture Press Publications, Used by permission; *Gaining Through Losing* by Evelyn Christenson, © 1980 Scripture Press Publications, Used by permission; *Lord Change Me* by Evelyn Christenson, © 1977 Scripture Press Publications, Used by permission; *He Leadeth Me* by V. Raymond Edman, © 1959 Scripture Press Publications, Used by permission; *Be Joyful* by Warren W. Wiersbe, © 1974 Scripture Press Publications, Used by permission.

Word Books, 4800 West Waco Drive, Waco, Texas 76796: *A Slow and Certain Light* by Elisabeth Elliot, © 1973 Elisabeth Elliot Leitch, Used by permission; *A Turtle on a Fencepost* by Allan C. Emery, © 1979 Word, Inc., Used by permission; *Salt for Society* by W. Phillip Keller, © 1981 W Phillip Keller, Used by permission; *Special Friends* by Twila Knaack, © 1981 Word, Inc., Used by permission; *Great Preaching* by Sherwood E. Wirt and Viola Blake, © 1963, 1965, 1966, 1967, 1969, 1970 Billy Graham Evangelistic Association, Used by permission; *Improving Your Serve* by Charles R. Swindoll, © 1981 Word, Inc., Used by permission.

Word Music, Inc., Winona Lake, Indiana: *He Lives* by Alfred H. Ackley, © 1933 Homer A. Rodeheaver, Renewed 1961 The Rodeheaver Co., All rights reserved, International copyright secured, Used by permission.

Word (UK) Ltd., Northbridge Road, Berkhamsted, Hertsforshire, England HP4 1EH: *The Best in Life* by Lindsay Glegg and John Fear, © 1972, Used by permission.

Zondervan Publishing House, 1415 S.E. Lake Drive, Grand Rapids, Michigan 49506: *Fearfully and Wonderfully Made* by Dr. Paul Brand and Philip Yancey, 1980 Dr. Paul Brand and Philip Yancey, Used by permission; *Fight for the Family* by Jill Briscoe, © 1981 Zondervan Publishing House, Used by permission; *Hush, Hush!* by Jill Briscoe, © 1978 Zondervan Publishing House, Used by permission; *The Fullness of Christ* by D. Stuart Briscoe, © 1965 Zondervan Publishing House, Used by permission; *Illustrations for Preachers and Speakers* by Keith L. Brooks, © 1946 Zondervan Publishing House, Used by permission; *Broken Things* by M. R. DeHaan, © 1977 Zondervan Publishing House, Used by permission; *Testimony of Triumph* by John M. Drescher, © 1980 Zondervan Publishing House, Used by permission; *A Step Further* by Joni Eareckson and Steve Estes, © 1978 Joni Eareckson and Steve Estes, Used by permission; *Knowing God's Secret* by John C. Hunter, © 1965 Zondervan Publishing House, Used by permission; *A Shepherd Looks at the 23rd Psalm* by W. Phillip Keller, © 1970 W. Phillip Keller, Used by permission; *A Thirst for Meaning* by Calvin Miller, © 1973 Zondervan Publishing House, Used by permission; *Woman to Woman* by Eugenia Price, © 1959 Zondervan Publishing House, Used by permission; *Prayer: Conversing With God* by Rosalind Rinker, © 1959 Zondervan Publishing House, Used by permission; *W W III* by John Wesley White, © 1977, 1981 Zondervan Publishing House, Used by permission.

Decision Magazine, 1300 Harmon Place, Minneapolis, Minnesota 55403: John Baillie, © 1965, Used by permission; Janice Barfield, © 1970, Used by permission; Dr. B. Clayton Bell, © 1975 B. Clayton Bell, Senior Minister, Highland Park Presbyterian Church, Dallas, Texas, Used by permission; The Right Reverend A. Jack Dain, © 1976, Used by permission; Millie Dienert, © 1967 Millie Dienert, International Consultant for Christian Women's Clubs of America, Community Bible Teacher and Retreat Speaker, Used by permission; Rev. Louis H. Evans Jr., © 1963, Used by permission; Jean Ford, © 1978, Used by permission; Ruth Bell Graham, Used by permission; Roy W. Gustafson, © 1973, Used by permission; Paul Little, © 1976 Marie H. Little, Used by permission; Anne Graham Lotz, © 1981, Used by permission; Dr. Robert B. Munger, © 1961, Used by permission; Harold J. Ockenga, © 1978, Used by permission; Stephen F. Olford, © 1978, Used by permission; Paul S. Rees, © 1970, Used by permission; Oswald J. Smith, © 1961; Bonnie Barrows Thomas, © 1981, Used by permission; D. Conrad W. Thompson, © 1974, Used by permission; Dr. John W. Williams, Minister, St. Stephen Baptist Church, Kansas City, Missouri, Used by permission; Sherwood E. Wirt, © 1973, Used by permission.

Individuals: Rev. Richard C. Halverson, Washington, D.C., Excerpts from *Perspective*, Used by permission; David Mullins, Excerpts from *Mary's Song*, Used by permission; George Beverly Shea, Excerpts from *Then Sings My Soul*, Used by permission; Gigi Graham Tchividjian, Excerpts from *Thank You, Lord, for My Home*, Used by permission; Sherwood E. Wirt, Excerpts from *The Cross on the Mountain*, Used by permission; Sherwood E. Wirt, Excerpt from *Living Quotations for Christians*, Used by permission; Winola Wells Wirt, Excerpts from *Interludes in a Woman's Day*, Used by permission.